ROYAL BABYLON

Broadway Books

NEW YORK

Royal Babylon

THE ALARMING

HISTORY

OF

EUROPEAN

ROYALTY

KARL SHAW

Broadway Books
1540 Broadway
New York, NY 10036

Broadway Books titles may be purchased for business or promotional use or for special sales. For information, please write to: Special Markets Department, Random House, Inc., 1540 Broadway, New York, NY 10036.

BROADWAY BOOKS and its logo, a letter B bisected on the diagonal, are trademarks of Broadway Books, a division of Random House, Inc.

The original edition of this book was originally published in 1999 by Virgin in the U.K.
First Broadway Books trade paperback edition published 2001.

Book design by Gretchen Achilles

Library of Congress Cataloging-in-Publication Data

Shaw, Karl.
Royal Babylon: the alarming history of European royalty / Karl Shaw.
p. cm.
Originally published: London : Virgin Pub., 1999.
Includes bibliographical references.
1. Royal houses—Europe. 2. Europe—Kings and rulers—
Biography. 3. Monarchy—History. 4. Courts and courtiers. I. Title.

D412.7 .S53 2001
940.2′8′0922—dc21
[B]
00-069800

ISBN 0-7679-0755-8

01 02 03 04 05 10 9 8 7 6 5 4 3 2

CONTENTS

9.

DUTY, DIGNITY, DECENCY

The Windsors

273

EPILOGUE

321

BIBLIOGRAPHY

323

INTRODUCTION

♔

ABOUT 200 YEARS ago, England's greatest republican confidently predicted the imminent downfall of the House of Hanover. "Hereditary succession is a burlesque upon monarchy," he wrote. "It puts it in the most ridiculous light, by presenting it as an office which any child or idiot may fill. It requires some talents to be a common mechanic, but to be a king requires only the animal figure of a man—a sort of breathing automaton. This sort of superstition may last a few years more, but it cannot long resist the awakened reason and interest of men."

Thomas Paine had good reason to believe that he was on fairly safe ground. The reigning King of England was evidently insane and reduced to conversing with long-dead friends and indecently exposing himself to servants. The King's brother Henry had just become the first member of the British royal family to be sued for adultery. The rest of the royals, especially the King's seven sons, were reviled throughout the land. One of them was even suspected of having murdered his manservant and raping his own sister. The heir to the throne, an unstable, bloated philanderer unable to step outside his front door without risk of being pelted by the London mob, was locked in the most publicly disastrous royal marriage since Henry VIII was obliged to remove Catherine Howard's head.

Those of Her Majesty's subjects who saw the blitz of British royal embarrassments of the mid-1990s and concluded that the British monarchy had never been worse represented were presumably ignorant of standards set by earlier generations. In the realm of royal behavior, Prince Charles's devotion to his mistress, Camilla Parker Bowles, probably qualifies as fidelity. Most of the men who have held the title "Prince of Wales" were an embarrassment, none more so than Prince Charles's great-great-grandfather, Edward VII, a man who took the family motto, "I serve," into another dimension.

From the day the Hanoverians first set foot on British soil in 1714, apart from during the reigns of George V, George VI and Queen Elizabeth II, the British royal family has never been popular, nor does it deserve to have been. Throughout the eighteenth and nineteenth centuries, British kings and queens—Shelley's "royal vampires"—were subject to regular attacks from the press for their profligacy, their indolence, their stupidity or for their squalid private lives. And then a curiously repressed minor royal from Germany, Prince Albert of Saxe-Coburg-Gotha, made the situation of his family even more difficult by forcing them into a straitjacket labeled MORAL FIGUREHEADS TO THE NATION, dooming the British royals to an endless struggle to keep up appearances and keep a lid on their family scandals.

The British royal family's rise in popularity was not a straightforward linear development from the much-hated Hanoverians to the widely respected Queen Elizabeth II, more a 300-year roller coaster of highs and lows.

British republicanism was a more potent force in Queen Victoria's reign than at any time since. Victoria herself conceded that the monarchy was so unpopular it would probably not survive her by more than a generation, and she saw no point in giving the Prince of Wales anything useful to do to prepare him for rule.

Then, in 1871, as in August 1997 with the death of Diana, there was one of those rare, defining moments for the British monarchy. Queen Victoria's playboy eldest son, Bertie, experienced an almost fatal attack of typhoid. The Prince emerged from his brush with death bemused to find his mother's subjects bursting with spontaneous gratitude for his recovery and, although his family hardly dared believe it, pro-monarchist sentiment. It was as though their popularity had been transformed by magic. For the first time in nearly three centuries, there was a sea change in public opinion and the tide had turned in the British royal family's favor.

Gladstone and Disraeli, the first royal "spin doctors," built on this slice of royal good fortune, skillfully turning the image of Queen Victoria round from that of greedy old recluse to the "Grandmama of Europe," cultivating her as a great empress looking down on an all-conquering British imperialist system. The new, more sympathetic public attitude toward the monarchy was as ever underpinned by the British press, as the politicians still had to rely heavily on the fact that the popular journals of the day—even *Punch*, which had laid ridicule on Prince Albert with a trowel—had suddenly become embarrassingly servile.

As an exercise in marketing, there is no doubting the House of Windsor's near-miraculous success. Under King George V, the British monarchy, which had previously existed as little more than a convenience of constitutional legality with a dodgy past, was reinvented as a bulwark of traditional family values and of duty, dignity and decency. In the 1930s, without telephoto lenses to probe the gulf between the royal family's public face and the sordid romps enjoyed by some of the King's sons, the royal family were always seen in a highly favorable light. It is unlikely that the virtuous middle-class–family image touted by George V would have been so readily embraced if their subjects had been able to read the rumors that throughout his marriage the King visited prostitutes in seaside boarding houses, or if it had been generally known that Queen Mary was a kleptomaniac, or that one of her sons was an alleged Nazi sympathizer and another a bisexual cocaine addict.

During and immediately after the abdication of Edward VIII, popular respect for the British royal family dipped to a new twentieth-century low, although the issue was quickly buried by developments abroad, as Europe inched closer to another World War. From George VI to the Silver Jubilee of Queen Elizabeth II, the British royal family enjoyed the support of an adoring, grateful public and an uncritical British press. Fleet Street could not have been more supportive if the Windsors had been censoring coverage of the royal family themselves. For the best part of forty years, the Windsors were invincible. So it came to pass that an opinion poll as recently as 1971 showed that a third of the population of Great Britain believed that Queen Elizabeth II was chosen by God.

Compared to many of their royal cousins abroad, however, the British royal family, even the Hanoverians, although talentless, greedy, rather unpleasant and generally absurd, were neither very shocking nor particularly strange. For the greater part of the last 300 years, the great continental royal houses have been populated by philanderers, simpletons, sociopaths and tragic emotional cripples. Every monarchy in Europe has at some time or another been ruled over by a madman, although Bavaria alone had the good fortune to have a king crazy enough to remain marketable as a tourist attraction more than a century after his death. The Victorian constitutional expert Walter Bagehot pointed out in 1867: "History seems to show that hereditary royal families gather from the repeated influence of their corrupting situation some dark taint in the blood." He noted that "in 1802 every hereditary monarch [in Europe] was insane."

Spain's rapid economic decline coincided with the reigns of an almost unbroken run of mad men and women. From the mid-seventeenth century right through to the Civil War in the 1930s, Charles III was the nearest the Spanish had to a king who could be described as fairly normal. The Habsburgs, for centuries the most powerful family in central and southern Europe, allowed themselves to become monstrously inbred and reduced to physical and mental decrepitude. Similarly, the Braganzas and the Savoys, the ruling houses of Portugal and Italy respectively, were so grotesquely inbred that they became too stupid to avoid their own extinction. The outlandish royal families of Germany, the fatherland of the House of Windsor, excelled at producing princes and princesses with gross personality disorders. Prussia's rulers, the Hohenzollerns, bred a string of psychopaths and megalomaniacs. The Wittelsbachs were frequently certifiably insane. The grasping Saxe-Coburgs, who provided roughly one half of the Windsor gene pool and somehow managed to infiltrate most of the royal families of Europe, were an outstandingly debauched family riddled with syphilitics and adulterers. The kings of France were sex-fixated epicures, gross even by the standards of their own day.

Unlike the Hanoverian and Windsor queens and queen consorts, who were mostly shallow and materialistic, the continental royal houses produced extraordinary women with passions for violence or for men. The sexual license of the Russian empresses Elizabeth I and Catherine II were the wonders of the age. One of the arguments most often put forward for the British monarchy is that Europe's republics rue the day they got rid of theirs; but there is no sign yet of the democratized former Soviet states running to the genealogical tables to look for a Romanov to sponsor. The entire Russian imperial family tree was thick with lunatics and murderers, and the rulers, male and female, were either drunken, debauched or mentally unstable, and occasionally all three. The great wave of sympathy for the butchered Russian Czar and his family, and the decades of antipathy toward the regime that ordered their assassination, has glossed over the fact that George V's look-alike cousin, Nicholas II, although not especially foul by Romanov standards, was one of the most sinister and cowardly royal despots of the century.

Indeed, reflecting upon the demise of the Russian imperial family, the Czar's sister, the wizened old Grand Duchess Olga, observed, "The Romanovs cared for nothing but the unending gratification of personal desire and ambition." As we shall see, the Grand Duchess's scathing epitaph could have been fairly applied to almost any royal family in Europe.

A lucky few emperors and empresses were so venerated that historians have awarded them the epithet "Great," but not for any good works or lasting benefits to mankind. As far as history is concerned, psychopaths can still be great statesmen or -women. "Great" was generally a recognition of power or brute strength, no matter how they lived, how many people they had killed or how repulsive they were. Consider Frederick the Great of Prussia, a toothless, gouty, smelly little man with no concept of the word "pity," and an ambiguous sexuality including an alleged inclination toward bestiality. Peter the Great was particularly fond of sadistic torture sessions and capable of watching his son being racked to death before enjoying a marathon banquet. Catherine the Great was both insomniac and nymphomaniac, which was desperately bad news for the dozens of handsome young soldiers she continued to drag into her bed well into her late sixties.

When the last Bourbon king of France, Charles X, was seventeen, he began to show an interest in the Swiss Guards parade ground. A minister of the royal household rebuked him: "You have acquired a liking for drill, *Monseigneur*. That does not become a prince. Run up debts and we will pay them." Much of royal life is typified by long periods of enforced idleness, punctuated by briefer periods of meaningless formality. Princes were born to endless wealth and privilege and rarely expected to do anything that disagreed with them. Princesses were born to a lifetime of card playing and hopeful motherhood. Education was not usually part of the equation. Until the nineteenth century, royals were very often illiterate, as the early years of their schooling were continually undermined by court ritual and official functions which made study impossible. Russia's Empress Elizabeth, probably the most powerful woman on earth at the time, was unable to spell, considered reading bad for her health, and, although she was reasonably well informed about international affairs, went to her grave without ever being quite sure where England was.

King Louis XV understood nothing about money: when he heard that the workers were starving he sympathetically sacked eighty gardeners. The Bourbon Henry V never went anywhere without his valet because he had never bothered to learn how to tie his own cravat. The Italian-born wife of the Austrian Emperor Ferdinand V lived in Vienna for fifty years without picking up a single word of German. Italy's first king, Victor Emmanuel II, knew nothing of the Renaissance because he never opened a book in his entire life. On July 14, 1789, the day the *ancien régime* collapsed and the head of the Bastille's governor was paraded around Paris on a pikestaff, the dismal Louis XVI wrote in his diary the one word his grandfather always used when there was no hunting—"*Rien.*"

Royalty and scandal are as indivisible as plankton and the sea. The Austrians discovered royal kiss-and-tell stories more than a hundred years ago when the Emperor Franz Josef's niece negotiated the sale of intimate secrets about the Habsburgs, including the truth about the Emperor's adulterous relationship with an actress, and the Crown Prince Rudolf's suicide. The Emperor bought her silence, and the niece retired to voluntary exile in the United States on an annual pension of $25,000. King Edward VII's sister-in-law, Queen Alexandra's eighteen-year-old unmarried sister Thyra, became pregnant in 1871 by a Danish army officer. The princess was hidden away in a castle in Rumpenheim and not allowed to see the baby, which was handed over to a laundry maid. Two months later, after a couple of abrupt interchanges with the Princess's father, King Christian IX, the child's father shot himself. When Nicholas III of Este, Marquis of Ferrara, was informed that his young wife was intimately involved with his eldest son, he had them immediately beheaded before asking for proof.

History is as much about the folly and madness of men as it is about underlying social events. When a system is built around people with dangerously flawed personalities, it is entirely appropriate to look at those personalities. The Germans, for example, created an administrative, industrial and military machine of awesome efficiency, in which the kaiser himself was the loose cog. It would be pointless to discuss the rise of Russia as a modern power without referring back to the drink-sodden and murderous Peter the Great. No serious study of the origins of World War I could be complete without an understanding of the personal inadequacies of the men Churchill called "those stupid kings and emperors."

This book is an anecdotal and irreverent exposé of the last three centuries of Europe's most dysfunctional dynasties, from the reigns of Queen Anne in England, Peter the Great in Russia and Louis XIV in France. It may help to explain why most continentals can't get enough of royalty, provided it isn't their own.

1. LIE BACK AND THINK OF BELGIUM

The Perils of Royal Marriage

WHEN IDI AMIN became President of Uganda in 1971 after a military coup, the Western world was slow to react, believing him to be a harmless, posturing buffoon. It didn't dawn on the international community that he was also dangerously insane until, in the interests of better diplomatic relations with Britain, he volunteered to marry Princess Anne.

Royal fairy tales are brittle to the touch, especially alliances between blue bloods and the ordinary red variety. Until relatively recent times, few people lost much sleep over whether or not their royals were happily married. The success or otherwise of all royal marriages was measured solely by the participants' ability to produce a healthy heir. Until that first great organized cull of European royalty, World War I, for centuries it was more or less taken for granted that royal marriages were dynastic arrangements designed to test the strongest of stomachs.

When King George III went mad it was suggested that his condition may have been brought on by the trauma of having sexual relations with his exceptionally ugly German wife. Kings and queens went to bed together not as man and wife, but as country with country. Princesses were culture flasks for royal DNA: heir-producing material, served up as sacrifices to complete strangers as a matter of foreign policy, sentenced to a lifetime of massive privilege and marital misery in equal measure. Marriage for love outside royalty was forbidden. A Saxe-Weimar princess, told by her family that she couldn't possibly marry a Jewish banker, shot herself.

FRENCH DELIGHTS

The Bourbon kings of France, as members of the most powerful family in Europe, were forced to endure some of the most dreadful royal marriages of all. The Sun King, Louis XIV, ruled with powers given to him directly from God, but his marriage to the last available sane member of the Spanish royal family was not made in heaven. When he made his vows to Princess Maria Theresa at the Saint Jean-de-Luz near the Spanish border, it was the first time he had ever seen her, and he found her to be obese, dwarfish and almost hidden beneath a forty-foot train of blue velvet. He nevertheless alarmed her by insisting on consummating the marriage that evening. Indeed, although the King was consistently unfaithful to his wife, he made a point of spending at least part of every night in her bed, apparently to keep a promise he had made to his mother. Maria Theresa consoled herself by stuffing her face round the clock with chocolate and garlic sauces. At the age of forty-five, her health impaired by a vitamin-free diet and seven pregnancies, she was bled to death by her enthusiastically incompetent physicians.

Even the ugliest of princesses, who if not for their status would have remained permanently on the shelf, became queens. Princess Agnes of Hesse took ugliness to the extreme—she was lame and hunchbacked—but was widely regarded as the wealthiest catch of all the German princesses of her day. Royal betrothals were a hazardous business, especially as princes were routinely expected to select their life partners without ever having met them in the flesh. Usually a trusted courtier would be sent to view the prospective bride and report back on any obvious defects in character or physical appearance. It was the courtier's first impressions that could either make or break the engagement—some courtiers were blessed with more reliable critical faculties than others.

Louis XIV's son and heir, Louis the Grand Dauphin, inherited more than his fair share of the family eccentricity and could have been even stranger had he lived longer (his Habsburg maternal grandfather, Philip IV of Spain, didn't develop a taste for human breast milk until well into his dotage). The bride selected for the Grand Dauphin by his father was a Bavarian princess, Marie Anne Victoire. Although Marie Anne was perfectly eligible and had all the right bloodlines, the King, recalling perhaps the shock of his own engagement, attempted to spare his son any similarly nasty surprises by sending his ambassador, Croissy, to Germany to get a sneak preview of the prospective daughter-in-law. Croissy filed an ambiguous report. His general impression was favorable: the princess didn't have any obvious enormous physical deformities, he noted, apart from brown stains on her forehead, sallow skin, red hands, rotten teeth and a very large, fat nose. The King dispatched a portrait artist to Munich with instructions that he was to paint a truthful, warts-and-all likeness of Marie Anne. When the portrait reached Versailles, the entire French royal family gathered to pass judgment on it. After much debate, Marie Anne was given the thumbs-up.

The painting, however, was also accompanied by a note from Croissy which hinted that in his opinion the likeness was outrageously flattering. Croissy drew attention in particular to the artist's creative interpretation of her nose. Although negotiations were now at an advanced and delicate stage, the King of France was prepared to abort the engagement there and then. His son would hear none of it. The Dauphin considered ugly women erotic—the uglier the better. The more he heard about Princess Marie Anne, the more excited he became.

When Marie Anne was summoned to Versailles it became obvious that Croissy had not exaggerated, especially the bit about the nose. The Grand Dauphin, however, was more than satisfied with his new bride. Louis XIV let it be known that his new daughter-in-law was to be admired: her nose was never mentioned again. Marie Anne and the Grand Dauphin were married and had three children. When Marie Anne died, at barely thirty years old, Louis took up with her ugliest lady-in-waiting, Mademoiselle de Choin, a huge woman well known for her large mouth, her pendulous breasts, but especially for her huge nose.

Over a century later, Louis XVI's hideously bloated younger brother assumed the title of Louis XVIII after the Revolution and tuberculosis had combined to make him next in line to the French throne. At the age of fifteen he was compelled to marry the none-too-fragrant Maria Guiseppina of Savoy, daughter of the King of Sardinia. Maria was small, dark, ugly, and a complete stranger to personal hygiene. The bridegroom's grandfather, Louis XV, had to beg her parents, the King and Queen of Sardinia, to persuade her to wash her neck and clean her teeth. Her favorite hobby was catching thrushes in nets and having them made into soup. As Louis XVIII was homosexual, impotent and preoccupied with the consumption of food to the exclusion of almost everything else, their bedrooms occupied separate floors.

The last French Bourbon king, Charles X, didn't fare much better than either of his elder brothers. He was married at sixteen to a Sardinian princess, Maria Theresa, daughter of King Victor Amadeus III. The bride was a vacant-looking dwarf with a very long nose. Charles's sense of duty overcame his repugnance just often enough for them to have two sons, and two daughters who died in infancy.

FAT MARY

Although even the homeliest of royal princesses were never usually short of willing suitors, Queen Elizabeth II's great-grandmother, Princess Mary Adelaide of Teck, rewrote the rule book. She was born in 1833, the daughter of George III's seventh son, Adolphus Duke of Cambridge, and known as Fat Mary—on the face of it an unnecessarily cruel nickname to inflict on a young girl, but conferred in these circumstances with some understatement. She was extremely short and weighed about 252 pounds. Her favorite pastimes were gluttony and dancing, the two combining with often dangerous results. She would thrash about on a crowded dance floor, squashing any unfortunate prince who got in her way. She alone could turn a quadrille into something not unlike a football-stadium disaster. Fortunately, Mary was not the sensitive type, and was bumptiously oblivious of the stares and sniggers that followed her everywhere she went. When she and Queen Victoria met in 1866, Mary had to be accommodated by two chairs. "Mary is looking older," Victoria bitched in her diary, "but not thinner."

Fat Mary's matrimonial prospects were understandably slim, a situation not helped by the attitude of her absurdly hard-to-please parents, who went about applying criteria for possible suitors as though their daughter was a supermodel. One of the more realistic candidates was Louis Napoleon III's obese cousin, "Plon-Plon." Victoria's consort, Prince Albert, vetoed the love match when it became apparent that Plon-Plon was so dissolute that even the French, immunized by centuries of repellent royals, found him disgusting. Prince Oscar of Sweden was a hot favorite for a while, but his thoughts quickly turned to the first train home just as soon as he saw her. The British Foreign Minister of the day, Lord Clarendon, wondered whether any foreign prince in his right mind would be up to "so vast an undertaking."

By the time Fat Mary had reached her early thirties and almost resigned herself to spinsterhood, a husband was miraculously found in Franz, a prince of Teck. Franz's prospects in the royal-marriage stakes were poor because he was tainted by morganatic blood. His father, Duke Alexander of Württemburg, had forfeited his children's rights to the throne by marrying Claudine, a very beautiful but low-born Hungarian countess. Theirs was a blissful arrangement, tragically and abruptly terminated when she was trampled to death by horses at a military review.

Franz's family was also relatively poverty-stricken, which

made his eligibility even more flawed. These problems, however, combined to make him ideal marriage fodder as far as Mary was concerned, whose parents' search for a son-in-law had long since passed through a slightly more realistic stage, gone on to a much more realistic phase, and had by now taken on an air of grim desperation. When a union was suggested to Franz, he eagerly agreed, much to the astonishment of everyone, especially those who knew about his taste for willowy blondes. It was, he thought, an end to his financial problems. He didn't find out until it was too late that Fat Mary was also broke.

Franz had plenty of time for bitter reflection on his marriage. After several years of living in his wife's shadow, his behavior became increasingly erratic, and his blood pressure soared higher as his wife's girth expanded. One morning in 1884, he woke up completely paralyzed down one side of his body and unable to speak. His wife diagnosed slight sunstroke and skipped off to a light five-course breakfast. Only after a great deal of persuasion by her doctors did she come round to accepting that her husband had suffered a stroke. From that day on, Franz's mental health deteriorated and, although his wife's cholesterol count ensured that he actually outlived her, he spent the remaining three years of his life in isolation guarded by medical attendants.

THE DRAGON OF THE RHINE

Emperor Wilhelm I and his wife, the Empress Augusta, were locked into Germany's most enduring and most turbulent royal marriage. In 1885 the Empress Augusta lost the use of her legs and was confined to a wheelchair. By this point, the Emperor hadn't seen her legs for forty-odd years.

Augusta, sometimes known as the "Dragon of the Rhine," was highly strung and said to be the most argumentative woman in Europe. She became more unpredictable as she grew older, occasionally making passes at her ladies-in-waiting and often disappearing for months on end. The Emperor and Empress shared a lifelong mutual loathing and it was said that barely a single day of their marriage, which lasted nearly sixty years, passed without a fearful row. On their days off, they simply refused to speak to each other and conducted their arguments via a third party. If Augusta addressed the Emperor, even though he was directly in front of her, he would ignore her and ask some nearby aide to repeat what she'd said. Wilhelm did not even bother to inform his wife when he became Emperor: she got to hear about it from one of her black footmen.

The Empress, once envied for her perfect cheekbones and porcelain skin, was reluctant to acknowledge that the passage of time had long since relieved her of both assets. In old age she invested in vast quantities of industrial-strength cosmetics, with results that became increasingly difficult for squeamish visitors to behold, and a personal wig collection which was considered in some quarters to be the eighth wonder of the world.

The aged Augusta lived on and on, one part human and three parts makeup. No one was quite sure what kept her going. Immobilized by infirmity and the weight of her wig, she occasionally gave out signs that she was still alive by trembling with the palsy. In 1887 the invalid Augusta was wheeled out to break the ice at her husband's ninetieth birthday, looking, according to one of the lucky partygoers, "like someone dug up from the dead . . . something of a skeleton and something of a witch." The only visible parts of her body, her hands, head and shoulders, were so thickly encrusted in white enamel that when she moved some guests thought they were looking at an automaton, presumably one of the Emperor's birthday presents.

Later that year, when the Empress became seriously ill, Wilhelm became visibly upset. A puzzled visitor asked one of the Emperor's aides why this should be so: after all, the constant rancor between the two was common knowledge. "Wait till you have been married for fifty years and have quarreled with your wife every day," explained the aide, "and then, when you are faced with the alternative of this habit coming to an end, you will be unhappy too." Augusta finally expired from influenza in 1890 aged seventy-eight, outliving her husband by nine months.

HANOVERIAN VENGEANCE

Divorces within any social group in the eighteenth century were extremely rare everywhere in Europe. In Britain, divorce required an Act of Parliament, although it was impossible for a woman to sue for divorce because a man's adultery was not considered sufficient grounds. There is, however, nothing in the British constitution to prevent a divorcé from becoming king, or a king from becoming a divorcé—the Church of England was invented as a convenience by Henry VIII to allow his successors to do precisely that.

When the middle-aged King George I arrived from Hanover to claim the British throne, his new subjects couldn't help noticing that he hadn't brought his wife with him. In fact, George had discovered that, while he was in bed with his mother's lady-in-waiting, his wife, Sophia, was secretly sleeping with a Swedish count, Philip Cristoph von Konigsmarck, behind his back. She even had the bad taste to write letters to her lover that made unfavorable comparisons about George's performance in bed. George intercepted and read some of the letters, including one which mentioned that Sophia prayed nightly that her fat husband would die in battle. He divorced her in 1694 and had her locked up in a German castle, where she remained for the next thirty-two years—more than half her life.

Her paramour fared worse: years later his body was found chopped to pieces under her dressing room. It was strongly rumored that George was involved. The King never mentioned his wife's name again and his children were banned from discussing their mother or the divorce. When the King heard about his ex-wife's death, he went to watch a play, then set out to attend her burial with one of his mistresses in tow. He forbade anyone to mourn her or even acknowledge her death. It was never really made clear why he felt it necessary to be quite so vindictive toward his ex-wife, although it may simply have been that he wanted revenge because she had infected him with gonorrhea.

George IV's later attempts to divorce Caroline of Brunswick-Wolfenbüttel would have succeeded had his wife not been represented by such skillful lawyers. Prinny (as George was known) nearly fainted when he first clapped eyes on her, and after their wedding night they went their own separate ways, never once attempting to disguise their mutual hatred. When Napoleon Bonaparte died in 1821, a messenger rushed to inform the King, "Your Majesty, your greatest enemy is dead." George replied, "Is she, by God?"

Despite Prinny's problems, and compared to elsewhere in Europe, the British establishment's attitude to legal separation was relatively relaxed. Queen Victoria personally sanctioned the divorce of her granddaughter Princess Marie-Louise from Prince Aribert of Anhalt. For the rest of Europe's royal families, however, divorce was unattainable. When a Belgian princess attempted to break free from her brutal and perverted husband, she was confined to a sanatorium because her family were prepared to see her certified insane rather than contemplate the odium of royal divorce.

RUSSIAN ORTHODOXY

Until the eighteenth century, Russia used a unique method of securing the succession that did not rigidly exclude non-royals. The Czar's bride was selected from his country's most beautiful maidens, who were summoned to the Kremlin and subjected to *smotrinya*, an intimate internal and external examination which was a cross between a beauty pageant and a customs body search. Girls who didn't pass muster were one by one dumped outside the Kremlin gates.

The Russian royal family accepted adultery as a way of life, but their position on divorce was more orthodox. Nicholas II's mother, the Dowager Empress Dagmar, considered that the death of a close relative was infinitely preferable to the disgrace of legal separation. Her daughter the Grand Duchess Olga was forced into a marriage of convenience with the homosexual Prince Peter of Oldenburg. When she was twenty-two, the Grand Duchess met a Russian army officer, Nicholas Koulikovsky, and they began a passionate and indiscreet affair.

Her husband was not in the least bothered about his wife's infidelity. The one thing that he would never agree to, however, was divorce, because it would blacken the family name. Prince Peter had another suggestion: why didn't his wife's boyfriend move in and live with them? Thus, with the consent of all parties, a *ménage à trois* was established in the royal household. The fact that two men, one a homosexual, were now cohabiting with a Russian grand duchess was thought to be considerably less scandalous than legal separation.

The Romanovs' idea of a real scandal involved the Czar's brother Michael, who shocked his family by living with his twice-divorced mistress. When Michael later revealed that he had secretly married her, the Russian royal family were mortified. The Dowager Empress prayed that news of the marriage would never get out or she would never be able to show her face in public again.

Czar Peter the Great found his own way round the problem of divorce. When he became bored with his first wife, Eudoxia, he simply had her shut away in a convent: thus at the age of twenty-six the Czarina became Sister Helen, a penniless nun. Although they were never legally separated, the Czar reasoned that, since his discarded spouse was now a "bride of Christ," she couldn't be the Czar's wife as well and he was therefore quite free to remarry. For Peter this extraordinary leap of logic was the perfect solution to his marital problem and no one was prepared to argue any differently.

The Czar's plan, however, was not designed to work in anyone else's favor, as his first wife was to discover later. After eighteen years in the convent, Eudoxia, over forty years old and a little worse for wear and tear after braving several Russian winters in a spartan convent cell, fell in love with an army captain by the name of Stepan Glebov. He took pity on her and brought her furs to make her cell a little warmer. Eudoxia, still technically a bride of Christ, albeit a reluctant conscript, became Glebov's lover. They made no attempt to conceal their affair in the convent and Eudoxia bribed the other nuns to make themselves scarce while they copulated in her cell. Glebov thought that sleeping with an ex-czarina, even a toothless and arthritic ex-czarina, would not do his career prospects any harm at all. He couldn't have been more horribly mistaken.

Peter the Great heard of the affair and achieved the sort of U-turn that only a psychopathic six-foot-five-inch czar could get away with. He announced that, even though he hadn't clapped eyes on Eudoxia for eighteen years and had himself long since remarried, she had never legally ceased to be his wife, and her boyfriend was therefore guilty of adultery. To hammer the point home, the next day at precisely 3 P.M. a wooden stake was driven into Glebov's rectum. He lingered on in agony until the evening of the following day. Eudoxia escaped relatively lightly: she was ordered to be whipped by monks in front of the other nuns, then shipped off to an even more remote convent.

LESSONS IN LOVE

The business of royal procreation was far too important to be left to chance, and sex education for the male line was mandatory. The boyhood sexual experiences of the kings of France were documented in the minutest of detail. We know from the records of the French court physician, Monsieur Hérouard, that the young Louis XIII groped his governess in bed and showed off erections "which went up and down like a drawbridge." Louis was married at fourteen and placed in bed with his wife by his mother, to whom he returned an hour later "with his cock all red."

King George I's parents found a mistress for him when he was just sixteen years old, as was the royal custom of the day.

She was five years older, relatively disease free, and could be relied upon to go quietly when it was time for the Prince to get married. For the Austrian Emperor Franz Josef, court ritual in the Hofburg was so restrictive that there was no possibility of his ever going out to find a girl of his own. When he was eighteen, his mother arranged for his "official instructor" to go out and select a healthy-looking Bohemian peasant girl for Franz to practice on. A deal was struck with the girl's parents—she was to be married to a minor court official and would receive a large dowry if she would go to bed with the young Prince. The event was carefully stage-managed to give Franz Josef the impression that he had met the girl by chance and seduced her. We don't know whether he ever got to find out about his mother's deception, although many years later he had a chance meeting with her at a court function but wasn't allowed to speak to her.

The formal sex education of Franz Josef's son was different but no less extraordinary. In 1871 the thirteen-year-old Austrian Crown Prince Rudolf was taken by his tutor and two doctors to a fish-breeding farm in Salzburg, whereupon they explained to him the facts of life. When he was seventeen, the task of initiating the Crown Prince was entrusted to a close friend of his father, Captain Karl Karnauer, who made discreet arrangements with the owner of a Viennese brothel to introduce him to a carefully selected, healthy young girl. Rudolf would have found this highly amusing. What the Emperor Franz Josef and Captain Karnauer didn't know but half the women of Vienna did was that the Crown Prince's virginity was already ancient history.

Princesses rarely received any such instruction in the mysteries of sex. The second Queen of Belgium, a former Habsburg Archduchess, Marie Henrietta, had the misfortune of marrying one of the nineteenth century's most debauched monarchs, and went to bed with him for the first time without any idea of what might be expected of her. "If God hears my prayers," she confided to a friend after her wedding night, "I shall not go on living much longer."

It might have been expected that Marie Henrietta would pass on the benefit of her experience to her two daughters, but the Queen neither explained the facts of life to the two Belgian Princesses nor did anything else to prepare them for the loss of their virginity. The eldest daughter, Louise, was betrothed at the age of seventeen to the voluptuary Prince Philip of Saxe-Coburg, fourteen years her senior and the owner of one of central Europe's biggest collections of pornography. Louise went to her wedding bed armed only with instructions to submit to her husband's wishes. Her husband's wishes turned out to be such a shock to her that when he got up in the night to use the lavatory she threw a coat over her nightgown, fled downstairs, then dashed outside and hid in one of the palace greenhouses. A palace sentry found her cowering behind some shrubbery at dawn and led her back to bed.

In 1898 a nineteen-year-old German royal, Duchess Marie of Mecklenburg, became pregnant by the footman whose job it was to bring a night lamp into her bedroom. Her parents, after allowing their daughter to reach this age in complete ignorance of the facts of life, kicked her out of the castle. The scandal touched most of northern Europe's royal families because most of them were related. The concept of a royal princess consenting to sleep with a footman was quite beyond the British royal family: Queen Victoria said the girl must have been drugged with chloroform; the Duke of York's explanation was that she must have been hypnotized.

CATHERINE THE GREAT

Catherine the Great had about as much say in her choice of husband as most princesses did in the eighteenth century. At the age of fourteen she was summoned to St. Petersburg and informed that she had been selected to wed the heir to the Russian throne, the Empress Elizabeth's nephew, Grand Duke Peter, a short and profoundly ugly German teenager said to closely resemble a monkey. Catherine found him so repulsive that the mere thought of spending her life with him made her feel physically sick, but she was ambitious enough to keep her thoughts, and her last meal, to herself. During their engagement, Peter fell ill twice, first with measles, and later with smallpox. When it was safe for Catherine to meet him again, she found two sunken eyes staring at her from his skull-like and hideously scarred face. Most of his hair had fallen out and, as what little remained had been shaved off, he sported a large, ill-fitting wig that made him look even more deformed. Catherine congratulated him on his recovery, then went away and fainted.

When the royal couple married, she was sixteen years old and Peter barely a year older. She had no idea of the basic differences between males and females. Catherine consulted her ladies-in-waiting for advice. Amazingly, although the sole topic of conversation was gossip about the routine adultery in the Russian court, not one of them had the faintest idea what sexual intercourse involved either. None the wiser, Catherine decided to ask her mother, who quickly gave her a smack round the ear for asking such disgusting questions.

Catherine need not have worried. On the night of the wedding, she retired to their nuptial suite in wide-eyed ignorance of what might follow, dreading Peter's arrival. Hours later, her new husband crashed into bed dead drunk and lay corpse-like beside her.

In fact, the Grand Duke Peter found his collection of toys a much bigger attraction than his wife, preferring to play with his wooden soldiers, miniature cannons and toy fortresses under the bedclothes. While Peter fought battles under the sheets, imitating the sound of blazing cannons, his virgin wife, owner of the most hyperactive libido in the known world, lay motionless beside him. Later, Peter took to rearing hunting dogs in his bedroom, and soon Catherine found herself sharing their bed with ten spaniels.

Peter was incapable of sexual intercourse because he, like the young Louis XVI, suffered from phimosis. A simple circumcision would have corrected the problem, but the cowardly Grand Duke decided that celibacy was a much more attractive proposition. After years of sexless marriage, one day he drank himself into oblivion and finally consented to go under the surgeon's scalpel. The operation passed off without a hitch, but, to test that everything was in full working order, the Empress Elizabeth decided to organize a "trial run" for her nephew. A volunteer was found in the form of a poor widow, one Madame Groot, who duly allowed herself to be defiled by the ugly Romanov in anticipation of a large reward from the Empress. In fact she received not one single ruble. Ten years too late, Peter finally fulfilled his obligation and slept with his wife. It was an ordeal for both parties, especially for Catherine, who by this time was quite heavily pregnant by her lover, Serge Saltykov. Nevertheless, she had little trouble convincing her stupid husband that he was taking her virginity. This was the only time that Catherine and Peter had any sort of conjugal relationship. It is little wonder that she later opted for strangulation rather than marriage guidance.

HANOVERIAN LOVE MATCHES

Love or even affection within British royal marriages was an irrelevance. Royals didn't marry for companionship or even to start a family: all they required was one healthy offspring to occupy the throne, and the circle was closed. The Queen's uncle, Edward VIII, was the first British king of his dynasty to marry for love, and he lost his crown and was more or less punished with exile abroad because of it. Foreign princesses, usually German, were routinely exported to Britain as breeding stock to secure the continuity of the British royal family. It was a mechanical and impersonal business.

When it was time for George I's eldest son to get married, the King insisted on making sure that his son's fiancée, Caroline of Anspach, was as chaste as she claimed to be by personally giving her a physical examination. Precisely what the Princess thought about having her prospective father-in-law, the King of England, look up her skirts is not on record, which is a pity because by all accounts she swore like a trouper.

Years later, George II grew to hate his eldest son, Frederick the Prince of Wales—"Griff" as he was known to his family, or "Poor Fred" as he was to be known to posterity thanks to a sour Jacobite jingle that celebrated his premature death. The

King disliked his son so much he had even considered passing him over for his younger brother, whose gratuitous savagery in putting down the Jacobites had earned him the name "Butcher" Cumberland.

However, in 1734 the Prince of Wales asked his father for an increase in his income and a suitable marriage. The first request was completely ignored; the second met with the offer of Charlotte, a Danish princess who was both deformed and mentally backward. The King terminated the marriage negotiations, re-marking, "I did not think that grafting my half-witted coxcomb upon a madwoman would improve the breed." The search was widened until the King's eye fell on a miniature portrait displaying the smallpox-scarred features of Princess Augusta of Saxe-Gotha.

The seventeen-year-old Princess Augusta arrived in London in April 1736 in a state of sheer terror at the prospect of marrying into a family in which sons constantly quarreled with parents while the fathers introduced themselves to their prospective daughters-in-law by peering inside their panties. She wasn't even allowed time to get used to her surroundings since the wedding was arranged for that very evening. She was crammed into her wedding dress and marched off to the altar, where, literally sick with fear, she threw up over the Queen's skirt. The Prince of Wales set himself up for his honeymoon nuptials by downing several plates of jelly, which he believed to be an aphrodisiac, and retired to bed wearing an outlandish nightcap that resembled a guardsman's beaverskin.

When George II decided it was time to marry off his fat and desperate eldest daughter, Anne, the husband he chose for her was Prince William of Orange. The Dutch Prince was ex-tremely short and almost a hunchback. Lord Hervey wrote: "The Prince of Orange's figure, besides his being almost a dwarf, was as much deformed as it was possible for a human creature to be . . . his breath was more offensive than it is possible for those who have not been offended by it to imagine."

Prince William arrived in London in 1733 for his wedding, but immediately fell ill with pneumonia and was packed off to sample the recuperative waters at Bath. The Princess Royal's parents, now that they had met their prospective son-in-law for the first time in the flesh, were so shocked by what they saw that they quietly offered her the chance to withdraw. The stubborn Princess, however, had fallen in love with the idea of being married at last, and announced that she would marry a baboon if she had to. "Well then," replied her father, "there is baboon enough for you."

The big day took place five months later than originally scheduled, on March 25, 1734. At this time the royal family still observed the cruel ritual of public "bedding," and the wedding night was open to court spectators as usual. The King contrived to have his malformed son-in-law hidden behind a curtain with only the Princess in view, but his pathetic appearance in an oversized nightshirt drew sniggers from their audience. Queen Caroline said she pitied her daughter for having to go to bed with such a "monster." Lord Hervey reassured her that in time the Princess would get used to the idea. The Queen replied smartly, "I believe one does grow blind at last, but you must allow, my dear Lord Hervey, there is a great difference, as long as one sees, in the manner of one's growing blind."

BRITISH BIGAMY

A high proportion of the British royal family were alleged bigamists. The allegation persists to this day that George III secretly married a Quaker daughter named Hannah Lightfoot at Curzon Street Chapel, Mayfair, in 1759, and that they had a son, also named George, and the rightful heir to the throne. This story ran throughout the King's reign and threw up another popular madness theory: according to this version, the King's condition was repressed guilt for having dumped Miss Lightfoot.

George IV entered into a bigamous relationship with Princess Caroline of Brunswick-Wolfenbüttel while already married to Maria Fitzherbert—as she was a two-times divorcée, a Roman Catholic and a commoner, this marriage was conveniently ignored, although as far as the Church of England was concerned it was valid. It was similarly alleged that when William IV was a serving officer in the Royal Navy he secretly married one Caroline von Linsingen, the daughter of a Hanoverian infantry commander, in a chapel near Pyrmont.

It is highly likely that Queen Victoria's parents also had a bigamous relationship. While her father, the Duke of Kent, was stationed in the army at Quebec he may have secretly married a French-Canadian prostitute named Julie de St. Laurent. This was a charge that the royal family strenuously denied, although they accept that he lived with her for twenty-seven years. George V's reign was dogged by a persistent rumor that he had married the daughter of a British naval officer in Malta, and had several children.

WHY WASTE A GOOD WIFE?

Indeed, the British royal mating game arguably reached an all-time cynical low with the marriage of George V and his consort,

Queen Mary. George's elder brother and heir to the throne, the bisexual Duke of Clarence, or Eddie as he was known to his parents, was simple-minded, effete, and so prone to scandal wherever he went that he was even thought to be Jack the Ripper. Apart from his homosexual liaisons, there was also evidence of an illegitimate child born to a London girl at St. Stephen's Hospital, Fulham. The family's time-honored solution to this sort of embarrassment was a quick arranged marriage to some sensible princess who might create an appearance of normality and kill some of the rumors about his private life.

The first name considered as a possible bride was Crown Princess Margaret of Prussia, but she was dropped when Queen Victoria admitted that the Crown Princess was "not regularly pretty." In the context of royal doublespeak it is safe to assume that she was grotesque. Prince Eddie announced a preference for Hélène, daughter of the Comte de Paris, who was grandson of King Louis Philippe and Pretender to the French throne. Hélène's mother was an extraordinary woman who smoked a pipe and strode around the house with a riding crop which she used to thrash her servants. Her family, however, were Catholics, and Eddie was bound by a British Constitution which forbids Catholic monarchs.

After a few more unsuccessful sorties into the European marriage market they finally found someone else who would take him on—his cousin Princess Mary of Teck, the daughter of "Fat Mary" Adelaide. The Teck family, tainted by the dead hand of non-royal blood, were not in a position to turn down any reasonable offer of a royal marriage. Although Mary must have been aware of his reputation, he was after all heir to Europe's greatest throne and it is likely that Princess Mary would have bitten his matrimonial hand off even if he had been

Jack the Ripper. Shortly before the wedding, however, six days after the Duke of Clarence's twenty-eighth birthday, he developed inflammation of the lungs after a shooting party and was suddenly dead. The preparations for his wedding were deftly switched to funeral arrangements.

The British royal family then made an extraordinary decision. If Eddie's younger brother George was to take over his brother's role as heir to the throne, he might as well take his wife as well. George had no say in the matter. The only woman he really wanted to marry, Princess Marie of Romania, had already turned him down. Within weeks of the funeral, the family were matchmaking Prince George with his dead brother's fiancée. Mary never mentioned Prince Eddie in public again: it was as though he had never existed. After the wedding celebrations, Prince George displayed the full extent of his lack of imagination, tact and sensitivity when he chose as his honeymoon venue York Cottage, Sandringham, the very spot where his brother had expired eighteen months earlier, and which still housed all of his personal belongings including his clothes. Queen Victoria noted that the choice of honeymoon was "rather unlucky."

2. *REX NOSTER INSANIT*:
OUR KING IS INSANE

IN MARCH 1801 the sick and confused King George III was laced into a straitjacket and led away by his medical attendants to confinement at Kew Palace. Meanwhile, nearly a thousand miles away in Lisbon, the Queen of Portugal, Maria I, sat on her throne dressed in children's clothing, deranged and raving. In Vienna, the Austro-Hungarian monarch Francis II, head of the mightiest empire in central Europe, observed his cabbage-like son and heir Prince Ferdinand, a six-year-old epileptic born with a hydrocephalic head. In Madrid, the vacuous King Charles IV ruled Spain by default because his violently disturbed elder brother Philip had been declared insane and removed from the line of succession. In St. Petersburg, the psychotic Russian Emperor Paul I threw his dinner around the room for the fun of watching his servants scrape it up after him. Eight hundred miles to the west in Copenhagen, the King of

Denmark, Christian VII, ran around his palace smashing furniture and bashing his head against the walls until he drew blood. It was not a good year to argue the case for hereditary monarchy.

Whenever historians talk about "mad" kings they nearly always run into problems. "Madness" is not an exact medical term: it is a general description applied by laymen to any condition that results in profoundly aberrant or irrational behavior. Mental disorders can have a variety of causes, including physical damage or disease. Encephalitis lethargica, for example, is an acute infectious disease of the central nervous system which can result in mental illness. At least one Habsburg Emperor, Ferdinand I, suffered from it; Czar Peter the Great probably did too. The symptoms of encephalitis—hallucinations, headaches, violent antisocial behavior and insomnia—are unfortunately so very similar to schizophrenia that retrospective diagnosis can be very tendentious. Another problem for historians is that by definition royalty is an occupation in which eccentric or anomalous behavior occurs naturally, making the line between genuine madness and "normal" royal behavior a very thin one.

THE MADNESS OF KING GEORGE

One gentleman for whom 1801 was a particularly good year was the Reverend Francis Willis, rector of the parish of Wapping. Willis was born the son of a clergyman and became the vicar of Gretford, where he opened a private lunatic asylum. It was quite common in eighteenth-century England for this type of establishment to be run by churchmen who wanted to supplement their income. Occasionally the treatment offered was relatively humane, but more often than not mental derangement was cured by restraint and punishment; the insane were broken, like horses. Willis belonged to the latter school. In time he became rector of St. John's, Wapping, but continued to run the provincial asylum, assisted by his son John, as a lucrative sideline. Over a period of twenty-eight years, the Willises acquired a reputation for running the best little madhouse in Lincolnshire.

On December 5, 1788, Francis Willis and his son John were summoned to Windsor Castle. King George III, they were informed, had taken temporary leave of his senses and required their services. For the Willises it was the beginning of an astonishing career as quacks by appointment to the crowned basket cases of Europe.

After that of Queen Victoria, the reign of George III was the longest of any English king or queen. His reign was full of ironies. The greatest irony was that the only reasonably dignified monarch the House of Hanover ever produced is mostly remembered as the mad king who lost his American colonies and later his marbles. In fact, he was just about the only male member of the British royal family who wasn't reviled by his subjects. Unlike other members of his dynasty, he didn't take hordes of mistresses or waste vast amounts of public money on personal extravagances. He ate and drank little and even took exercise when he could because he didn't want to become freakishly obese like many of his close relatives. He was quite diligent in fulfilling his royal duties, and was still writing his own official and private correspondence until he was sixty-seven without any help.

Uniquely for a Hanoverian monarch, he was a likable man who was at ease chatting freely with commoners. Dr. Johnson met him and was impressed: "Sir, they may talk of the King as they will, but he is the finest gentleman I have ever seen." It was said that if only George had visited America the colonials would never have risen against him. But George never traveled to America, or anywhere else for that matter. Beyond his holiday jaunts to Weybridge, he hardly traveled at all, never once setting foot in Wales, Scotland or Ireland, and in England never any farther north than Worcester.

Like most of the Hanoverians, George III was far from clever, but he was naturally inquisitive and loved to dabble. He was an unlikely patron of the arts and sciences. He founded the Royal Academy, yet had no taste in art. He had little grasp of science, yet gave personal financial backing to the greatest astronomer of the age, William Herschel. He was certainly no scholar, believing Shakespeare to be "sad stuff," yet he amassed the greatest book collection of the day, now the King's Library in the British Museum. He also had a fairly enlightened attitude toward medicine and the treatment of the mentally ill. It is again ironic that in his later years he should have suffered so horribly at the hands of medical ignorance.

George III was not the first mentally unbalanced British monarch. King John was a deeply disturbed individual, probably the victim of a psychological disorder, according to a contemporary report "sent mad by sorcery and witchcraft." Richard II's most recent biographer believes that he showed signs of incipient madness consistent with schizophrenia. Henry VI suffered a complete mental breakdown and was evidently insane for the latter part of his reign. Henry VIII suffered from a severe and progressive personality disorder, possibly the result of brain damage, either from a severe blow to the head or tertiary syphilis.

Historians still do not agree on the cause of King George III's illness, or how many bouts of madness he had. There were at least four, and possibly six, periods throughout his reign during which he was apparently mentally unbalanced. He may have had a couple of early minor attacks in the 1760s which were kept secret by the court and passed off to the outside world as influenza. Even the Prime Minister didn't suspect that anything was wrong, and the King made a swift recovery on each occasion. The theory that these two early illnesses were connected with his later condition is disputed.

The King became seriously mentally unbalanced beyond doubt in 1788–89, then again in 1801, in 1804, and then permanently from 1810 until his death ten years later. In 1811 the King's physicians testified to Parliament that George III was irretrievably insane. By this time he was also seventy-three years old, stone-deaf, blind and almost certainly suffering from senile dementia.

The first serious attack of mental illness—and the events covered by the film *The Madness of King George*—began in 1788 and lasted just a few months. In June 1788 the King had what his doctor called "a smart bilious attack," and was sent to take the waters at Cheltenham. He returned to Windsor four weeks later apparently cured. Three months later, however, during the evening of October 17, the King fell ill with violent stomach cramps and complained of respiratory problems. His condition alarmed everyone who saw him. The veins in his face stood out; he became delirious and he foamed at the mouth. It is said that the King's old friends rallied around him with an astonishing display of loyalty by pretending to be mad themselves. The Duchess of Devonshire recorded in her diary: "The courtiers all affect to have been mad." The regular court physician, Dr. Baker, reported that the King's condition was deteriorating quickly. His speech became rapid and agitated, and he babbled feverishly and continuously. He became violent and abusive toward his family and his courtiers, and was generally "quite unlike his normal self." At one point he lapsed into a coma and appeared to be near death.

At first it was thought that the King was suffering from "flying gout"—the Georgian medical profession's stock-in-trade diagnosis for anything they couldn't explain, which covered pretty much everything. This mysterious affliction was thought to be relatively harmless unless one was unfortunate enough to get it in one's head. The King's flying gout, it was asserted, had originated in his feet but had traveled to his brain and become somehow stuck there. The answer was to apply blisters to the royal head to drive the gout back down again. When it became all too obvious that this was a painful waste of time, Dr. Baker administered large drafts of opium to his patient, but was otherwise completely baffled by the King's illness and at a complete loss what to do about it.

Six more doctors were called in to the King, none of them any wiser than the last, but each hoping to profit by finding a fluke cure for the royal affliction. They bickered among themselves, placed his head on a pillow made from a bag of warm hops, put leeches on his temples, gave him large doses of James's Powder to make him sweat, and stuck his feet in red-hot water to draw out the "humor." Sir William Fordyce was consulted on the strength of his well-known treatise, *Cultivating and Curing Rhubarb in Britain for Medical Uses*. Eventually the only thing that everyone could agree on was that the King was suffering from temporary insanity. Finally and very reluctantly, they agreed to stand aside and let a so-called expert on the

treatment of the mentally ill have a go. Enter the Willises of
Wapping.

Until the eighteenth century, madness had always been regarded as demonic possession. The in-vogue text on the subject
of madness, a book called *Anatomy of Melancholy* by Robert
Burton, had been published back in 1621. Burton taught that
madness was often caused by the retention of bodily excretions:
the best cure was to tie patients to a wall and literally beat the
crap out of them. Burton's work was soon to be usurped by the
crack French physician Jean Esquirol. Mental illness, explained
Monsieur Esquirol, was caused by a variety of conditions, including living in a new home, squeezing a pimple, old age,
childbirth, the menstrual cycle, a blow on the head, constipation, shrinkage of hemorrhoids, misuse of mercury, disappointment in love, political upheavals, shock, thwarted ambition,
excessive study, masturbation, prostitution, religion and bloodletting (the last item was particularly confusing to a medical
profession who had been brought up to believe that bloodletting was the best cure for everything, including insanity).
Doctors of the mad French king Charles VI tried to cure him
by trepanation—the sawing of small holes in his skull to relieve
pressure on his brain—and an early fifteenth-century version of
shock treatment, when ten men with blackened faces hid in the
King's room, then leapt out at him. Charles VI died completely
insane seventeen years later. Until the early twentieth century,
most English doctors were taught that much mental illness was
a result of large quantities of phlegm: the standard treatment
was to force the patient to throw up three or four times a day.

By King George III's day there had been a slight shift toward a more enlightened approach, and doctors were prepared
to recognize madness as a physical problem which was theoret-

ically open to treatment. Unfortunately, treatment had not kept pace with theory, and much of it still depended upon confinement and punishment. Many physicians continued to consider treatment of the mentally ill as beneath them and fit only for attendants. Basically, the medical treatment that George III received hadn't changed much in 200 years.

The Willises had at their disposal a complete, in-depth, contemporary understanding of how to treat the mentally ill. That is, they hadn't a clue either. Willis Senior confidently asserted that the King's illness was the result of "severe exercise, weighty business, severe abstemiousness and too little rest" and set about preparing his cure. The King, who had no idea what was coming to him, was at first quite relaxed about the arrival of Willis and in his lucid intervals was even able to joke with him about his treatment. "A parson and a doctor too?" the King enquired when he saw Willis's dog collar. "Our Savior, sir, went about healing the sick," replied Willis. "Yes, yes," said George, "but He didn't get seven hundred pounds a year for doing it." The King even dubbed the dreadful iron contraption which Willis forced him into every day his "new coronation chair."

Of course, if the official records of such events are to be taken seriously, royal patients are a lot braver and more courteous than the rest of us. After George IV had a sebaceous cyst removed from his head in 1821, entirely without the aid of any sort of anesthetic, he casually inquired of the surgeon, Astley Cooper, "So, what do you call these tumors?" Queen Victoria had a particularly nasty axillary abscess drained when she was fifty-one years old. When she came round from the chloroform, she is supposed to have opened her eyes and remarked, "A most unpleasant task, Professor Lister, most pleasantly performed." The price of failure for a royal medic, however, has always been high, as demonstrated by Bohemia's blind King John. When his surgeons failed to restore his eyesight he had all of them drowned in the Danube.

The royal knockabout banter didn't last. The Willises' state-of-the-art equipment for the treatment of mental illness comprised a straitjacket, iron clamps, a chair and a length of rope. Additional treatment was in accordance with conventional guidelines: frequent bleedings, forced vomiting, a starvation diet, salivations, and afterward a cold bath. To divert "morbid humors" from the King's head they applied blisters— various types of irritants—to the skin on his legs. These humors were supposed to be drawn through the serum of the blisters and through the pus that formed as they became infected, thus creating running sores that lasted for weeks. For the final eight years of the King's life, his medical bill was a staggering £271,000.

The King soon learned to dread the Willises and their torture-chamber techniques. The regular court physicians observed with unintentional irony that they were nothing more than a couple of dangerous quacks, and not much saner than the people they locked up in Gretford. Doctors from all over the country flocked to denounce their methods and to offer their own equally useless remedies. Although the treatment the Willises offered was both shocking and brutal, they were only working to the standard theory and practice of the day, doing the best they knew how with the best techniques available to them. If they hadn't taken the King's money, someone else surely would have done.

This is the point at which King George III's reign starts to drown in myth. Many of the best-known stories about the King's outlandish behavior stem from a pamphlet published in 1789 by

Philip Withers, "History of the Royal Malady by a Page of the Presence." The document was full of false or greatly exaggerated anecdotes about the King's eccentricities which are still repeated to this day, including the one about how he was supposed to have shaken hands with an oak tree, having mistaken it for Frederick the Great. Many other eyewitness accounts of George's odd behavior were tainted by political prejudice. William Pitt's promonarchist friends tended to play down the King's problems and exaggerate his remissions. The opposing Whigs, on the other hand, found more than adequate proof that he was mad in just about everything George said or did.

In 1789, in spite of taking on the chin everything that enlightened medical science could offer him, the King's condition improved. In February he was able to walk arm in arm in Richmond Gardens with his wife, Queen Charlotte. The Lord Chancellor visited him and reported back to his Prime Minister that the King was completely recovered: "There was not," asserted the Chancellor confidently, "the least trace or appearance of disorder."

The Willises claimed full credit for this temporary remission. Parliament responded with a fit of generosity, striking official medals to celebrate and voting Willis Senior an annual pension of £1,000 and his son John £550 pounds for life. Reverend Willis meanwhile had some medals struck of his own for promotional purposes. On one side of the medallion there was a profile view of Willis, while the other bore the legend "Britons Rejoice Your King's Restored—1789." News of the Reverend Francis Willis's triumph spread all over Europe. It was received with particular interest in Lisbon at the court of the royal House of Braganza, home of the mad Queen Maria I.

In February 1801, King George III suffered a relapse. By this time, Willis Senior was over eighty years old and retired, and his son had taken over the family practice, but both Willises were brought in again. They advised that the King should be forcibly removed to Kew Palace for further treatment. Again the King lapsed into a coma and was thought to be dying. This, however, was a much briefer illness, and by March 4 he was well enough to receive his Prime Minister Pitt, and to attend a meeting of the Privy Council. In spite of his apparently complete recovery, the King's sanity could no longer be taken for granted, and the royal family lived in constant expectation of a relapse. The Willises were retained as permanent consultants to oversee his aftercare.

In January 1804 George III was again seized with a short attack. By this time the King had such a morbid dread of the Willises that it was recognized that their presence might be counterproductive and make him permanently mad. Samuel Foart Simmons, physician to St. Luke's Hospital for Lunatics, was appointed in their place. Unfortunately for the King, Dr. Simmons also favored a regimen that wouldn't have looked out of place in the Spanish Inquisition and was not appreciably any less ruthless than that of his predecessors. After a few more weeks of hell, however, the King was apparently well again.

The final attack came in October 1810, shortly after celebrations to mark the seventy-two-year-old King's golden jubilee. Simmons was recalled, and the old King was laced back into his royal straitjacket.

The strain of the King's illness took a dreadful toll on his wife, Queen Charlotte. When George first came to the throne in 1760 as an unmarried twenty-two-year-old, there was then, just as there would be now, great public interest and speculation surrounding his choice of partner. A small army of emissaries was dispatched abroad to assess marriage potential and report back, and George was invited to sample the obligatory short list of ugly, stupid, mad, loose and smallpox-scarred German princesses. A princess from Brandenburg was a front-runner for a while, but was rejected when it became known that her adulterous mother had been locked up as punishment for having an affair with a courtier. Princess Frederica of Saxe-Coburg was struck off the list because she was deformed and believed to be incapable of bearing children: she died a spinster aged thirty-five. The fifteen-year-old Princess Caroline of Hesse-Darmstadt was considered, but her chances of becoming Queen of England vanished when it emerged that her father, the Landgrave of Hesse-Darmstadt, was mad. Finally, George settled for his third cousin, the seventeen-year-old Princess Charlotte. Ironically, he made his choice because he dreaded the possibility of introducing mental instability to the blood-line.

None of the female members of the House of Hanover were noted for their good looks. Queen Charlotte, however, was by all accounts extremely ugly. Contemporary descriptions of her range from "plain" to "hideous." When the German Princess arrived in England to take her throne, Londoners greeted her with cries of "pug-face." Charlotte requested a translation, and was told that it meant "God bless Her Majesty." The King wisely chose his own wedding night to put an end to the British court ritual of "bedding," to spare her the indignity of being stared at by a crowd of smirking strangers. After she had been in England for some time, Horace Walpole paid her the nearest thing she was ever going to get to a compliment when he noted, "The bloom of her ugliness is beginning to wear off."

The King and Queen were out driving through a turnip field in an open carriage one day when George overturned it, smashing the Queen's nose. This accidental reworking of her features was noted to have been a significant improvement.

Whether there was a physical attraction or not, King George III and his wife bred like flies. In spite of her dainty build, the Queen was a tough woman who endured her fifteen pregnancies bravely, although she suffered frequently and horribly from postnatal depression. All but two of her children survived infancy. The first to die was Prince Alfred, who was a congenital invalid and survived less than two years. It was a sad comment on eighteenth-century child mortality that, according to a popular saying of the day, the Queen was not considered "a proper mother" until she had at least one dead child. Less than a year later, her three-year-old son Octavius was also dead, probably from the aftereffects of his smallpox vaccination—a dangerous procedure at that time.

While the rigors of almost continuous childbirths had destroyed her health, the King's mental illness broke Queen Charlotte's spirit. By the age of forty-four, her blond hair had turned white and she looked at least twenty years older. In middle age Charlotte was afflicted by attacks of erysipelas, causing her face to swell and turn an alarming shade of purple. Although she was naturally quite thin, by 1807 she had become so bloated that a courtier recorded that she looked as though she was carrying all fifteen children simultaneously.

Although the King and Queen—uniquely for a royal couple—had apparently enjoyed many long years of almost touching domesticity, the King's illnesses effectively ended their marriage. At first Queen Charlotte had been worried and a little embarrassed about her husband's condition, but in time her concern turned to sheer terror as his behavior became more unpredictable. During the day she made sure that she was never alone with the King, and at night she moved to a bedroom as far away from his as she possibly could and kept the door locked. This rejection made the King extremely upset and he became even more violent.

Queen Charlotte had every confidence in the Willises and was quietly relieved that she didn't have the responsibility of looking after her husband. She colluded with the so-called kidnapping of the King in April 1801 when the Willises had him tied up and taken to Kew. After his third illness of 1804, the King and Queen ceased to have anything to do with each other more or less permanently. Although he had always been known as the only monogamous member of his dynasty, the King's mental state played tricks with his libido. He propositioned one of his wife's ladies-in-waiting, Lady Elizabeth Pembroke, with love letters and obscene suggestions. Lady Pembroke was seventy years old at the time.

The King did not recover from this last attack of illness. In 1811, his physicians testified that his mental incapacity was irreversible. Dr. Richard Warren informed Parliament, "*Rex noster insanit*: our king is mad."

The old King spent the last eight or nine years of his life blind and deaf, alone in the north side of Windsor Castle. He lived in complete silence, white-haired and bearded, now and then picking at his harpsichord, or talking to dead friends, or occasionally indecently exposing himself to his servants.

THE THEORIES

Historians down the ages have offered their own verdicts on the King's condition, and madness theories have come in and out of fashion. The *London Chronicle* asserted that the King's problem "was owing solely to his drinking the waters of Cheltenham."

Nineteenth-century royal biographers attributed the King's mental illness to his failure to take a mistress. For more than 150 years after his death the most popular interpretation of events was that George III had a manic-depressive or schizophrenic personality which sometimes tipped him over the edge into complete mental breakdown. The strange and excitable letters he wrote as a young man to his mentor, Lord Bute, were cited as evidence of an unstable and neurotic character. As a young king he was highly strung and often prone to bouts of depression—twice he became so depressed that he considered abdicating. The loss of the American colonies was regarded by contemporaries as the greatest disaster in British history, and the King's reputation suffered accordingly on both sides of the Atlantic. Many believed—an old theory hinted at again in the 1994 film—that his trauma over the loss of his colonies may have been behind his first breakdown, although by the time of his first illness the war in America had been over for six years.

For many years the central participants in the debate over George III's mental state were two medical historians, Richard Hunter and Ida Macalpine. In the 1960s they published a retrospective diagnosis of the King's illness in a book called *George III and the Mad Business*. They argued that the King's condition was largely consistent with the characteristics of variegate porphyria, a hitherto obscure metabolic disorder which attacks the central nervous system. Symptoms of this disorder include delirium and hallucinations, paralysis, fits, stomach cramps, pains in the limbs and cataracts. The most persuasive evidence to support their argument could be found in the King's chamber pot. Porphyria takes its name from the brownish-purple porphyrins, not discovered in blood until more than half a century after George III's death, which are often passed in the victim's urine. The early medical notes on George III reported a discoloration of the King's urine on four occasions: once it was described as "bluish" and on another occasion as "bloody." Hunter and Macalpine concluded that George III was not clinically insane but was suffering from an inherited metabolic disorder.

Hunter and Macalpine went on to make a connection between George III's illness and similar physical problems encountered in previous royal invalids. In all, they found evidence of an inherited illness afflicting fifteen generations of the British royal family, traceable back to Mary Queen of Scots. If Hunter and Macalpine are correct, George III could blame his bad luck on the Stuarts, who transmitted the disease to the Hanoverians via James I's granddaughter (and George I's mother), the Electress of Hanover.

If the King suffered from porphyria it is reasonable to assume that he could have passed it on to some of his progeny. Hunter and Macalpine's medical detective work claims at least four of George III's sons as porphyria victims, including George IV, Augustus the Duke of Sussex, Frederick the Duke of York, and Queen Victoria's father, Edward the Duke of Kent. George IV's wife, Caroline of Brunswick, is also listed as a candidate for the disorder, as some aspects of her medical history were also consistent with porphyria. If the latter assumption is correct, porphyria was probably the only thing she ever had in common with her husband. Their only daughter, the tragic Princess Charlotte, would almost certainly have inherited it also, an extrapolation that could be applied to account for her mysterious death during childbirth.

The case for porphyria is tempting, but it is not now quite as fashionable as it was in the 1960s. For the historian, the crucial question must be to explain how porphyria, which supposedly existed in a relatively benign form for generations, should suddenly manifest itself in the third George with such devastating virulence.

Much more is now known about the disorder, which, although quite rare in Europe, occurs frequently in South Africa, and recent research exposes serious flaws in the porphyria theory. Temporary mental illness of the type displayed by George III is not a proven symptom of porphyria. Most cases in this century have been preceded by barbiturate abuse—a substance unheard of in George III's day. Even if temporary insanity was a characteristic of porphyria, this retrospective diagnosis runs into another serious problem. George III and his wife had fifteen children whose descendants went on to populate virtually every royal household in Europe. If the King had porphyria there can hardly have been a royal family in Europe that was not tainted by it. The South African model shows that there should have been a far greater concentration of porphyriacs in the British royal family, and a much greater distribution throughout the royal families of Europe. Widespread evidence of the illness would surely have been very easy to detect. Hunter and Macalpine's scholarly research turned up several royal invalids displaying some of the lesser symptoms of porphyria, including stomach cramps, cataracts, painful joints and the like, but these were common ailments which could have any number of simple explanations. Even the discoloration of the King's urine, the most important evidence underpinning Hunter and Macalpine's theory, could have been caused by overprescription of purgatives.

The precise nature of George III's illness is essentially unprovable, but it continues to be a talking point for medical historians and within the British royal family. The present heir to the throne, Prince Charles, who for obvious reasons doesn't favor any theory suggesting an inheritable disorder, metabolic or otherwise, was once persuaded to contribute the foreword to a biography of George III, and apparently believes that his predecessor's illness could have been caused by lead poisoning. Many historians, however, are now returning to the pre-1960s assessment that George III suffered from a psychiatric disorder, a condition which was aggravated by the bestial medical treatment meted out to him by the Willises and others.

Although the war with America was long over by the time of his illness, political stress could have been an important factor. The cumulative stress of a long and difficult reign could have brought about the onset of mental illness. Many of the King's symptoms were compatible with schizophrenic or manic-depressive mental illness. Schizophrenia is not always a permanent or a degenerative condition, and it can often lead to temporary remission or even complete recovery. Manic-depressive insanity can often reveal itself in incoherence and gastrointestinal problems. It is very likely that George III had a genetically flawed central nervous system which made him predisposed toward manic-depressive illness, and his incompetent doctors subjected the weakened King to so much pain and humiliation that they just broke his spirit and caused him to have a complete mental breakdown. His final illness at the age of seventy-three was in any event almost certainly senile dementia, a natural condition unconnected with his earlier attacks.

Whatever the cause of George III's illness, it was bad news for his family. The fear that the madness that afflicted the King might resurface was, in the words of Hunter and Macalpine, "a possibility which hung over them like the sword of Damocles."

Although George III's ghastly eldest son, "Prinny," could barely contain his glee at being proclaimed Regent, he nevertheless lived in permanent dread that his father's condition would strike him down too. In fact, every one of the seven sons secretly feared that they might also be tainted by hereditary mental illness. It was never mentioned in public, but the Prince of Wales's letters to his brothers show that they were all comparing notes about it and were arriving at their own conclusions.

Indeed, the subject of mental instability was undoubtedly a big conversation killer around the royal dining table at Windsor long before George's illness took hold, because the King had a brother-in-law who was evidently stark raving mad.

CHRISTIAN OF DENMARK

King Frederick V, ruler of Denmark from 1746 to 1766, was a vain and eccentric man who bizarrely had his portrait painted at least seventy times by the same artist, Carl Pilo. He was also a dedicated philanderer whose unfortunate lifestyle led to his premature death, aged forty-three, from the effects of syphilis and delirium tremens. It was in his dwarfish son Christian VII, however, that syphilis had the most marked effect.

For most of King Christian VII's long reign he was obviously insane, although for the best part of forty-two years the people of Denmark were completely unaware that they had a lunatic on the throne. Little was known of the King's mental condition outside royal circles, most Danes believing that their King's conspicuous aversion to public appearances was excused by the fact that he was being kept a prisoner and was being maltreated or drugged. Even when the full story broke years later, the Danish establishment put out an official version of the King's mental condition which avoided mention of either hereditary insanity or mental illness caused by syphilis. Danish history books taught that King Christian VII had simply become a little odd because he had been sexually abused by pageboys when he was a child.

Christian acquired a royal prince's taste for bad company, liquor and whores at a very early age. He demonstrated a keen intellect but was subject to extreme mood swings—a symptom often associated with dementia praecox or schizophrenia. He was extremely aggressive. At night he stalked the streets of Copenhagen with a gang of equerries, brandishing a spiked wooden club. He and his friends ran riot, often completely destroying shops and brothels. He also acquired a fascination for public executions, secretly watching dozens of them in disguise. Occasionally he would play at mock executions. He was a sadomasochist and had a rack made for himself, on which he lay while his friend Conrad Holcke beat him until he bled.

When he was only seventeen years old and already an alcoholic roué, Christian was betrothed to George III's sister, the fifteen-year-old Princess Caroline Matilda. Although she was a plain-looking girl, she charmed everyone who met her with her natural grace and innocence; everyone except her deranged husband that is, who treated her from the first with undisguised hostility by hanging her portrait in the royal lavatory. Caroline Matilda quickly found out about some of her husband's more loathsome habits, which according to the eminent Danish psychiatrist Christiansen included habitual overindulgence in masturbation, although not such complete overindulgence that he couldn't find energy to spend at least some of his time with his mistress or his boyfriends.

In 1768, soon after Caroline had done her duty by giving birth to a bouncing Crown Prince, the Danish King was required to make an official state visit to England and France—a tricky operation as Christian was already obviously losing his mind. King George III had heard all the stories about his brother-in-law and anticipated his visit with barely concealed dread. To the immense relief of all concerned, especially the Danish government, Christian behaved relatively normally: normally enough at least for both Oxford and Cambridge Universities to award him honorary degrees, and for him to be loudly cheered on the streets of London. In fact, during his visit Christian and his gang had conspicuously frequented a number of London brothels and wrecked the lodgings provided for them at St. James's Palace. From a Danish point of view, however, things could have been a lot worse.

For most of this foreign tour Christian had been accompanied by his traveling court doctor, a forty-year-old Prussian, Johann Friedrich Struensee. Dr. Struensee took a lot of the credit for the success of the tour, especially for Christian's restrained behavior, and was rewarded with unlimited access to the King. What most people were not aware of at this time was that the ambitious doctor had also become Queen Caroline's lover.

As soon as King Christian returned to Denmark, however, he lapsed back into insanity, suffering from hallucinations and delusions that he was illegitimate and not Denmark's true king. He spent his days running around his palace, bashing his head against the walls until he drew blood, smashing his windows and furniture.

The opportunist Struensee enjoyed complete control over both the mad King and his young, impressionable Queen. With the mad Christian's acquiescence, Struensee became in effect the most powerful man in Denmark—a Danish-royal-family version of Rasputin. The doctor had such a mysterious hold over the royal couple it was rumored in the Danish court that he was also the King's lover. Christian had in fact once confided to his doctor that he didn't want to be King anymore and suggested that he and Struensee run away together.

Although Struensee spoke little Danish, he began to throw his newfound political weight about. He quickly made enemies, including the old Dowager Queen Juliane, who was ambitious for her own mentally infirm and physically malformed son, Christian's half-brother Frederick. In 1771 Queen Caroline gave birth to a daughter, Princess Louise. The paternity of the child was one of Denmark's most poorly kept secrets, and the Danish press named Dr. Struensee as the father. Struensee was arrested in January 1772 and charged with high treason and adultery. He was tortured into confession and three months later sentenced to death. On April 28 his right hand was chopped off while he was still fully conscious, then he was decapitated and his body was quartered and exposed on a wheel. The Dowager Queen Juliane watched the execution, grinning, through an opera glass. She complained later that the only detail that had spoiled her otherwise perfect day was that Caroline Matilda's body hadn't been tossed into the death-cart as well.

Queen Caroline might have very easily lost her head as well if her brother hadn't been King George III. The British envoy, Sir Robert Murray Keith, informed the Danish court that England would declare war if King George's sister was harmed in any way. With ten Royal Navy ships already heading in her direction, Denmark backed down and Caroline was sent into comfortable exile at Celle in Hanover. She never returned to Denmark or saw her children or her family again, and died in 1775 aged twenty-three.

King Christian lived on for another twenty years, completely mad and unaware of either the banishment or subsequent death of his estranged wife. He was dragged out to make the odd ceremonial appearance when affairs of state demanded it, but was otherwise immured in his palace.

HEREDITARY INSANITY

In November 1995, Diana, the Princess of Wales, created a media sensation when she admitted adultery and doubted her estranged husband's suitability to be King. The Princess used a controversial TV interview before an estimated fifteen million in Britain alone to discuss her bulimia, self-inflicted harm, the pressures of being a royal, her husband's adultery with Camilla Parker Bowles, and hinted that it might be better for her eldest son, Prince William, to succeed the Queen. Although most neutral observers found her TV performance to be reasonably restrained and self-controlled, at times she struggled to contain her emotions and the establishment went on the attack. Government minister Nicholas Soames, a personal friend of Prince Charles, described the Princess as showing "the advanced stages of paranoia" to the point of "mental illness." Harold Brooks Baker, editor of *Burke's Peerage*, said the interview showed Diana to be unsuited to her role as Princess and future Queen, and that she had shown herself to be "very mentally disturbed," adding, "There is no possibility that she is capable of the duties she took on when she married Prince

Charles . . . I feel sorry for this woman but it does not make sense to allow her to destroy the monarchy."

It was grotesquely ironic that the Prince of Wales's supporters should have accused Diana of being mentally ill, given that insanity is something of a Windsor family tradition.

The theory that the British royal family suffers from a form of hereditary insanity has a long and interesting history. The strange behavior of at least two, and possibly three, of George III's immediate successors points to a far more widespread family problem. In 1788 the royal physician, Dr. Zimmerman, was the first to dare hint at this in public when he wrote, "It has come to our knowledge that several members of the Royal Family and in particular his Royal Highness the Duke of York and Prince Edward [the Duke of Kent, Queen Victoria's father] are subject to the same paroxysms, and this arouses our suspicion of a hereditary predisposition." At the parliamentary inquiry into George III's illness in 1810, the Windsor physician Dr. William Heberden concurred that the royal family was probably genetically blighted.

In the palaces of Europe it was widely believed that the British royal line of succession was tainted with hereditary insanity. There were extraordinarily few proposals for the hands in marriage of George III's six eligible daughters. The second U.S. President, John Adams, misunderstood the business of royal dynastic purity and was briefly determined to marry his son to one of George III's daughters, but in the end he too was scared off by the family mental illness.

The King's eldest son, Prinny, looked at his world through a more or less permanent fog of alcoholic intoxication. Many people who were personally acquainted with him, including a few doctors and several close friends, thought that the Prince of Wales, apart from being a dissolute and totally irresponsible drunk, was also quite mad. The Duke of Wellington for one was convinced that he was mentally deranged, and made comments to that effect several times. The King's own younger brother, the Duke of Cumberland, also believed Prinny was mad.

After the birth of his daughter Charlotte, the Prince had a nervous breakdown and made a will leaving everything he had to "Maria Fitzherbert who is my wife in the eyes of God and who is and ever will be such in mine." As soon as he recovered he had the will put aside and forgot all about it.

There were many such occasions when George IV convinced himself that he was dying. He would fake a terminal illness over the most trivial ailment, and intermittently threatened suicide. He regaled Maria Fitzherbert with forty-page suicide notes to get her to agree to marry him. When he became Prince Regent in February 1811 he suffered three epileptic fits; he was almost exactly the same age George III was when he had his first mysterious "attack." In fact, many of his symptoms were uncannily similar to those experienced by his father, but he was always very careful to keep quiet about them. When he was given news of victory at Waterloo in 1815, he became hysterical and had to be tranquilized with a large quantity of brandy.

Although he had never set foot abroad throughout the war with Napoleon and spent most of it cowering in his Brighton Pavilion, years later he would embarrass his ministers by claiming he had fought at Waterloo. He would also describe how he had helped to win the Battle of Salamanca by leading a charge of dragoons disguised as General Bock. A favorite anecdote was how he had ridden the horse Fleur-de-Lys in the Goodwood Cup, an astonishing claim given that he was so obese that he was incapable of mounting a horse at all without being lifted into the saddle with a complicated mechanism involving cranks, winches, platforms and rollers. Were these fantastic stories the lies of a drunken braggart, or were they, as Wellington and others believed, the fantasies of a madman?

George IV was an incredibly thick-skinned individual. Most of the time his powers of self-delusion served him well because it helped him avoid the painful truth about his own massive unpopularity. He was, however, like Bavaria's mad Ludwig II, uncharacteristically sensitive about speculation that he might be insane. When *The Sunday Times* speculated that he might be suffering from a hereditary mental illness, George went berserk. He demanded that the Attorney General prosecute them immediately and pressed the Home Secretary to treble the duty on all Sunday newspapers. He became increasingly paranoid about rumors that his father's condition was hereditary.

We can make informed guesses about the nature of George III's illness because his medical history was written down in great detail, but this was not the case with George IV. Although he consistently feigned illness to get his own way, whenever he became genuinely ill the details were always deliberately hidden from the public. He banned royal health bulletins because, he said, they only led to gossip.

At best, George IV's brother King William IV, the former Duke of Clarence, was a transient eccentric who left no mark on the monarchy. Many of his contemporaries, however, were privately convinced that he was as mad as his father. He frequently made a fool of himself in the House of Lords with rambling, muddled speeches in defense of slavery and, perversely for a man with at least ten bastards, pious attacks on adulterers. Most of the politicians who had dealings with the ill-educated and boorish "Sailor King" were of the opinion that he was an inadequate and embarrassing old man who was completely out of his depth and should have been left at sea. A large minority, however, took the more serious view that his confused behavior was another sign of the hereditary family insanity.

QUEEN VICTORIA

William's niece Queen Victoria displayed obvious signs of manic-depressive illness after the death of Prince Albert. Her mourning was so intense and her behavior so erratic that some of her ministers thought her ghoulish cult of Prince Albert was a sign of something more sinister and that she, like George III, had lost her mind. The widowed Queen contemplated suicide and then spent the best part of forty years wearing black mourning clothes. She once scolded her eldest son for writing to her on paper that had insufficiently thick black borders. The Queen retained all of Albert's personal equerries and grooms to keep his rooms exactly as he had left them. Every evening hot water was taken to his chambers and fresh clothes were laid out on his bed. She commissioned a portrait of her daughter Alice painted as a nun in the presence of a vision of the recently deceased Albert.

Her closest adviser and mentor, Baron Stockmar, was convinced that Victoria had become mentally unhinged. He recalled that on the death of her own mother the Queen's reaction had been similarly intense, albeit more briefly. The Queen was also a hypochondriac—a classic symptom of a manic-depressive personality. She would summon her personal physician up to half a dozen times a day with various imaginary complaints, usually concerning her digestive system. When her doctor was on his honeymoon he was surprised to receive a note from his Queen informing him "the bowels are acting fully."

Queen Victoria was known to have been highly sensitive about her grandfather George III. Both she and Prince Albert lived in perpetual dread that the hereditary illness would strike against their own children. When they had their eldest son's bumps felt by a leading "expert" in phrenology, it appeared to confirm their worst fears. Sir George Combe examined the Prince's cranium and gravely pronounced that their poor boy had inherited the shape of his brain from the "mad" King George III "and all that this implied."

TWENTIETH-CENTURY WINDSORS

No one has yet suggested that Edward VII was insane, although considering the disastrous education he received it is a wonder that he wasn't driven mad. Quite what modern psychoanalysis would have made of his compulsive-obsessive behavior, including his record of sleeping with over 1,500 women, or his shooting or his eating habits, not to mention his lifelong hobby of recording the weight of everyone who visited Sandringham, is another question.

Edward VII and his wife, Alexandra, raised lackluster children whose general educational standard was well below average. The eldest, Prince Eddie, was by any standards a half-wit. The royal family were desperate to conceal the fact that the heir to the throne was mentally infirm, but recognized that he couldn't be hidden from the world forever and went to great lengths to prepare him for Cambridge. England's finest tutors were hired and quickly concurred that a university education would be a complete waste of effort. Their report concluded damningly: "He hardly knows the meaning of the words 'to read.' "

After a predictably disastrous spell at Cambridge, Eddie was made a lieutenant in the Tenth Hussars, where his stupidity quickly became all too apparent. One day, while he was in dinner conversation seated next to his great-uncle the Duke of Cambridge, Commander-in-Chief of the British army, Prince Eddie casually revealed that the Crimean War was something of a mystery to him and that he had never actually heard of the battle of Alma. His brief military career was, like his academic training had been, in the words of his father, "simply a waste of time."

Queen Elizabeth II's uncles all grew up to be either physically or psychologically challenged. The youngest, Prince John, showed signs of mental infirmity from an early age and was isolated from the rest of the royal family until his death at the age of fourteen. Prince Henry, the Duke of Gloucester, also had diminished mental faculties. He was neurotic, physically very frail and knock-kneed, had a squeaky voice and was prone to giggling fits or bursting into tears for no apparent reason. Known in family circles as "Poor Harry," he was politely described as "slow." In old age the Duke took refuge in his favorite pastime, watching children's television. He once kept King Olav of Norway waiting for half an hour because he couldn't be torn away from an episode of *Popeye*.

The Prince of Wales, later the Duke of Windsor, was in appearance like a slightly more neurotic version of Buster Keaton. The Prince was a heavy drinker, moody, bad-tempered and liable to fits of depression. Prime Minister Stanley Baldwin noted that he appeared to be in a permanent state of arrested development. His Private Secretary, Alan Lascelles, agreed with Baldwin: "For some hereditary or physiological reason," Lascelles wrote in the 1940s, "his mental and spiritual growth stopped dead in his adolescence." Edward's character defects were attributed by some members of his family to childhood mumps.

The Queen's father, George VI, was the most psychologically damaged of George V's sons. He was born on what was cheerfully known in the family as "Mausoleum Day," the anniversary of the death of Prince Albert and coincidentally the death of Albert's third child, Princess Alice, some seventeen years later. He was a cripplingly shy neurotic, and suffered from facial twitches. From childhood to the age of thirty, George suffered with a pronounced stammer in his speech, which exacerbated his natural shyness. The stammer was possibly the result of his father's attempts to "cure" him of left-handedness and knock-knees. (The old King had forced him to wear iron braces on his legs, from the age of eight, for several hours a day and all night, although the young boy had begged his parents to be allowed to sleep without them.)

According to one of his biographers, George VI had a secret drinking problem which grew steadily worse with age. When he became King by default, he probably had a nervous breakdown. It was so widely doubted that he would even turn up for his own coronation that London bookmakers took odds against it. At times he appeared to be dangerously out of touch with reality. In 1939 he astonished his Prime Minister by twice offering to write to Hitler "as one ex-serviceman to another" in an attempt to avert war. The letters he wrote to his family showed that he alone believed that conflict with Hitler was avoidable even days before war broke out. On April 20, 1939, he sent congratulations to Hitler on the occasion of his fiftieth birthday.

In September 1940, Buckingham Palace was bombed. Although large chunks of London had already been blitzed by German bombers, the King took this bomb very personally. He claimed it had been deliberately dropped on his house by a distant Spanish cousin, the fifth Duke of Galliera. This Duke, claimed the King, was involved in a German plot to restore his brother on the throne. Only a close relative of the family, he explained, could have known exactly where to drop it. It hadn't occurred to him that German intelligence might have been clever enough to acquire a map of central London. The King practiced firing his revolver, vowing that he would defend the palace to the death. Fortunately, no such defense was necessary.

Unfortunately, some of the precious little new blood that has been introduced to the royal line also came from tainted stock. The mostly German-and-Danish bloodline of Queen Elizabeth II's husband, the Duke of Edinburgh, is shot through with mental instability. When his father deserted him and his family for the nightlife of Paris and Monaco, Prince Philip's eccentric mother, Princess Alice, became mad, believing herself to be a nun, and gave away the little money they had to Greek refugees.

The Queen Mother, Elizabeth Bowes-Lyon, represented the first ever injection of truly non-royal blood into the family. Ominously, in 1941, five members of the Bowes-Lyon family were confined to a Surrey mental hospital on the same day. They were forgotten by the world until 1985, when the British press revealed that two of the Queen Mother's nieces,

Katherine and Nerissa Bowes-Lyon, had been left to rot for more than forty years in an NHS ward of the Royal Earlswood Mental Hospital in Redhill. Nerissa, a first cousin of Queen Elizabeth II, died in 1986 aged sixty-seven and was buried in a pauper's grave marked only with a cheap plastic cross. Equally disturbing were the royal family's attempts to hush up the facts. The Palace had lied to *Burke's Peerage*, leading them to print that Katherine Bowes-Lyon had died in 1940. Her sister was listed as having died in 1961, yet was still alive in 1985. Two other close female relatives of theirs were also in the hospital; also mentally handicapped. The editor of *Burke's Peerage* told journalists that their condition was undoubtedly the result of inbreeding.

3. A BREED APART

A Lesson in Royal Inbreeding

THE FAMILY CREST of the Habsburgs, the rulers of the Austro-Hungarian Empire, was a double-headed eagle. According to legend, one day the Austrian Emperor Ferdinand I shot an eagle and, when the dead bird was brought to him, he was puzzled and inquired why it had only one head. The remarkable thing about Ferdinand I, considering the extent of inbreeding in his family, was that he was the only Emperor of the Austro-Hungarian Empire who can be positively identified as mentally handicapped.

Long before genetics became a science, common sense dictated that incest was not a good idea. People could see for themselves that the children of related couples were less likely to grow up healthy and normal. Europe's royal families, however, are exceptions to the rules of common sense or even good taste. Kings and queens exist to breed, whether they are genetically flawed or not. Being a prince meant going to the family reunion to meet women.

One of George V's courtiers once observed that as far as the King was concerned "there are only three kinds of people in the world: blacks, whites and royals." Royalty has always considered itself to be quite literally a breed apart. When Princess Diana was described in the press as a "commoner" in the early 1980s it caused some public confusion, as her relatives, the Spencers, had great hereditary wealth and a direct lineage going back at least as far as the present Queen's. This is because royalty does not acknowledge any gradation between non-royals; any distinction between a waitress and a non-royal duchess. As far as they are concerned, the rest of us exist in an equal but separate parallel dimension. British non-royal aristocrats have always been looked down upon by European royalty as being quite inferior to even the most minor of continental princes, even though the British aristocrat may have considerably more wealth. In matters of precedence, emperors came first, kings second, princes third, and the rest nowhere.

The remaining royal families of Europe today are a concentration of centuries of inbreeding and congenital deficiencies. All too often, the royal way of improving the breeding stock was to import some new blood from someone else's inbred royal family. Thus the great hereditary monarchies of Europe were doomed to slowly drown in their own gene pool. By the start of the twentieth century, every ruling sovereign of Europe, apart from Albania, including the deposed monarchs of Germany, Russia and Spain, could trace descent from Britain's King James I. By the beginning of World War I, the major royal families of Europe and even some of the new Balkan monarchs were all intimately related to each other either by blood or by marriage. The British royal family, through Queen Victoria and her nine children, was related to the German Emperor, the Czar of Russia, and the kings of Spain, Portugal, Belgium, Bulgaria and Romania; and via Edward VII's wife, Alexandra, they were linked to the royal families of Greece, Denmark and Norway.

In normal circumstances, hereditary diseases are quite rare because people who exhibit obvious physical signs of genetic deficiency are less likely to find a mate, reproduce and thus pass on the defect to their children. In a closed society, however, there is always much more risk of a married couple each receiving copies of harmful genes from their common ancestors. The biggest danger comes from marrying cousins, because their children can inherit a double dose of a recessive gene. The dangers of royal inbreeding are greatest where there is the highest frequency of repeated ancestry. The present-day Count of Paris, for example, is related to his ancestor the sixteenth-century French King Henry IV in 108 different ways.

As the royal families of Europe rigidly excluded outsiders, the effects of social isolation were just as great as if they were living in some remote ancient village. The blue-bloods may have lived hundreds, even thousands, of miles apart, but they were still in effect marrying the girl next door. In fact, the choice of marital partners was even more exclusive, thanks to the taboo of religion. After the Reformation and the religious wars which followed, the royal houses of Europe tended to divide themselves into two camps: the Catholic south and the Protestant north. The kings and queens of England, Holland, Russia and Scandinavia married among themselves or from the pool of Protestant German dynasties. The French, Austrian, Spanish and Italians bred among themselves or with German Catholics.

Marriages between Catholics and Protestants did take place, but very rarely.

The British royal family has a few genetic skeletons in its cupboard. Queen Victoria was worried about the quality of the British royal-family bloodstock. Her concerns for what she called the "lymphatic" blood of her royal house were voiced in her letter to her daughter Vicky:

> I do wish one could find some more black eyed Princes and Princesses for our children! I can't help thinking what dear Papa said—that it was in fact when there was some little imperfection in the pure Royal descent that some fresh blood was infused . . . For that constant fair hair and blue eyes makes the blood so lymphatic . . . it is not as trivial as you may think, for darling Papa—often with vehemence said: "We must have some strong blood."

It is unlikely that at the time of writing this letter the Queen had any idea precisely what was wrong with her family's blood. In fact, the woman whom history reveres as the Matriarch of Europe was its unwitting scourge.

QUEEN VICTORIA'S GIFT

Through repeated intermarrying, Victoria bequeathed the potentially lethal affliction hemophilia, a recessive genetic disorder that causes failure of the normal blood-clotting mechanism. Until recently it was untreatable and few hemophiliacs survived to reproductive age because any small cut or internal hemorrhaging after even a minor bruise was fatal. Hemophilia affects males much more frequently than females.

The "Royal Disease"—as it became known, due to the fact that it spread to the royal families of Europe through Victoria's descendants—first became apparent in the British royal family in Victoria's eighth child, Prince Leopold the Duke of Albany. Leopold was the least known, the brightest and the most unfortunate of the Queen's four sons. As a hemophiliac, every trivial bruise or scratch in the routine rough-and-tumble of the nursery would have given him acute pain and exposed him to mortal danger. When he was six his mother recorded in her diary, somewhat cruelly: "He walks shockingly and is dreadfully awkward—holds himself as badly as ever." Throughout his relatively short life Leopold suffered severe hemorrhages and was always described as "very delicate." In spite of all the usual precautions, he bled to death aged thirty-one in Cannes in 1884 after slipping on a polished tile floor and cutting his knee.

The appearance of hemophilia in one of her sons was both upsetting and confusing for Queen Victoria, and she protested that the disease could not have originated on her side of the family. Yet the legend of the "curse of the Coburgs," from whom she was directly descended, was well known to her. This curse was supposed to have dated from the early nineteenth century, when a Coburg prince married the Hungarian Princess Antoinette de Kohary. A monk, a member of the Kohary family, was jealous of the wealth inherited by the couple from the bride's father, and cursed future generations of Coburgs with the disease. The scientific view, however, is that there was a mutant gene in Queen Victoria herself, or in the genes of her father, Edward the Duke of Kent.

THE SPREAD OF HEMOPHILIA IN THE ROYAL HOUSES OF EUROPE

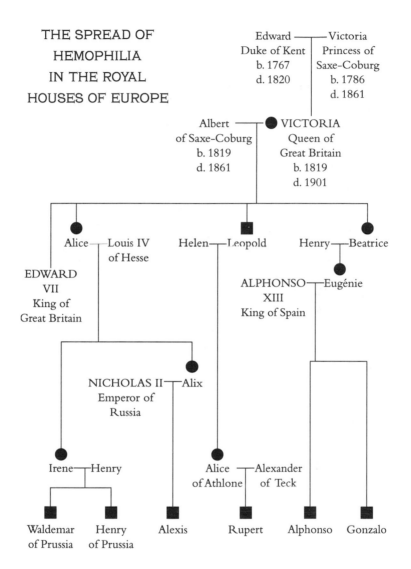

Edward ——— Victoria
Duke of Kent | Princess of
b. 1767 | Saxe-Coburg
d. 1820 | b. 1786
| d. 1861

Albert ——— VICTORIA
of Saxe-Coburg | Queen of
b. 1819 | Great Britain
d. 1861 | b. 1819
| d. 1901

Alice ——Louis IV   Helen——Leopold   Henry——Beatrice
of Hesse

EDWARD
VII
King of
Great Britain

ALPHONSO——Eugénie
XIII
King of Spain

NICHOLAS II——Alix
Emperor of
Russia

Irene——Henry   Alice ——Alexander
of Athlone | of Teck

Waldemar   Henry   Alexis   Rupert   Alphonso   Gonzalo
of Prussia of Prussia

● Carrier for hemophilia

Victoria also transmitted it to three of her daughters, the Princess Royal and Princesses Alice and Beatrice. Queen Victoria's third child, Alice, passed hemophilia to the German and Russian imperial families. Of Alice's six children, two were carriers and one was a victim. Her three-year-old son Frederick suffered a minor cut to his ear and very nearly bled to death before the flow of blood was stanched. A few months later, while playing in his mother's room, he charged headlong through an open window and died later that evening from massive internal bleeding. Alice's daughter Irene married her first cousin Prince Henry of Prussia and gave birth to two hemophilic sons. Desperate attempts were made to conceal the fact that the dread disease had manifested itself in the German imperial family, but, at the age of four, Waldemar, the youngest of the Princes, bled to death.

Alice's daughter Alix was also a carrier. She declined offers of marriage from two of Edward VII's sons, the Duke of Clarence and his brother George, thus preventing hemophilia from reintroducing itself into the reigning branch of the British royal family. Alix, however, married Czar Nicholas II and carried hemophilia into the Russian imperial family instead. Within a few months of the birth of their son Alexis, his parents realized that he had hemophilia. The first sign was some unexpected bleeding from the navel. Much more serious was the bleeding into his joints, which caused terrible pain and crippled the affected limbs. As Alexis grew older he was obliged to spend weeks in bed or to wear a heavy iron brace. Alexis did not die from hemophilia: at the age of fourteen he was executed with the rest of the family.

Victoria's youngest daughter, Beatrice, had two hemophilic sons, and a daughter, Ena, who was a carrier. When Ena married

King Alphonso XIII of Spain, the disease spread to the Spanish royal family. They stumbled upon the fact that their firstborn and heir to the Spanish throne was a hemophiliac when the old Spanish court custom of circumcising the royal children almost caused him to bleed to death. From then on the Spanish royal family padded the tree trunks in the royal gardens to stop the heir from bruising himself. He survived childhood, but years later was involved in a car crash and bled to death.

Of Queen Victoria's children, grandchildren and great-grandchildren, thirty-six were either sufferers, carriers or suspected carriers of the disease. The disease was never mentioned because official royal policy was to hush it up. Nor was Victoria ever aware that she was the source of the disease, and she went to her grave blaming her husband's Coburg side of the family. There are still hemophiliacs among Queen Victoria's 300 living descendants today.

ROYAL EUGENICS

One of the most common congenital disorders, caused by the wrong number of sex chromosomes, produces unfortunate physical defects that can result in exceptionally ugly women. We know from contemporary descriptions that many princesses of central and northern Europe were very ugly. Ordinarily such a woman would probably not marry and have children, but if she was a royal princess in the eighteenth or nineteenth century she was quite likely to find herself the next Queen of England.

The Hanoverian kings of England were renowned for their own ugliness, and also for the plainness of their wives and their mistresses. Thomas Lawrence was commissioned to paint the portrait of George III's exceptionally ugly wife, Queen Charlotte, but because the results were more honest than flattering the King refused to pay him and he in fact never received his fee. George IV was less than fussy about whom he slept with, preferring quantity to quality, but he nearly fainted when he first clapped eyes on his squat fiancée, Princess Caroline of Brunswick.

Congenital plainness was not exclusively a problem of the German courts. The male members of the Spanish royal family were notoriously ugly; the female line mostly obese and dwarfish. The royal family of Sardinia also produced a high proportion of female dwarfs. The Austrian royal family with their "Habsburg Lip," the Bourbons with their huge noses, the squat Hanoverians with their slack chins and protuberant pale-blue eyes, all looked as though they came from different sections of a horse-breeder's stud book.

In the nineteenth century the British royal family, like nearly all of the great royal houses of Europe, was slowly choking to death in ever tightening spirals of royal DNA, but until quite recent times consideration of genetic problems and the need for outbreeding rarely influenced their marriages. King George III's Royal Marriages Act of 1772 was an exercise in royal eugenics. The objective was to make the British royal family a closed caste which would never again be polluted by inferior local stock. It was a remarkable success. In the three centuries that have passed since the Hanoverians came to Britain, the bloodline of this almost exclusively German royal family has only twice been breached by commoners—George VI's wife Elizabeth Bowes-Lyon, and by Diana Spencer. In genetic terms it is too little too late because, although new genes dilute the effects of recessive genes, the bad effects of inbreeding can resurface in the descendants of mixed marriages many generations later. The present heir to the British throne, Prince Charles, is every inch the Frankenstein creation of a European monarchical system that has been in place for a thousand years. At least, some might say, the policy of more or less hermetically sealed royal pond life prevented their genes from leaching out into the community at large.

If everything had gone according to plan, Princess Elizabeth's marriage to Phillipos Schleswig-Holstein-Sonderburg-Glücksburg would have marked the last time a princess of the British royal family lost her virginity to a distant cousin. However, the subsequent disastrous marriages of the Queen's children may force the House of Windsor to reconsider whether it is yet safe to let their sons and daughters loose on partners they are not already related to.

Mental instability as a direct result of genetic malformation due to chronic inbreeding existed until recent times. As the constitutional crisis in nineteenth-century Bavaria demonstrated, inherited insanity is one of the obvious pitfalls of absolute monarchy, as quite often one madman was removed from the throne in order to substitute another. Nowhere were the disastrous biological events which have warped European history more apparent than in the House of Habsburg, rulers in central Europe from the thirteenth century until World War I.

THE HABSBURG INHERITANCE

The Habsburgs suffered from a monstrous genetic mutation as a result of generations of inbreeding. The disorder known as acocephaly produces distinctive physical and mental abnormalities, in this case the famous "Habsburg Lip," first noticed in the mid-fifteenth century. In the sufferer, the lower jaw protrudes so that the lower teeth lie in front of the upper ones and the mouth often hangs open. The Habsburg Lip became even more frequent in the sixteenth and seventeenth centuries, when the Austrian and Spanish Habsburgs interbred so frequently that they tied reef knots in their bloodlines.

Emperor Ferdinand I's parents were first cousins. His father, the Emperor Francis, had an abnormally large sexual appetite and married four times. He was known as the "wife killer" because according to family legend he had finished the first three off with his awesome libido. He advised his son Ferdinand I to "Rule, and change nothing." Ferdinand was born with a hydrocephalic head, and grew up to be epileptic. He could just about sign his own name but was otherwise incapable of performing the simplest of tasks. His tongue was too large for his mouth—another inherited Habsburg defect—and he found it virtually impossible to string a sentence together. The historian A. J. P. Taylor recorded that Ferdinand's only known coherent remark on any subject was "I am the Emperor, and I want dumplings." The Emperor's idea of a good time was to wedge his backside in a wastepaper basket and roll around the floor in it. Indeed, on encountering Ferdinand, the Russian Czarina Alexandra wrote in her diary, "I had heard so much about him, about his small shrunken ugly figure and his huge head void of any expression except that of stupidity, but the reality beggared all description." The Austrian statesman Metternich described him as "a lump of putty."

Nineteenth-century medical science wrongly believed that epilepsy was hereditary, and it was therefore with some astonishment that the rest of Europe received the news that the Emperor's physicians had allowed him to marry and attempt to produce an heir. The unfortunate bride was twenty-eight-year-old Sardinian Princess Maria Anna. There were no children: during the wedding night alone he had five epileptic attacks. Although more or less everyone in Vienna was aware that the Emperor was backward, he was regarded with sympathy and affection by his people for most of his thirteen-year reign. When revolution broke out in 1848, however, men in white coats whisked him away from Vienna to Olmütz in Moravia, and persuaded him to abdicate in favor of his eighteen-year-old nephew Franz Joseph. Ferdinand died in 1875 in his eighty-third year.

CHARLES "THE BEWITCHED"

Spain suffered more than most from the genetic mutation of inbreeding. Although the royal line was predominantly Bourbon, the debilitated Habsburg blood also ran profusely through the veins of the Spanish royal family. King Philip IV fathered fifteen children by his two wives. All of these Spanish Princes and Princesses, unlike his numerous healthy bastard offspring, were born physically degenerate and most did not live to see their fourth birthdays. In his successor, Charles II, centuries of inbred Habsburg physical and mental abnormality combined to reveal the laws of genetics at their cruelest. A sickly four-year-old when he succeeded his father, he reigned for thirty-five years, mad, illiterate, incapable of governing, living his life in complete ignorance of even the basic geography of the empire he ruled. He had been a virtual invalid from the day he was born. When he came to the throne he was still being breast-fed by relays of fourteen wet nurses. His Habsburg underbite was so enormously pronounced that he could barely use his jaws to chew food; his tongue was so big that his speech was unintelligible. The King's condition was also degenerative: by the time he was in his late thirties his legs were too weak to carry him, and he was an emaciated, mentally ill wreck. As he grew older he also succumbed to bouts of madness with increasing frequency. He had himself exorcised as it was believed he was possessed by a devil: hence he became known as Charles "The Bewitched." These exorcisms apparently gave him some temporary relief. As the attacks grew worse the whole Spanish court became preoccupied with witchcraft, to the great amusement of Spain's neighbors.

In spite of his physical and mental incapacity, his station naturally required that he should be married and sire children to secure the future of the Spanish state. A "volunteer" was found in the French Princess Marie Louise, a niece of Louis XIV. It seems that Louis had been forewarned that the King of Spain was physically monstrous and that his poor seventeen-year-old niece was in for a nasty surprise, but the Sun King gave his blessing to the marriage anyway because he thought the union would favor French interests. Marie Louise did her best as a dutiful wife, but Charles was incapable of fatherhood. In 1689 she died, childless, after a riding accident. When she had been dead for about ten years he insisted on seeing her corpse. He descended by torchlight into the royal vaults beneath the church where several generations of Spanish kings and queens lay. He took one look at his first wife's remains and ran screaming from the vault, and it was said that he was permanently crazed from that day on. The King spent the rest of his reign being led like a prize chimpanzee from one ceremonial function to another.

In 1770 Charles II died heirless and the Spanish Empire passed to Philip Anjou, the grandson of Louis XIV of France, thus plunging Europe into thirteen years of bloody war. Thousands died on the battlefields of Europe before the great powers finally accepted him as Philip V of Spain by the Treaty of Utrecht of 1713.

KING PHILIP'S LIBIDO

Genetically speaking, King Philip V had little going for him. Charles II was the last Spanish king of pure Habsburg descent, but the Habsburg legacy was to linger on in the Spanish blood-line for generations. Apart from Philip's Habsburg blood, which was obvious from his long, melancholy features and jutting jawline, his mother, Mary Anne, was a Bavarian Wittelsbach and his father was a Bourbon. The result of this blue-blood cocktail was that for nearly half a century Spain was ruled by a mentally unbalanced sex maniac.

Philip was unfeasibly oversexed even by Bourbon standards. Only two things mattered to him—sex and God. On the one hand he was a complete and utter slave to his libido, and on the other he was a religious maniac. The combination of the two meant that he spent most of his life darting between his bed and the confessional. According to his minister Alberoni, all he needed in life was "a couch and a woman." Unfortunately, as the King's deeply held Catholic views would not allow him to take mistresses, his wives bore the full brunt of his libido.

King Philip V married twice. His first wife, Queen Maria Luisa, died aged twenty-six after a long illness. She was only fourteen years old when they married but she handled her new husband with an astuteness which belied her tender years. To teach him a lesson after they were married, she made him wait two whole days before she would let him sleep with her. Philip's grandfather Louis XIV let it be known that he considered this a gross insult to Bourbon manhood.

The King's first serious mental breakdown occurred in 1717. He shut himself away for days, refusing to see anyone except the Queen, and only then when he required sexual intercourse. Philip complained to his doctors that he was being consumed by a fire from within his stomach. His doctors examined him but found no sign of illness and advised that the King was suffering from delusions. By this time, Philip had convinced himself that he was dying in mortal sin. The King was aware of the history of mental instability on both sides of his family and arrived at the conclusion that he too was going mad and was unfit to govern. After seeking divine inspiration, he decided to pass over the reins of government to someone else before his mind went completely. In January 1724 the King of Spain, to the astonishment of every court in Europe, suddenly abdicated in favor of his seventeen-year-old son Louis I.

After a reign of only eight months, however, Louis was suddenly dead from smallpox, naming his father as successor. King Philip V resumed the throne very reluctantly. Throughout his brief, eccentric retirement he had taken to dressing up as a humble Franciscan friar, but had otherwise managed to retain all the trappings of luxury he had enjoyed as King. As before, the burden of responsibility caused him to have a mental breakdown. Although only thirty-eight years old, Philip was stooped, shrunken and bowlegged, shambling around the palace like an octogenarian. The French ambassador reported back to Versailles that the Spanish King's sexual addiction had wrecked his health and driven him to madness.

By 1727 his mental state had deteriorated so completely that his second wife effectively took over the rule of Spain. King Philip refused to change his clothes and wandered around the palace clad only in filthy, stinking rags, his hair long and wild. He believed that his personal filthiness was the only thing holding him together and that he would die if he changed his clothes. He bit chunks out of his arms and hands, and through the night alternately screamed and sang. Philip took on a permanently vacant expression and lapsed into lethargy, hardly ever eating, lying motionless in his own excrement for days on end in complete silence. On July 9, 1746, His Catholic Majesty's miserable life was brought to an abrupt end by a massive stroke.

THE SPANISH LEGACY

The only surviving son of Philip V, by his first marriage to Maria Luisa of Savoy, the vacant and pasty-faced Ferdinand VI, became king at the age of thirty-three. He was severely paranoid and lived in constant dread of assassination. Eventually he too became completely insane. Like his father, he was addicted to sex and became a slave to his short, very plain wife, Queen Barbara of Braganza, daughter of Portugal's King John V. Queen Barbara was also a neurotic and lived in constant fear of being left a penniless widow. Her confidence that she would outlive her husband was, however, misplaced. In 1757 she took to her bed in terrible pain and became covered in boils. She died after a horrible and lingering eleven-month illness. It was discovered that her private apartment was crammed to the ceiling with Spanish currency which she had stashed away to see her through a comfortable widowhood.

With his Queen dead, Ferdinand's mental state went quickly downhill. He alternately starved himself and binged on food, and randomly attacked his servants. The last few months of his life were marked by a series of increasingly desperate suicide attempts. He tried cutting his wrists with scissors, hanging himself with bedsheets, and strangling himself with table napkins. When all else failed he begged his doctors to give him poison. King Ferdinand died in his sleep of natural causes aged forty-six.

By and large, genetics took a holiday with King Charles III, ruler of Spain from 1759 to 1788. He inherited the Bourbon family nose, which cast a shadow over his mouthful of rotten teeth, but was otherwise a dull but perfectly sane king. Charles III was lucky to have escaped the effects of tainted heredity, but the family curse skipped just one generation and struck at his children. His eldest son and heir, Philip the Duke of Cabaria, was a raving psychopath, subject to fits from infancy and mentally unstable by the age of twelve. The King had him examined by specialists and declared insane, and had the law changed so that he could be removed from the line of succession.

The Duke lived on until he was thirty years old, stalking the Spanish court like a royal Jack the Ripper. A team of chamberlains was detailed to watch him round the clock, and special care was taken to keep him away from women. On a few occasions, however, he eluded his keepers and attacked and raped female courtiers. During his more placid moments, his favorite form of amusement was to have one of his hands held up by an attendant while increasingly larger gloves, up to sixteen pairs at a time, were placed on his hand one over the other. In 1777 he died of smallpox after the King refused on religious grounds to allow him to be vaccinated.

Charles III's preoccupation with the family's inbreeding and his concern for the mental health of his offspring led him to make some well-intentioned but unfortunate decisions about their upbringing. The King of Spain gave express instructions to the royal tutors that none of his children, especially his second and third eldest sons, should be mentally exerted in case it put too great a strain on their minds and tipped them over the edge. This regime more or less guaranteed that both of them grew up to be ill-educated morons who between them ruled most of southern Europe, the elder as King of Spain, the younger as King of Naples and the Two Sicilies.

The younger son, King Ferdinand, spent his days leapfrogging, fondling the ladies of court, and shrieking obscenities at the top of his unusually high-pitched voice. When the Emperor Joseph II of Austria attended a court ball at the Palazzo Reale in 1769, he found the young King to be "a complete idiot." In a letter home he described an incident he encountered in the palace. The King and Queen, accompanied by two chamberlains, were making a dignified approach to an antechamber, where they were awaited by several officials, when Ferdinand suddenly began to gallop around the room, kicking out at his courtiers. When the King wanted to play, Joseph discovered, the whole court was expected to join in. Soon the entire throng, including elderly men and quite senior ministers, were galloping through the corridors of the Neopolitan court.

The French ambassador, who unhappily found himself in the path of Ferdinand, received a punch in the face and his nose collided with a wall.

Ferdinand insisted on having a crowd around to keep him amused while he labored on the toilet. The Emperor Joseph related: "We made conversation for more than an hour, and I believe we would still be there if a terrible stench had not convinced us that all was over." Joseph then declined an offer to view the fruits of Ferdinand's labors. The King's wife, Maria Carolina, sister of Marie Antoinette, ruled the kingdom in everything but name until she herself went mad on hearing of her sister's bloody death at the hands of the French revolutionaries.

The disastrous and tyrannical King of Spain Ferdinand VII was known for his sadism and his religious bigotry. In a royal family renowned for their congenital ugliness, Ferdinand was known to be outstandingly hideous. He was married four times, twice to his own nieces. Three of his wives died young, two of them in highly suspicious circumstances. His first wife, his consumptive niece Antonia, died aged twenty-two and was rumored to have been murdered by her mother-in-law. The second wife, Isabel, died in childbirth aged twenty. His third wife, Maria Josepha, was a religious fanatic who never put down her rosary beads for long enough to procreate, and also died suspiciously, aged twenty-six. During her lying in state, her face quickly turned black, hinting strongly at the possibility of arsenic poisoning.

The King's first three wives had all failed to produce a male heir. By the time Ferdinand was in his forties and was ready to marry for the fourth time, he was already an old man, crippled with gout, massively obese and prone to fits. His fourth wife was another niece half his age, the precocious Maria Christina, daughter of King Francis I of Naples. The Neopolitan prisons, it was said, were full of young men who had dared flirt with the young Princess. The marriage did not produce the required male heir, but two daughters. When Ferdinand VII died, Maria Christina took to throwing extremely lavish court balls, but always invoiced her guests for the food and drink they consumed.

Ferdinand VII had announced that his daughter Isabel should become Queen after he died, a decision which plunged Spain into seven years of bloody civil war. There was some confusion as to whether or not a female was allowed to succeed to the Spanish throne. The first Bourbon king of Spain, Philip V, had introduced Salic Law, which prevented women from succeeding. When his son became King he reversed this law, but for one reason or another didn't bother to make it public. Queen Isabel was later married to both her first cousin and her nephew on the same day—not difficult for a Bourbon because they happened to be one and the same person, the homosexual Duke Francis of Cadiz. Their son King Alphonso XII later compounded the inbreeding problem by marrying his first cousin Maria.

THE HOUSE OF BRAGANZA

The English traveler and diarist William Beckford arrived at the Portuguese court in 1794, just as the Queen was having one of her turns: Beckford reported "the most horrible, the most agonizing shrieks . . . inflicting upon me a sensation of horror such as I never felt before."

Through generations of intermarrying, the Portuguese royal family had become one of the most dangerously inbred in Europe. The situation took a considerable turn for the worse in 1760 when King Joseph decided to have his daughter and heir to the throne, Maria, incestuously married to her half-wit uncle Pedro. The flawed logic behind this peculiar arrangement was that the Portuguese crown would be kept securely in the family. One of the more obvious results was that the House of Braganza became even further corrupted by inbreeding.

In 1777, the old King Joseph died and Portugal found itself ruled by young Queen Maria, already displaying signs of incipient insanity, and her feeble-minded husband, King Pedro III. In 1786 Pedro died and, thanks to the complicated domestic arrangement ordained by the late King, Maria found herself in the unusual position of mourning the double loss of a husband and an uncle who shared the same coffin.

Two years later, a smallpox epidemic carried away several people who were close to Queen Maria—her confessor and a few of her immediate family, including her son José. The latter loss could have been avoided if only she hadn't forbidden her son to be inoculated. It was generally believed that the combined shock of these deaths tipped her mind completely over the edge. Queen Maria took to wearing children's clothes and became violently unstable.

The Braganza family felt it necessary to send to London for a specialist in the treatment of insanity, and the "expert" they chose was the Reverend Francis Willis, fresh from his inept but apparently successful treatment of George III. Willis demanded and received a consultancy fee of £10,000. Needless to say, none of his advice worked. The Portuguese people were kept in ignorance about the Queen's condition, and in 1807 she was quietly smuggled off to Brazil so that her subjects wouldn't discover that insanity had once again struck their royal family.

When Maria died she was succeeded by her second son, King John VI. He was a very ugly, fat little man, and a martyr to his piles, while everyone else within spitting distance was a martyr to his abysmal table manners. The new King's heredity was heavily stacked against him from the start, and the Portuguese court held its breath, fearing that the new King might also be mad. As the fruit of an incestuous relationship between his mad mother and a half-wit father, who also happened to be his grandfather's brother, he was entitled to be confused, but King John took it all in his stride. When someone dared suggest to him that he was a little strange, the King shrugged—"How can I help it? I have Braganza blood in my veins. I take after my ancestors."

His wife was the ugly Charlotte, a daughter of the Spanish court. She demonstrated the touching bond which had grown between them by attempting on several occasions to have her husband declared mad and locked up. Unfortunately for Queen Charlotte, although King John VI was weak and inept he wasn't, strictly speaking, certifiably insane. He was, however, prone to frequent mental breakdowns, which he tried to pass off as a "fear of horses." Although his mental processes were always suspect, conclusive proof that the King wasn't clinically insane came in 1808, when he displayed a keen sense of self-preservation and fled to Brazil on a Portuguese man o' war at the first hint of trouble from Napoleon's armies.

4. THE SPORT OF KINGS

The Secret of Royal Adultery

IN MOST EUROPEAN courts, charades always came a poor second to adultery. Frederick, an eighteenth-century hereditary prince of Baden-Durlach, had around 160 *Gartenmagdlein* ("Garden Girls") for his pleasure. They were dressed in hussar uniforms and, when they made a mistake during their exercises, the Duke liked to punish them personally. Just over a hundred years ago, the Victorian constitutional expert and royal apologist Walter Bagehot argued that it was unreasonable of us to expect royalty to behave otherwise: "It is not rational to expect the best virtue where temptation is applied in the most trying form at the frailest time of human life."

AUGUSTUS THE STRONG

When King Augustus II of Poland lay on his deathbed in 1733, his last words were "My whole life has been an unceasing sin— God have mercy on me." From anyone else this could be considered a touch melodramatic, but not from the behemoth of royal adulterers. The king of whom it was said he "left no stern unturned" was known to his subjects as Augustus "the Strong" for his exceptional physical size and strength, his gluttony, his drinking prowess and his lechery, but most of all for his astonishing virility. Over a period of half a century he fathered 365 bastards, give or take a dozen. It is probably only fair to record that there was also one legitimate heir.

Augustus presided over an enormous warren of concubines. Some enjoyed official status; others he preferred to keep quiet about—his own daughter, the Countess Orzelska, for example. One of his favorites was the Swedish Countess Aurora of Königsmark; another was Fatima, a captured Turkish slave girl. Some of his more ambitious mistresses negotiated legal contracts and annual salaries for themselves: one earned herself a large palace in Dresden.

Karl Ludwig von Pollnitz's book, *The Amorous Adventures of Augustus the Strong*, records that the most unusual of all his many conquests was his liaison with the jilted mistress of the British ambassador to Saxony. What made this affair so remarkable was that she was the only woman the King failed to impregnate in half a century of indiscriminate sexual congress.

Although Augustus the Strong's libido was one of the great marvels of the age, it didn't go down well with his Polish subjects, who were outraged by his private life, nor with his wife,

Eberdine, daughter of a German margrave. She was so disgusted and embarrassed by his flagrant infidelities that she refused to set foot in Poland throughout her husband's reign. He was also a fairly disastrous king because, unlike his spermatozoa, his political ventures rarely produced a result.

Try as he might, Augustus found it impossible to keep track of his bastards. Some argued that the King didn't try quite hard enough—if you were going to give him the benefit of the doubt you'd have to say that his incestuous relationships with at least one of his daughters was down to sloppy bookkeeping rather than deliberate bad taste. Augustus the Strong's progeny went on to populate most of Europe and some of them became famous in their own right, including Maurice de Saxe and his daughter George Sand.

FRUITS OF THEIR LABORS

The Hanoverian kings sired a whole string of bastards, although no one came near to equaling the personal record set by Charles II, who fathered about twenty illegitimate children, of whom fourteen were acknowledged by him. George IV accepted paternity of only three illegitimate sons throughout his life. He was also widely credited with, but refused to acknowledge the existence of, a daughter by a boardinghouse keeper from Weymouth, Mrs. Mary Lewis. It was only because of his terrible state of health that there weren't many more—after years of alcoholic and gluttonous excess he had become a grossly flatulent wreck and was rendered prematurely impotent. In ten years, William IV fathered ten illegitimate children, five sons and five daughters, by an Irish actress, plus a child by another woman, identity not known. His greedy and ungrateful bastards, known as the little Fitzclarences, dogged him to the end of his days.

The last reigning British monarch to acknowledge a bastard was Queen Elizabeth II's great-grandfather Edward VII, but it was widely rumored that the Queen's uncle, Edward VIII, fathered at least one illegitimate son by the wife of one of his best friends. The child in later years openly boasted of his uncanny physical resemblance to the then Duke of Windsor. Given the amount of recreational sex still indulged in by the male line of the British royal family, the fact that there haven't been any more recent cases of royal illegitimacy says more about the effectiveness of modern birth control than anything else.

CATHOLIC GUILT

Southern European monarchs in particular found it difficult to reconcile their sex lives with their religious beliefs. The mad Spanish King Philip IV fathered about thirty bastards, but being a good Catholic always felt bad about it. Spain's King Philip V made astonishing demands on his wife by insisting that she sleep with him three times a day for the whole of their marriage, but always atoned for his abnormal sexual urges by yelling for his confessor every time he'd had sex in case he died suddenly in eternal damnation. France's King Louis XV didn't see any conflict between his debauchery and his sincere religious convictions. Before he penetrated his adolescent whores in his exclusive brothel, the Parc du Cerfs, the King would demand that they kneel and pray beside him. Louis would pray silently that this time he wouldn't be visited with the dreaded syphilis.

King John V, Portugal's self-styled "Most Faithful King," was anything but. He considered himself an extremely pious man and his lifelong passion for the Catholic Church led him to lavish ruinous amounts of money on religious establishments. Portugal should have become rich from the discovery of Brazilian gold in the eighteenth century. Instead the people got poorer and poorer while the King squandered his country's wealth on fantastic follies, most of them religious: the chapel of St. Roque, for example, was built then taken to pieces and reassembled in Lisbon. When he wasn't building solid-gold coaches, he was perpetually endowing monasteries; eventually Portugal had about eight thousand of them. By the time of his death in 1750, one in every ten Portuguese was either a monk or a nun.

John V found a unique way of combining his two greatest, but on the face of it mutually exclusive, interests—namely prayer and sex—by copulating with nuns. The King had long-standing and quite open sexual relationships with nuns of Odivelas Convent, an arrangement that was widely known and talked about. His charity work in the nunnery resulted in the birth of three illegitimate sons, known as "the children of Palhava" after the palace in Lisbon where they grew up: Antonio, born in 1714 to a French nun; Gaspar, born in 1716, who became an archbishop; and José, born in 1720, who went on to become Grand Inquisitor.

THE BOURBON APPETITE

More often than not, the Bourbon name was synonymous with debauchery. Nearly all of the great Bourbon monarchs were known for their extraordinary appetites. The greatest of them all, the Sun King, Louis XIV, was only five feet and four inches tall, but his libido was twelve feet tall in its stockinged feet. He strutted around clutching his golden snuff box, devouring food and women like a latter-day Elvis Presley. He employed every artificial aid in the known world to make him look taller, including six-inch red high heels and a twelve-inch-high, full-bottomed periwig, either of which could have accounted for his extraordinary gait: maintaining his balance, let alone his dignity, was a daily trial.

Apart from near the very end of his life, when the promise of death suddenly made him very God-fearing, Louis XIV was utterly promiscuous and very easily pleased. If one of his four official mistresses wasn't available he would seduce any female within easy reach. If a mistress kept him waiting he would molest her ladies-in-waiting. Pretty chambermaids strayed too near to the tiny King at their peril because he was likely to launch himself at them without warning.

During his wife's first pregnancy he took a fancy to her seventeen-year-old lady-in-waiting, the blond, club-footed Madame de Soubisse. The affair lasted for several years: the King didn't completely go off her until her front teeth went black and fell out. She later fell seriously ill with a glandular disease known as "King's Evil." This was the name given to scrofula, or tuberculosis of the lymph glands, which causes swellings in the neck and was originally associated with Edward the Confessor. It was believed that all royals could cure the disease by touch. In England "touching" died out with George I, but it was still practiced by the French monarchy until the middle of the nineteenth century. Madame de Soubisse's illness was not, it was noted, for want of being touched by the King.

The King's affairs followed a predictable pattern. When he grew tired of his current mistress he would extend his search for a replacement no further than her immediate circle of friends and acquaintances, including her servants. Louis was at one time enamored of his new sister-in-law, the buxom Austrian Princess Henrietta. Even at Versailles, where marital fidelity was a novelty, the King's carnal interest in his own brother's wife was beyond the limits of acceptability. When his infatuation became too obvious and began to attract adverse comment, he pretended that he was having an affair with one of her ladies-in-waiting, Louise de La Vallière. The King's mother, however, saw through his ploy and warned him to keep out of his sister-in-law's bed or risk a major court scandal. King Louis decided to cut his losses by sleeping with Louise the diversionary lady-in-waiting. She was to introduce him to his long-standing mistress, Madame de Montespan, and she in turn led him to her replacement, Madame de Maintenon.

Louis XIV's relentless sexual activity produced an unusually large brood of illegitimates, who became a massive drain on the French treasury. Sibling rivalry at Versailles often spilled over into factional in-fighting. Louis also bucked the system by having his bastards married into the legitimate royal family, thus polluting the true Bourbon bloodline. The King's nepotism was deeply resented in the French court.

In 1686 Louis XIV endured a terrible operation for anal fistulas. Twice he was sliced open without any form of anesthetic. The press releases said, as they always did of kings, that he endured the operation heroically. A group of French nuns at the cloister of Saint-Cyr heard of his recovery and celebrated by writing a song, "Dieu Sauvez le Roi." A traveling Englishman heard the tune, copied it down, and when he got home translated it into "God Save the King": thus the British National Anthem evolved from a hymn written to celebrate a successful operation on the French King's derrière.

PITFALLS OF THE JOB

Louis XIV had seven illegitimate children by the grubby Madame de Montespan, a formidable woman with an equally formidable personal-hygiene problem. She was the King's regular mistress for thirteen years, but she had to work hard at keeping him. When Louis met her she was said to be a sensational beauty, dark and sensuous. Later she dyed her hair blond to keep up with the fashion. She already had two children by her first husband, so she dieted hard, unusually for the time, and had her body massaged for two or three hours a day to keep her figure. A regular bath, however, was not part of the beauty treatment. As sleeping with the King was an ambition shared by almost every woman in the court, one of the accepted occupational hazards attached to the enviable status of *maîtresse en titre* was a large number of enemies. Madame de Montespan's savage tongue and vile temper helped attract more than the usual amount of venom. Inevitably, the King began to grow weary of her. She was found, however, to be a poor loser who would try anything to retain her position, including black magic. It was said that she held a Black Mass during which a baby was sacrificed over her naked body. Sadly there was nothing she could do—not even feeding the King toad excrement as an aphrodisiac—that could prevent her inexorable slide toward redundancy. By the time she lost him to his eventual second wife, she had grown almost as fat as the King: her thigh was said to have been as thick as a man's waist. Madame de Montespan ended her days in a convent.

About twelve months after the Queen died, Louis secretly married a friend of his mistress, a matronly widow in her forties named Madame de Maintenon. Louis XIV had a habit of granting audiences to people while he was sitting on his close-stool: some visitors, including the English ambassador Lord Portland, even regarded it as a special honor to be received by the Sun King in this manner. Louis announced his betrothal to his second wife while in the middle of a bowel movement.

He was attracted to her statuesque figure, but what he found even more attractive was that she refused to sleep with him. For Louis this was an irresistible novelty: women did not play hard to get with the King. His new morganatic wife was accepted by the royal family, many of them quietly relieved that perhaps at last in old age the King had given up on his relentless philandering and was settling down to become a model husband. The truth was less romantic. True love hadn't slowed him up; syphilis, however, had.

Although Madame de Maintenon was a middle-aged woman, she was probably a virgin when King Louis first slept with her: her previous marriage with a disabled poet had not been consummated. Even if she had been sexually experienced, the unflagging virility of her syphilitic little husband would have been a major shock to her system. When she was seventy-five years old and Louis was seventy, she complained to her confessor that she found the effort of making love to him twice a day rather tiring.

The King's health was badly weakened by assaults from the popular medicinal cures of the day, including indiscriminate bleeding, purging, enemas and massive doses of opium and qui-nine, but they barely dented his appetite for food or sex. In

1715, sores broke out on the King's left leg, and soon the leg began to stink and turned black with gangrene. It led to a slow and agonizing death. The whole country rejoiced: his coffin, as it traveled to Saint-Denis, was hooted at by a drunken mob, and people drank and sang along the route.

PHILIP, DUKE D'ORLÉANS

Louis XIV's nephew, Philip, Duke d'Orléans, was Regent to the boy-king Louis XV for nine years and ruled the country in all but name. The myopic little Regent was generally considered to be the most debauched man in French history. Although he had demonstrated himself to be an intelligent and very gifted politician, his chief interests were women and wine. At the age of fourteen he became the father of a baby girl when he raped the head porter's daughter at the Palais Royal. He made an actress and his wife pregnant at about the same time, mistress and wife simultaneously giving birth to an illegitimate son and a legitimate daughter.

His mistresses were legion; it was reckoned that he kept over a hundred at a time. His choice of women drew comment too, as all of them were very plain. When he was chided by his mother for his lack of taste, he famously replied, "Bah, Mother, all cats are gray in the dark!" His personal harem and his "daily filthiness" were the talk of France, but he was similarly famous for his drinking binges. The Regent was a desperate alcoholic, particularly partial to the new fizzy champagne recently invented by Dom Pérignon. To the very end he continued to consume seven bottles of champagne almost every evening.

The Regent's regular orgies in the Palais Royal scandalized

Paris. Every evening he would shut himself away with a few male and female companions, then get himself wildly drunk and sleep with whoever took his fancy, while naked prostitutes were served upon silver dishes for his guests. Even more controversially, he was an atheist and proud of it: he held orgies on Good Friday and it was alleged that he dabbled in the occult. The single most shocking allegation against the filthy old Regent, however, concerned his incestuous relationship with his eldest daughter, the Duchess de Berri. The abominable Elizabeth, short, obese and badly marked from smallpox, was almost as debauched as her father. Married at the age of fourteen to her cousin the Duc de Berri, the youngest grandson of Louis XIV, within four years she became a wealthy teenage widow interested only in drinking herself senseless and running up huge gambling debts. Daily she drank herself into a stupor and could often be found rolling in her own vomit on the carpet. Eventually she became so fat that she found it impossible to mount a horse.

It was widely rumored that she was sleeping with her father, gossip which the Regent encouraged by inviting her to his all-night orgies and painting her in the nude. She died aged twenty-four, most probably from cirrhosis of the liver and weakened by a difficult and illegitimate childbirth, although her death certificate stated that she ate herself to death. It was commented at her funeral that the Regent's unusually intense display of emotion at his daughter's early demise was motivated by something other than parental grief.

In his forties, the Regent took on the appearance of a senile and purple-faced old man. When he first showed himself in England, London's bookmakers offered odds that he would be dead within three months. In 1723, against the advice of his physicians, he took a new mistress thirty years his junior. The effect on his heart was predictably disastrous. They were sitting by the fireplace of his drawing room at Versailles one December evening when he had a massive stroke and slumped unconscious. When a doctor tried to bleed him, a lady courtier warned, "No! You'll kill him . . . he has just lain with a whore." Two hours later he was dead, aged forty-nine. Most people thought it was a miracle that he had lived that long. Although it was quite obvious to everyone what had killed him, court etiquette demanded that there should be an official postmortem. Unfortunately, while the physicians were carving him up, the Regent's favorite dog snatched his master's heart and ate it.

DANGERS OF THE SPORTING LIFE

There were risks attached to royal free love. In the eighteenth and nineteenth centuries, syphilis replaced the battlefield as the slayer of princes. Most forms of venereal disease, including gonorrhea, soft chancre and syphilis, were collectively known as "the foul disease" or "the pox." In the early part of Queen Victoria's reign, doctors were still unable to differentiate gonorrhea from syphilis.

Gonorrhea was also known as the "Preventer of Life" because, although it rarely led to death, it frequently resulted in sterilization in both sexes. Syphilis was the more pernicious of the two and a far more dangerous disease than it is today. It remains live in human tissue for a lifetime unless it is destroyed by treatment. When primary syphilis goes untreated it develops into the second stage, resulting in hair loss, gum disease and loss of teeth, painful joints, indigestion, fever, headaches, circulatory problems and cardiac palpitations. The third stage can lie dormant in the system and erupt anything up to thirty years later. It can damage vital organs, including the heart, and cause paralysis, blindness and deafness. Without treatment it results in paresis, a softening of the brain. The brain-damaged victim may not quite qualify for modern psychiatry's precise meaning of the term "insane," but the victim nevertheless appears to be mad.

In 1909 the commendably persistent Paul Ehrlich discovered Salversan, the first ever treatment for syphilis. It was also known as "Treatment 606" because it was Ehrlich's 606th attempt to find a cure. In the nineteenth century there was no treatment except massage with mercury, a medication which was sometimes worse than the disease. The risks of prolonged mercury use were great: gums became swollen; teeth fell out; mouths became terribly ulcerated. These side effects were considered to be appropriate because they were likely to deter syphilitics from further reckless sexual adventures. This unfortunately did not allow for the various other ways that syphilis could be passed on independently of sexual intercourse: in England, for example, the custom of kissing a Bible when taking a judicial oath often led to syphilitic infection.

Syphilis was able to rampage through most European courts assisted by the filthy conditions that even royalty lived in. The eighteenth-century Prussian King Frederick William I was considered by his contemporaries to be most eccentric, not because he was a demented, vicious psychopath, but because he washed his hands regularly. Eighteenth-century English nobility, when faced with newfangled ideas about disease and personal hygiene, clung to the belief that washing was decidedly not for them. A duchess at a society dinner once sat down to eat with noticeably filthy hands. When the grubbiness of her fingers was remarked upon, she replied, "Madam, you should see my feet." When Queen Victoria inherited Buckingham Palace in 1837 it didn't even have a bathroom. Her predecessors, the Georgian royals, believed it was "sweat, damn it, that kept a man clean."

Versailles was considered to be the very pinnacle of fashion and culture. It made a quite different first impression on the Austrian-born Duchess of Orleans, who wrote home in 1694: "There is one thing at court that I shall never get used to . . . the people stationed in the galleries in front of our rooms piss into all the corners. It is impossible to leave one's apartment without seeing someone pissing." Although Louis XIV was an enthusiastic lover, the King's advances must have been a trying time for his mistresses: he took only three baths in his lifetime, and each of those under protest. His great-grandson Louis XVI was the first French king to use a knife and fork, take a regular bath and brush his teeth. An Italian ambassador noted the King's "peculiar" interest in hygiene. After the first Spanish civil war, the Carlist Pretender Don Carlos and his wife lived briefly in exile in London at Gloucester Lodge, Brompton. The Duke of Wellington visited them and was appalled by the stench, complaining that they could at the very least have brought with them "a little soap and water."

The Russian court was the dirtiest of all, a mixture of fantastic extravagance and medieval squalor. Catherine the Great noted that it was not unusual to see a woman exquisitely dressed and covered in jewels emerging from a courtyard ankle deep in sewage "and horrors of every sort." The Winter Palace of St. Petersburg during the reign of Czar Nicholas I was considered to be one of the biggest and most opulent royal residences in the world, with 1,600 rooms and 4,000 inhabitants. It was, however, perpetually alive with vermin, mostly because of the Czar's reluctance to get rid of the herd of cows he always kept on the top floor to ensure a regular supply of milk for his family. When the Imperial Annanhof Palace in Moscow burned down, bystanders were amazed by the mass evacuation of rats down the grand staircase.

The crowned heads of Europe held their breath when Peter the Great became the first ever Russian czar to travel west in 1697. The filthy Czar was noted to be blissfully unaware of rudimentary personal hygiene, table manners or even basic potty training. When Peter's son Alexis went to Dresden in 1712 to marry a German Princess, the Elector of Hanover, Ernst August, noted with distaste in a letter to his wife that the Czarevitch defecated in his bedroom and wiped his backside with the curtains. The assembled throng of "civilized" Europeans were also amazed by his lack of familiarity with the handkerchief. The Electress Sophia wryly observed that, if the King of France took to blowing his nose on his fingers, it would immediately be considered the height of fashion by all Europe.

THE COST OF SYPHILIS

In the first half of the twentieth century, students of history were always told to look out for signs of syphilis at the onset of premature physical or mental decrepitude. Frederick the Great suffered badly from it, as did King Christian VII of Denmark. The Romanovs were particularly hard hit by syphilis. Catherine the Great contracted syphilis despite taking elaborate precautions to avoid it by screening her myriad sleeping partners through a committee of female courtiers and doctors. Catherine's mad son Paul I showed all the classic signs of congenital syphilis, including a saddle nose.

The British royal family has from time to time also found itself to be venereally challenged. Medical historians speculate that Queen Anne's Danish consort, Prince George of Denmark, may have been congenitally syphilitic, resulting in his wife's catalogue of disastrous pregnancies. The "water on the brain" from which one of her sons died suggests a low-grade congenital syphilitic meningitis. The premature death at twenty-eight of Edward VII's eldest son, the Duke of Clarence, was officially attributed to pneumonia, but was rumored to have been caused by syphilis of the brain. King George V's cousin Prince Alfred of Saxe-Coburg-Gotha caught syphilis and was subsequently shunned by the royal family and his regiment. He lived in exile in Romania attended by only one servant and his tutor, and died of cerebral syphilis aged twenty-four in 1899. According to *The Times* he "had been suffering from a chronic cerebral affection." *The Complete Peerage* recorded that he shot himself.

As far as retrospective diagnosis will allow, it is possible to judge that the family history of schizophrenia wasn't the only factor in the devastation of the Bavarian and Austrian royal families in the nineteenth century. The mental breakdowns of Bavaria's "Mad" King Ludwig II and his brother King Otto may have been partly attributable to syphilis. Ludwig's post-mortem referred to a non-specific organic disease of the brain. Ludwig's father was believed to have died of typhoid, but he caught syphilis as a young man during a fling with a Hungarian prostitute: he could easily have passed it on to his sons.

Syphilis also provides one of the more plausible motives for the Austrian Crown Prince Rudolf's suicide in 1889. There was considerable speculation that the Crown Prince might have decided to take his own life rather than face a slow and lingering death from venereal disease. The health of Rudolf and his mad Bavarian cousins Ludwig and Otto deteriorated markedly when they were still quite young men. Each aged prematurely; each suffered early tooth loss. In his early thirties, the narcissistic Ludwig became very flabby, began to lose his hair and could no longer bear to be seen in public. He shunned court dinner parties, and when he was absolutely forced to attend he hid behind huge flower arrangements so that the other guests couldn't see him. These are classic signs of untreated syphilis.

LOUIS XV

King Louis XV of France had more reason than most to live in perpetual fear of syphilis. Of all the Bourbon monarchs, his sex life was the most astonishing. The King had started his reign with the epithet "Louis the well beloved," but this undeserved popularity waned when the stories about his relentless debauchery began to circulate. Even the relatively small amount of sexual congress that his subjects got to hear about—in actual fact only the tip of the iceberg—led to rumors that the King had to bathe daily in children's blood to renew his exhausted body.

Louis XV was a king at five, a husband at fifteen and a father at sixteen. By the time he was in his early twenties his valets were regularly procuring whores for him, although he continued to keep in touch with his drab Polish wife, Maria, by

sleeping with her when the mood took him. The King's pecca-
dilloes became the talk of Versailles, not for the sheer quantity
of sexual activity he enjoyed, but because of whom he was doing it with. Remarkably, he took five of his mistresses from the
same family, all of them sisters.

His first official mistress or "left-handed queen" was a twenty-
seven-year-old married woman, the Comtesse de Mailly, one of
five daughters of the Marquis de Nesle. A contemporary court diarist described her as "well built, ugly, stupid looking but with
good teeth." Her plainness surprised many foreign visitors to
Versailles, who naturally expected a flamboyant Bourbon king to
keep a glamorous mistress. As the Comtesse's mother was one of
the Queen's ladies-in-waiting, her four sisters were all attached to
the French court. To the Comtesse's everlasting horror, the King
slept with all of them.

The first sister to be seduced was Madame de Vintimille, a
huge woman described as having "the face of a grenadier, the
neck of a stork and the smell of a monkey." She died in childbirth
while giving him an illegitimate son who bore such an obvious
resemblance to the King that he was to be known as Demi-Louis
for the rest of his life. Louis then transferred his affections to her
obese and even more repulsive sister Adelaide, who held his attention briefly before it strayed to the next sister, Hortense. By
this time the King's soft spot for the incredibly ugly Mailly sisters
en masse had become the inspiration for a number of lewd popular songs. Having gone thus far, Louis figured he might as well
go for the full set. The last member of the family to be visited
upon by the King was Marie-Anne. She was more attractive and
considerably more ambitious than her sisters. She ruthlessly
evicted the rest of her family from the court, and considered her
position so unassailable that she dared to be openly abusive to the

Queen. Unfortunately, this mistress was struck down with peritonitis and died in her twenty-eighth year.

The King's sister Louise caused a sensation when she walked out of the palace to become a Carmelite nun, announcing as she left that she would shut herself away to pray for the King's soul. As no member of the French royal family had been anywhere near a convent since the Middle Ages it was a damning indictment. Soon half of France was talking about how the evil, dissipated King had turned Versailles into a huge brothel.

His next mistress, the grandly styled Madame de Pompadour, was suspected of having an undue amount of political influence over him, and consequently made more than the usual amount of enemies at court. The King met her at a masked ball in Versailles's famous Hall of Mirrors. He had taken elaborate precautions to remain anonymous, arriving dressed as a yew tree, just like eleven of his friends. Although the King was completely enraptured with his ravishing new *maîtresse en titre*, she wasn't very keen on sex. This was naturally a handicap for someone whose position depended upon her ability to guarantee the royal pleasure, especially when the lover happened to be the most libidinous of a long line of oversexed Bourbons. Madame de Pompadour was not a strong woman and she found the King's sex drive physically exhausting. To make matters worse, Louis had finally stopped sleeping with the Queen, who had become prematurely aged and paunchy, and increased his demands on his mistress's time to satisfy his needs. When the King remarked one day that Madame de Pompadour was "as cold as a coot," it dawned on her just how precarious her privileged position was.

Consumed with the fear that she might lose her royal lover and her gilded lifestyle, she stuffed herself with aphrodisiacs, living for months on chocolate, truffles, vanilla and celery soup. Instead of increasing her ardor, however, this particular F-plan diet merely made her vomit. The royal mistress finally arrived at the conclusion that the only way to retain her position and get a decent night's sleep now and then was to turn a blind eye to the King's indiscretions. A sensible solution to her dilemma was found in the infamous Parc du Cerfs.

Previously, the girls procured for the King by his trusted valet, Lebel, would be taken to a small apartment in the palace of Versailles known as the "Bird Trap." If the King liked what he saw, they were then lodged at the apartment, usually one or two at a time, under the supervision of a housekeeper, Madame Bertrand. The girls were nearly always "high-class" whores, but the only firm rule was that they had to be young and disease free. As the King's popularity declined and the stories about his private life increased, Louis felt it necessary to keep some of his seedier affairs away from the prying eyes of his courtiers, especially as he had acquired an unhealthy taste for very young girls, sometimes bedding several at a time. So he set up the Parc du Cerfs in a discreet little building with just five or six rooms set in a quiet street in Versailles.

Most of the post-revolutionary stories about the Parc du Cerfs were wildly exaggerated: tales of naked underage girls being hunted through the woods by the King and his hounds; Thomas Carlyle wrote of the King as "a fabulous Griffin, devouring the works of men, daily dragging virgins into thy cave." But the truth did not require embellishment.

The Parc du Cerfs was not a unique concept. Many wealthy Frenchmen of the period kept their own private brothels. Louis XV's personal harem, however, was probably the grandest ever to service the needs of one man, costing £200,000 a year to maintain. Lebel and others were expected to make available to the King a constant supply of healthy girls aged between nine and eighteen years. Only from the age of fourteen years upward were they obliged to be "in active service." Louis, fortified by an opium-based mixture known as "General Lamotte's Drops," would sneak off to his private brothel in the early evening and return to the state bed at dawn.

Madame de Pompadour did not, as was popularly alleged, become his procuress, but she accepted the existence of her lover's private brothel as the lesser of two evils: at least if he was sleeping with peasant girls it would keep him out of the beds of her rivals at court. As for the prostitutes in the Parc du Cerfs, Madame de Pompadour assured a friend, "All those little uneducated girls would never take him from me."

It may have been due to Louis's fear of catching syphilis that he took to sleeping with very young girls, believing it would lessen the risk. When the girls outstayed their welcome by reaching the ripe old age of nineteen, they were either married off or dispatched to a convent. There was apparently no shortage of volunteers. Parents considered that a relatively brief period of dishonor was a price well worth paying for the guarantee of lifelong security for their daughters. Little is known about who, or even how many girls, passed through the Parc du Cerfs, but over a period of thirty-four years it probably ran to several thousands. Remarkably, most of the girls had no idea at all who they were sleeping with. They were usually told that the man they worked for was a foreign dignitary. More often than not their client passed himself off as a wealthy Polish nobleman.

A few we do know about. The most famous was Louise O'Murphy, a fourteen-year-old, half-French, half-Irish girl, her bare backside immortalized in several paintings by Boucher. She was resident in the Parc du Cerfs for four years until she was dismissed for making an unflattering remark about Madame de Pompadour. Miss O'Murphy had at least two, possibly three, children by the King. Another, Madame de Romans, was one of the King's personal favorites. She objected to being hidden away in the Parc du Cerfs and was rewarded with her own residence. The son she gave him was the only illegitimate child he ever acknowledged as his own. All things considered, he fathered very few bastards—probably only about twenty.

Lebel found it increasingly difficult to maintain a steady intake of fresh young girls. It also became even more difficult to excite the King's jaded appetite. As a result, the building was finally sold off in 1771. From then on, the King's new official mistress, Madame du Barry, monopolized his sexual requirements to the end of his days. For, by 1756, time and tuberculosis had destroyed the health and the looks of the proud Madame du Pompadour. She had been severely weakened by several miscarriages and she also suffered from bronchitis, which caused her to cough blood incessantly. Her gaunt, ravaged features were masked behind several strata of highly toxic lead-based cosmetics which were also slowly killing her. The court diarist, D'Argenson, recorded that her skin was yellow and withered. "As for her bosom," noted D'Argenson, "it is kinder not to mention it." In 1764, the King's mistress of some twenty years standing coughed her last.

At this time there operated in Paris an infamous pimp named Jean Baptiste du Barry, widely known as "Mahomet" because of his huge harem of prostitutes. He specialized in picking up good-looking shop-girls and unemployed actresses, and grooming them into courtesans for his rich clients. It was his dream that one of his more upmarket protégées would eventually strike it lucky and become the mistress of an aristocrat. His star pupil was to exceed even his wildest expectations. Marie Jean Bécu was the illegitimate daughter of an unmarried seamstress; her father was a friar. After a brief spell working as a Paris shop assistant she was spotted by Monsieur du Barry. She took her pimp's surname and, via a string of noblemen, bedhopped her way to Versailles.

Jean du Barry had already slept with several members of the French court before King Louis met her. Finally she was ushered into the royal presence. She made the obligatory three curtsies, then walked up to the King and kissed him full in the mouth. The sexual chemistry for the old Bourbon was immediate, especially as she also came complete with a health certificate which stated that she was free from venereal disease. Louis XV began sleeping with his new official mistress as his wife, Queen Maria, lay on her deathbed.

Madame du Barry was immediately written off by the French court as a shallow girl whose good looks alone would not hold the King's attentions for long. They had underestimated her considerable sexual expertise. Richelieu once dared to ask Louis what he saw in her. The King replied, "She is the only woman in France who has managed to make me forget I will soon be sixty." Louis confided to the Duke d'Ayen that thanks to Madame du Barry he had "discovered some pleasures entirely new to him." The Duke replied that this was probably because the King had never been to a decent brothel. Madame du Barry stayed with the King for the next four years, until his death. She chose his ministers, dictated French foreign policy, and used the royal treasury as though it was her own personal expense account. She was in effect the uncrowned queen of France.

The King had aged prematurely—his doctors complained that the new official mistress left the sixty-four-year-old Bourbon "sucked dry." Alarmed by his decline, they appealed to him to take an older, less energetic mistress who would be less of a strain on his heart. The King reluctantly promised that he would "rein in the horses." The doctor replied, "You'd do better to unharness them."

The King's doctors had always mistakenly believed that Louis had survived a slight attack of smallpox when he was young and was therefore immune. In 1774, however, the King developed a severe headache which was swiftly followed by a sinister and familiar rash. As no one dared admit the mistake, they kept him away from mirrors, but the King became suspicious. One morning he saw spots on his hands. He cried, "This is smallpox . . . at my age one doesn't recover!" In spite of the obvious high risk of contagion, he insisted that his mistress stay by his bedside and mop his forehead. His face quickly became black, covered with encrusted scabs, and swollen to twice its normal size. On May 10, 1774, Louis died painfully, but not before making his first confession in thirty-eight years. A courtier timed it at a suspiciously brief sixteen minutes. Nineteen years later the French revolutionaries remembered Madame du Barry's four-year spree of power and profligacy, and removed her head.

CHARLES X

The grotesquely bloated Louis XVIII was probably the only homosexual Bourbon king of France, but his successor, the last reigning Bourbon, was truer to family form. The charming but useless Charles X came to the French throne in 1824 and abdicated six years later. As a young man he was a violent and abusive drunk, was known in almost every brothel in Paris, and had seduced half the ladies in court. In time he was transformed from an oversexed lout into a witless dandy. When the Austrian Emperor Joseph visited the French court he described Charles as "a fop" and his wife as "a complete imbecile." Louis XV and his mistresses had long since left the French monarchy in a state of near-bankruptcy and Charles blew what little was left on an unfeasibly large personal wardrobe which included a new pair of shoes for every day of the year. His biggest single expense was the Etruscan-style building known as the Bagatelle, which existed as a result of a bet: he wagered 100,000 livres that he could build, decorate and furnish a house in Bois de Boulogne in nine weeks.

Charles X's son Ferdinand, the Duke de Beri, was also a notorious libertine. After his assassination in 1820, his wife, Caroline, was visited by a score of women from Nantes, every one of them claiming to be pregnant by her husband. The Duchess couldn't believe it, and asked one of her household how long her husband had stayed there. She was informed that the Duke had been in Nantes for one week. "Ah, then," said the Duchess, "in that case it's quite possible."

THE ALPHONSOS OF SPAIN

At the end of the nineteenth century, Spain was ruled by another Bourbon in the person of the promiscuous King Alphonso XII, whose life was brought to a premature end in 1885 when he was only twenty-eight years old. Officially he died from consumption, but there was little doubt that the real cause of death was venereal disease. At the age of seventeen, Alphonso had fallen in love with the beautiful Princess Mercedes, daughter of the Duke of Montpensier. Although his bride was also his first cousin it was a rare royal love match. Within six months of their wedding day, however, she was struck down dead with gastric fever. As she was also related to the unfortunate Austrian Emperor Franz Joseph, superstitious Spaniards blamed her death on the so-called Habsburg Curse.

Alphonso plunged into an almost suicidal depression from which he never quite recovered. He regained his poise sufficiently to honor his dynastic obligations, and a year later was remarried to Maria, daughter of the star-crossed Austrian Archduke Franz Ferdinand. In private, however, he submerged his grief in the beds of other women.

The King's philandering produced one of the great secret royal scandals of the nineteenth century. One of Alphonso's regular mistresses was the wife of a young army officer. The King discovered, to his irritation, that the husband was a jealous and naturally suspicious type, and so he pulled a few strings to put him permanently out of the picture. The cuckolded young officer suddenly found himself dispatched to Cuba on a series of dangerous and life-threatening assignments. Inconveniently for King Alphonso XII, the young officer survived. Worse still, someone had tipped him off as to the real reason he had been posted 3,000 miles from Madrid. He deserted and returned home. When the King next arrived at his mistress's house, he found her husband armed and waiting, intent on revenge. This time, however, Alphonso had taken the precaution of bringing along an armed bodyguard. The jealous husband was put to the sword and his body secretly disposed of.

Another of Alphonso's favorites was a dancer called Elena Sanchez, who bore him two bastards. On his deathbed, she and his wife, Maria Christina, stood side by side to pay their final respects. When the King died his wife was pregnant. The baby was born King Alphonso XIII in May 1886, under the Regency of the Queen Mother.

The boy-king grew up to be odd-looking even for a Spanish Bourbon. He was physically puny, tubercular, unnaturally pale, and in addition to his huge Bourbon nose he had a very pronounced jawline. In spite of his runtish appearance it quickly became apparent that there was very hot Bourbon blood coursing beneath his corpse-like complexion.

The Spanish court had long since decided that it was time to address the problem of the royal family's genetic stock, as too many centuries of marriage partners from Catholic southern Europe had resulted in a family that was dangerously inbred. Accordingly, in 1906 Alphonso was married to Princess Victoria of Battenberg, who had been raised in England as a Protestant and was a granddaughter of Queen Victoria. Although she had converted to Catholicism, the marriage to Queen Ena, as she became known, was controversial and bitterly resented by Spanish conservatives.

Although the King suffered from debilitating heart and chest conditions he was an aggressive adulterer. He surrounded himself with a gang of like-minded friends and pimps and together they cruised Madrid's brothels. According to the mistresses who kissed and told, the King was a voracious but selfish lover. His private life was an open secret at court and his conquests were discussed freely. One evening a young nobleman was about to leave a Madrid brothel when the proprietress stopped him and made an unusual request: she recognized him as an acquaintance of the King—could he please return His Majesty's signet ring, which he'd left in the brothel the night before? The young courtier returned it discreetly to Alphonso, who made him kneel then jokingly dubbed him "Duke of Loyalty."

King Alphonso was also a frequent visitor to Paris, where he had several people on the payroll at the Spanish Embassy whose sole job was to procure women for him and ensure he had a regular supply of fresh black satin sheets.

For all but the first two or three years of their marriage, the King and Queen lived virtually separate lives, appearing together only when protocol required it. For many female courtiers, flirting with the King was almost a reflex action. Queen Ena suffered her husband's infidelity in silence, even when he was cruelly indiscreet—his conquests included several of her ladies-in-waiting, and even her first cousin Beatrice. The King sired countless bastards, few of whom could look forward to royal patronage or any sort of acknowledgment. Alphonso had seduced a young Irish governess who was employed briefly in his court. When she became pregnant by him and gave birth to a daughter, she was simply sacked and kicked out of the royal household in disgrace.

ROMANOV ROMANCE

Czar Peter the Great was one of history's all-time heavyweight royal adulterers. The Czar took pride in the fact that he was the father of countless bastards: he considered it part of his patriotic duty. Whenever the Czar wanted sex, his wife's ladies-in-waiting were his mainstay for instant gratification. When Peter and his wife visited Prussia in September 1717, they had in tow about 400 ladies-in-waiting, who acted as cooks, chambermaids and washerwomen for the party. A German princess noted that about one in every four women was carrying a very well-dressed child. When pressed about the whereabouts of the fathers, each replied with a smile, "The Czar did me the honor."

Foreign ambassadors would pretend not to notice while Peter openly fondled the breasts of his wife's ladies-in-waiting. The Prussian King Frederick William I witnessed Peter greeting his niece the Duchess of Mecklenburg. The Czar swept her up in his arms, carried her to an adjacent room, tore off her underclothes and had sex with her right there on the spot, not even bothering to shut the door to prevent her husband from watching.

Both of the Czar's wives were aware that he regularly took prostitutes as well. Unabashed, he boasted that he spent less money on his mistresses than any other monarch in Europe. When he visited France the thing he looked forward to more than anything else was the promise of the Parisienne brothels. At Versailles it was recorded that he slept with a streetwalker, upset her with his legendary stinginess, then sent her packing.

Husbands sensibly learned to turn a blind eye when it became apparent that their wives had taken the Czar's fancy. One of Peter's mistresses was married to an army captain named Tchernichov. She gave birth to seven children, and no one was quite sure, not even their mother, which were the husband's and which were the Czar's. When she gave Peter syphilis, however, the Czar was furious and instructed the husband to give her a sound whipping.

The Czar had a long-serving mistress named Mary Hamilton, a Russian-born girl descended from a Scottish family. When Peter became bored with her, she consoled herself by sleeping with several of Peter's aides. She found herself with a series of unwanted pregnancies, which she resolved by systematic infanticide. One of Mary's lovers was a courtier named Orlov who bullied her and demanded money from her. To keep Orlov happy, she pilfered from the Czarina's jewelry collection. Mary's access to the jewels made her the prime suspect, and when she was questioned by the Czar she quickly broke down and confessed all, including the murder of the newborn babies. Peter was incensed, not because she had slain innocent children, but because it was just possible that one of them might have been his, and Mary Hamilton was duly sentenced to death. The Czar was present at the execution. He kissed her, then watched as her head was cut off by the executioner. He picked up the bloodied head, pointed out to the crowd below how expertly the axman had severed her neck, kissed her full on the lips, dropped the head in the mud and then walked away for a beer.

The Czar demanded fidelity from his wives. His second wife, the Czarina Catherine, had an affair with her husband's chamberlain, William Mons. She was indiscreet and everyone at court got to know about it except the Czar. When word of the affair finally reached him, he was both furious and sorely embarrassed. His ego would not allow him to admit that his wife had preferred to sleep with another man, and so he could not bring himself to confront her. Without any reference to the alleged adultery, Peter had his chamberlain arrested and condemned on trumped-up bribery charges. Catherine watched as Mons was beheaded, but her nerve held and she was very careful not to show the slightest sign of emotion that might betray her. The Czar was exasperated by his wife's display of inscrutability. One evening Catherine returned to her room to find her ex-lover's head pickled in alcohol in a jar by her bed. She retired to bed without flinching. Night after night, Catherine went to sleep beside her grisly bedside ornament, but still she kept her composure. Finally Peter gave up and had the head removed. Half a century later when Catherine the Great was reorganizing Russia's Museum of Fine Art she found two jars containing the pickled heads of Mary Hamilton and William Mons, which had been on display in the gallery since 1724.

Like Peter the Great, Czar Alexander I was fêted abroad as a great enlightened liberator but feared at home as a ruthlessly oppressive autocrat. As a teenager he had been sickened by the senile sexual frolics of his grandmother Catherine the Great, but it didn't diminish his robustly healthy interest in women. Soon after he married thirteen-year-old Princess Louisa of Baden, Alexander took up with the wife of his master of the hounds, a beautiful Polish woman named Maria, who flaunted her position as the Czar's favorite mistress as blatantly as she possibly could. He also seduced the wives of two of his best friends, plus a whole string of wives of minor court officials.

The Czar's interest in women took a less healthy turn when his attentions focused on his sister. The Grand Duchess Catherine Pavlovna was a petite, vivacious woman with "eyes of fire and the figure of a demi-goddess," according to one of her many admirers. Unfortunately, her greatest admirer was her brother. Alexander and his sister became almost inseparable, and when they were apart he showered her with passionate letters written in French: "I am mad about you . . . I love you like a madman" and "I rejoice like a maniac to be seeing you again . . . after having run like a man possessed, I hope to take delicious rest in your arms."

His lust for his favorite sister ended abruptly at about the time of Napoleon's retreat from Moscow, when the Czar's life took a strange and unexpected turn. He unaccountably became involved with an obscure religious cult, and surrounded himself with shadowy "priests." The Czar's death at the age of forty-seven was shrouded in mystery and myth. Some Romanovs believe to this day that Alexander faked his death and lived out the rest of his years as a religious mystic. According to the official version, however, he was already weakened by an acute liver condition and his doctors finished him off by giving him two enemas and applying thirty-five leeches to his neck.

When Alexander died childless, the Crown should have passed to his vicious brother, the Grand Duke Constantine, who had inherited both his insane father's looks and his sensitivity. The Grand Duke, however, committed the unpardonable royal sin of entering into a morganatic marriage, and was so widely unpopular that he was forced to waive his rights to succession, in favor of his younger brother Nicholas.

Czar Alexander's vigorous and handsome brother and eventual successor to the throne, Nicholas I, was considered to be a bit of an eccentric because he didn't take a mistress until he had been married for twenty-five years, and only then when his wife's health failed. His choice of mistress, however—one of his wife's ladies-in-waiting, Varvara Nelidova—was not in the best possible taste. His younger brother Mikhail had an even stranger relationship with his very beautiful young wife, the grand Duchess Elena Pavlovna. On their wedding night, instead of escorting his new bride to the royal bedroom, he suddenly jumped on his horse and galloped off to review a guards regiment. It was, as they say, the talk of St. Petersburg.

As a young man, Czar Alexander II flirted with, and greatly impressed, Queen Victoria, and under different circumstances could even have become her husband. In 1839 the heir to the Russian throne visited England. The young Victoria was besotted with the tall, striking, twenty-year-old Romanov. When she met him again thirty-five years later, even though he was much altered and England and Russia had fought each other in the Crimean War, Queen Victoria confessed that she had never quite lost her infatuation for him.

The Czar was certainly no Prince Albert. Alexander II managed to shock even the jaded sensibilities of the Russian court when, at the age of fifty, he suddenly ditched his loyal wife, Marie, after twenty-seven years of marriage and took up with an eighteen-year-old St. Petersburg schoolgirl named Catherine Dolkuruka. The middle-aged lovelorn Czar installed her as one of his wife's ladies-in-waiting and promised her that he would get rid of his wife at the earliest opportunity. The young mistress bore him four children over the next fourteen years, three of whom lived in the palace. This brought the Empress Marie enormous grief. When she fell terminally ill and lay alone and dying, it was said that she could hear the laughter of her husband's bastards as they played in the room above.

Russian law obliged the Czar to observe the minimum requirements of decency and good taste by waiting one full year after his wife died before he remarried. The Romanov family were shocked to discover that Czar Alexander had secretly married his young mistress within forty days after the Empress's death. There were few expressions of regret on either side of the Kremlin wall in 1881 when Alexander II was blown apart by a terrorist bomb.

THIRD-REPUBLIC MORALITY

In the nineteenth century, French court morals sank to an all-time low. However, this time the chief culprit was not a

Bourbon. Napoleon Bonaparte's nephew Louis Napoleon became Emperor of France in 1852, taking the title Napoleon III. He married a year later. His wife, Eugénie, a beautiful Spanish countess, had attempted to commit suicide after an unrequited love affair in her youth by breaking the heads off phosphorus matches and drinking them dissolved in milk. It is unlikely that the Emperor was faithful to her for more than the first six months of their twenty years of marriage.

Emperor Napoleon III was the unlikeliest of lady-killers—four feet and six inches tall, with an overly large head, little hair, one dilated eyeball, a beaky nose, a music-hall waxed mustache and a rheumatic limp. He appeared in public on horseback whenever possible because of his stumpy legs and his peculiar waddling gait, which was largely due to the fact that the Emperor wore nappies. Neither his appearance nor the testimonies of countless women to his less than extraordinary performances between the sheets dented his unwavering belief that he was an irresistible seducer.

In England in the late 1840s he slept with a succession of actresses, most famously Elisa Felix, who under her stage name Rachel was one of Europe's best-known actresses. She boasted that she had slept with almost every prominent man in London. In 1847 Louis Napoleon and Miss Felix were in a first-class train compartment traveling from London to Birmingham, with his cousin "Plon-Plon." During the journey his cousin fell asleep. He awoke to see Louis and the actress fornicating on the seat opposite him, but judiciously closed his eyes.

One of Louis Napoleon's most rewarding relationships was formed with a blond English courtesan who subsequently financed his election to the French Presidency. Elizabeth Ann Haryet, also known as Mrs. Howard, was the twenty-four-year-old daughter of a Brighton cobbler. At one time she was the mistress of the jockey Jem Mason, rider of the winning horse in the 1839 Grand National. Later she had a son by a major in the Life Guards, and slept with at least three other titled English gentlemen, the Duke of Beaufort, the Earl of Chesterfield and the Earl of Malmesbury. By the time she met Louis Napoleon she had acquired a large fortune through various generous financial settlements from her ex-boyfriends.

Louis Napoleon installed her in a house in Berkeley Street, not far from his own residence in St. James's, and as soon as he became President of France he took her with him and put her up in a house near the Elysée Palace. He was still sleeping with her when he suddenly announced his forthcoming engagement to Eugénie. The first his English mistress knew about it was when she casually picked up a copy of a newspaper in a hotel lobby on the morning the news broke. She dashed back to her home to find that Louis Napoleon's secret police had already ransacked her rooms to make sure that there was nothing incriminating that could link him to her.

While his wife was pregnant with their son, the Emperor embarked on his most scandalous affair yet, taking a nineteen-year-old Italian mistress, the Comtesse de Castiglione. She was said to be Europe's most accomplished and most beautiful courtesan. The English Lord Hertford, allegedly the most tight-fisted man in Paris, paid her a million francs (about $30,000) for the pleasure of one night in bed with her, providing she promised to indulge his every whim. As a result she was confined to bed for three days. Thereafter they gave each other a wide berth, it was said, out of mutual respect.

Napoleon gave his Comtesse a new pearl necklace worth

about half a million francs and a monthly salary of 50,000 francs. Little did he suspect that his new mistress was spying on behalf of her boyfriend, the Italian King Victor Emmanuel II, and the Italian government. The plan worked perfectly in every detail but one. The frothy Comtesse neither knew nor wanted to know anything about politics, and although she made considerable inroads into Louis Napoleon's bank balance she failed to extract any useful information or exert one iota of influence over his policies.

Louis Napoleon's health was undermined by his unflagging sex life, but he had a few other problems besides, including neuralgia, sciatica, dyspepsia, insomnia, gonorrhea and syphilis. He was in agony for much of the time from a combination of rheumatism and the stone in his bladder. The Emperor had some success in keeping his health problems a secret from the press, and even from his wife, who didn't find out the true extent of his illnesses until after he was dead. Before the Battle of Sedan in 1870, he had his cheeks carefully rouged so that his men couldn't see he was white with fear and ravaged with dysentery. He commanded with towels stuffed inside his breeches to act as king-size nappies. He was too ill to attend the opening of the Suez Canal in 1869, and so Eugénie, who also happened to be the cousin of Ferdinand de Lesseps, stood in for him. The royal doctors tried to explain the Emperor's nonappearance at this prestigious event by claiming that he had rheumatism. Napoleon soldiered on with his bladder stone, stubbornly refusing the urologist's probe.

His poor health further restricted his performances in bed. One mistress, the Marquise Taisey-Chatenoy, left a detailed description of his seduction technique, beginning with his ludicrous appearance at the foot of her bed in the middle of the night "looking rather insignificant in mauve silk pajamas." The Marquise continued, "There follows a period of brief physical exertion, during which he breathes heavily and the wax on the ends of his mustaches melts causing them to droop, and finally a hasty withdrawal."

5. GOD'S BAILIFFS

Absolute Power in Hohenzollern Germany and Romanov Russia

THE HOUSE OF Hohenzollern, the royal family of Prussia, and ultimately kaisers of Germany, believed in a family ghost. According to legend a "white lady" would appear before the head of the household when it was time for him to die. One night, Frederick of Prussia's mad young wife charged headfirst through the glass door to his bedroom and appeared before him in her white underclothes splattered in blood. The old King took her for the family ghost, had a heart attack and died a few days later. The Queen, a complete lunatic, had to be maintained at huge expense for another twenty years.

Although the British royal family was blighted by mental illness it was by and large a personal, rather than a political, tragedy. As constitutional monarchs, the amount of damage they could do was limited: executive power lay in the hands of politicians and prime ministers. Elsewhere in Europe the circum-

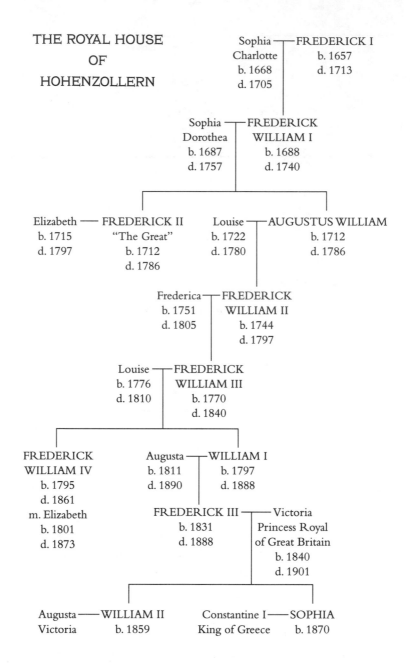

THE ROYAL HOUSE
OF
HOHENZOLLERN

Sophia ——— FREDERICK I
Charlotte
b. 1668
d. 1705

b. 1657
d. 1713

Sophia ——— FREDERICK
Dorothea
b. 1687
d. 1757

WILLIAM I
b. 1688
d. 1740

Elizabeth ——— FREDERICK II
b. 1715
d. 1797

"The Great"
b. 1712
d. 1786

Louise ——— AUGUSTUS WILLIAM
b. 1722
d. 1780

b. 1712
d. 1786

Frederica ——— FREDERICK
b. 1751
d. 1805

WILLIAM II
b. 1744
d. 1797

Louise ——— FREDERICK
b. 1776
d. 1810

WILLIAM III
b. 1770
d. 1840

FREDERICK
WILLIAM IV
b. 1795
d. 1861
m. Elizabeth
b. 1801
d. 1873

Augusta ——— WILLIAM I
b. 1811
d. 1890

b. 1797
d. 1888

FREDERICK III ——— Victoria
b. 1831
d. 1888

Princess Royal
of Great Britain
b. 1840
d. 1901

Augusta ——— WILLIAM II
Victoria   b. 1859

Constantine I ——— SOPHIA
King of Greece   b. 1870

stances were not quite so fortunate. The last official act of Prussia's King Frederick William IV, just before he was officially declared insane, was to consider and ratify thirteen death sentences. The private trauma of George III and his relatives pales into insignificance beside the mental problems of the Houses of Hohenzollern and Romanov, problems which were often harbingers of great political calamity.

Apart from blood ties, the Hohenzollerns and the Romanovs had much in common. The most charismatic figure of each dynasty, King Frederick and Czar Peter, each known by the epithet "Great," were both driven by deep-seated personality disorders. Some of the key figures in both families suffered from a rare condition known as paradomania—an unhealthy obsession with militaria. Both dynasties ended within a couple of years of each other while in the custody of two of their weakest and most ineffective rulers, both of whom were cousins of King George V.

THE KINGS OF PRUSSIA

The home and birthplace of the Hohenzollern dynasty was the frontier region or "Mark" of Brandenburg, an area of about 10,000 square miles of northeastern Germany. At the turn of the seventeenth century, they were still minor rulers of a relatively obscure little principality, looked down upon by neighboring royal households. Within a couple of centuries, however, the upstart Hohenzollerns had transformed their homeland into the most powerful state in Europe, thanks to a knack for awesome administrative efficiency and a disproportionately huge standing army.

A study of any European monarchy would reveal a few

kings and queens with bizarre behavioral problems, but the Hohenzollerns had a remarkable capacity for breeding psychopaths and madmen. The first member of the House of Hohenzollern to take the name King of Prussia, Frederick I, was a dwarfish hunchback who tried to disguise his physical deformity by wearing high-heeled shoes and growing his curly hair long over his hump. Frederick was unlucky in love. His first marriage ended after four years with the death of his twenty-two-year-old wife, Elizabeth. His second wife was Sophia Dorothea, the Hanoverian sister of King George I. She died in her thirty-eighth year. Their son, the Crown Prince Frederick William, married another member of the British royal family, his first cousin Sophia Dorothea, sister of George II.

Crown Prince Frederick William was at first a major disappointment in the business of producing heirs. Although he and his wife fornicated "night and day" to secure the succession, the few sons that they were able to produce all died young. Frederick I had serious doubts about his son's ability to sire a healthy male heir and feared that he could go to his grave with the Hohenzollern succession in doubt. At the age of fifty-one the sickly and weak old King decided to take matters into his own hands: he came out of "retirement" to rut for Prussia. Frederick I remarried again, this time to a German princess less than half his age, Sophia Louise of Mecklenburg-Schwerin. As it turned out, the old King's noble act of self-sacrifice wasn't necessary. His concerns about the Crown Prince's procreative abilities dissolved as his daughter-in-law went on to produce a string of children—fourteen of them in all, including a healthy male heir apparent.

Unfortunately for the King, his new young bride very quickly went mad and ran raving around the palace. Frederick, by now a frail, tired and white-haired little man, tried to keep out of her way as much as possible and simply let her get on with it, although it killed him in the end.

THE DRILL MASTER OF EUROPE

Frederick's son, the darkly psychopathic Frederick William I, "the drill master of Europe," was a dangerous sadist known to posterity for his freakish army of giants and the way he terrorized everyone, including his own children. Some historians believe that the King inherited the genetic disorder porphyria from his mother, Sophia Charlotte. Like King George III, Frederick William was afflicted with a variety of prolonged illnesses, including gout, piles, migraine and terrible stomach cramps. Unlike George III, whose illness was sporadic until he succumbed to senile dementia, Frederick William was a seething, raging bully for almost his entire life, highly unpredictable and potentially murderous. Although he was very short, he weighed nearly 280 pounds and had a 102-inch waist. He knew that his blotchy, purple-brown features and his wild bulging eyes gave him a truly menacing appearance, and he played up to it by deliberately smearing bacon fat on his face, apparently to make it look more weather-beaten and intimidating.

Most feared was the King's ever-present rattan stick, which he used to thrash anyone in sight: on the streets of Berlin he would smash passersby in the face. Anyone who attempted to defend themselves risked provoking even more anger and possible death. The city became deserted as people fled at news of the crazed King's approach. Once he caught hold of a terrified man who was too slow to get away and asked him why he was running. When the poor man truthfully replied that he was afraid, the King screamed, "You are supposed to love me, scum!" Then he laid into the man with his stick.

The King was vicious but fair: everyone got the same treatment, including members of his own household. At mealtimes he threw plates and cutlery and attacked his servants. He starved his children or spat in their food. He beat and degraded his son Prince Frederick, often in front of the servants. When the Prince rebelled, the King taught him a lesson by forcing him to watch the execution of his best friend, then ordered that the severed head and body be left to lie for hours beneath his son's window to let the message sink in.

As his reign continued he became progressively more violent. By his side he kept two pistols loaded with salt which he would fire at his servants if they didn't move quickly enough. One valet had his eye shot out; another was crippled. His courtiers were so fearful of him that when one of them was summoned to the King's private quarters he dropped dead with fright. The King's punishment on the parade ground was even more intimidating. One of his army majors, humiliated by a thrashing from the King, drew his gun and shot himself through the head. Frederick William regularly drank phenomenal amounts of beer, and when he was drunk he amused himself by taunting his court fool, named Gündling. The inebriated King and his cronies would play practical jokes on Gündling, or would beat him up, torture him and even set fire to him. One of their favorite drunken pranks was to throw Gündling from the castle walls into the moat below. One winter's day they threw him over the side, too drunk to notice that the moat was frozen, and cheered as Gündling bounced on the ice. When the poor court fool finally expired aged fifty-eight, the King had his former employee amusingly pickled inside a wine cask and buried in the castle grounds.

Frederick William despised all forms of art, culture or finery. On a state visit to the court of the Saxon King Augustus II he smashed an entire Meissen dinner service on a whim. As soon as his father was buried he ripped down all of his fine palace draperies and curtains and threw out the most expensive furniture and carpets. He was a dedicated Francophobe at a time when France dominated European culture. Prussian noblemen copied everything in the French style, including buildings, furniture, clothes and food. The King let his noblemen know exactly what he thought about their precious fashions by dressing criminals up in the finest French clothes before he hanged them.

Apart from beer, the King's only pleasure, and chief obsession, in life was his regiment of very tall grenadiers known as the Potsdam Giant Guards. The minimum height requirement for the Potsdam regiment was six feet, although most were over seven feet and the tallest were almost nine feet tall. All of them wore special pointed headgear which sometimes reached a height of ten feet. Height was the only criterion; many of them were mentally infirm. Frederick William was insanely proud of his Potsdam Giant Guards. Wherever he traveled, his giants would march alongside his carriage holding hands over the top of it. His favorite giants were immortalized in life-size oil paintings. When one exceptionally tall Norwegian grenadier died, the King had him sculpted in marble.

The recruits were press-ganged from his own country, or were bought or kidnapped from all over the world. The Prussian King was prepared to spend any amount of money, and go to any length, even at the risk of war, in his pursuit of tall men. His army of recruiting agents had instructions to use whatever force was necessary. A giant carpenter was once tricked into lying down in a box then found himself locked inside and shipped to Potsdam. As his captor had forgotten to drill air holes in the box, however, the carpenter was found dead on arrival. The King was furious: the agent who captured him was charged with causing the loss of a recruit and imprisoned for life.

Even foreign diplomats weren't safe from King Frederick William's press gang. An exceptionally tall Austrian diplomat was seized in Hanover, but was able to escape. An Irish giant called Kirkman was kidnapped on the streets of London and delivered to Potsdam at a cost to Frederick William of a thousand pounds. A tall priest was kidnapped from Italy in the middle of Mass, and a monk was spirited away from a monastery in Rome. They kidnapped Portuguese, Hungarians, Slavs, Russians, Englishmen, Turks, even Ethiopians and Americans. They were men of every profession, including doctors, lawyers, accountants and teachers. The rest of Europe observed the King's hobby with amusement until his agents began to trespass on their soil. One of Frederick William's less reputable tactics was to induce tall men in the armies of foreign countries to desert.

Many of his recruits, however, were gifts from other European courts. Whenever the King went on a state visit he would broadly hint that the sort of farewell gift he would most appreciate would be a giant or two. The Austrian and Russian courts were particularly obliging benefactors. Peter the Great, another great admirer of freaks, sent the Prussian King hundreds of Russians, all over six feet four inches. Other European courts found that they had hit upon a novel method of bribing

Frederick William. Tall men became diplomatic bargaining chips as word spread through diplomatic circles that the King of Prussia would agree to virtually anything if you gave him a few tall freaks. The British government persuaded him to sign a pact that was highly biased in their favor by slipping him a "gift" of fifteen very tall Irishmen. The Saxon Foreign Minister sent Frederick William a birthday present of two expensive Turkish pipes and a load of high-grade tobacco. The package was delivered by a seven-foot-tall messenger complete with a note which contained a birthday greeting—at the bottom it read, "PS, keep the delivery boy."

The King acquired an eight-foot-tall Swede from Augustus the Strong of Saxony. Frederick William was delighted with his new plaything, but was frustrated when the Swede turned out to be so mentally infirm that he couldn't be drilled, despite many beatings. The King despaired and threw him out of the guards, probably the only time that anyone ever left the Potsdam Grenadiers freely. The poor childlike giant drifted into Berlin, where, unable to support himself, he died a beggar on the streets.

When the procurement of conscripts by abduction became too expensive and too dangerous, the King turned to crude genetic engineering. Every tall male in Prussia was forced to marry a tall woman. When this breeding program proved too slow and unreliable, he went back to kidnapping. Eventually Frederick William acquired 2,000 of his precious giants.

The price in human suffering was high. Living conditions for members of the Potsdam freak show were pitiful and morale was dreadful. Almost all of the men who passed through the regiment were held against their will. They mutinied regularly, and several times they tried to burn down the whole of

Potsdam in the hope of killing the King in the process. About 250 giants successfully deserted each year, but violent deaths during escape attempts were commonplace and reprisals brutal. The King dispatched bounty hunters on manhunts to track them down: those who were recaptured had their noses and ears sliced off and were locked in Spandau Prison. Many of the giants resorted to self-mutilation or suicide, or took part in mercy killings of their fellow soldiers to end their misery.

What was, potentially, the greatest basketball team in history was disbanded when King Frederick William I died, aged fifty-two. He was irascible to the end. On his deathbed he called for his physician and demanded to know how much longer he had to live. The doctor took his wrist and after a few moments gravely replied that he feared the worst as the King no longer had a pulse. "Impossible," he roared, waving his arm in the air. "How could I move my fingers like this if my pulse were gone?" Frederick William had made his point, but the effort killed him.

FREDERICK THE GREAT

The rise of Prussia reached critical momentum under Frederick William I's successor. Frederick "the Great" was the third son born to his parents, but the first named Frederick to survive infancy. Two earlier Fredericks were dead, the first from having his fragile head crammed into a crown at the time of the christening, the second from shock when the guns saluting his birth were fired too near his cradle. The young Prince was the antithesis of his father: physically small and frail, with a taste for French fashion, literature and music.

As with the neighboring Hanoverians, relationships between father and son in the Prussian royal household were dreadful. Frederick William saw his son's yearning for culture as a sign of latent homosexuality. The Crown Prince, raged Frederick William, was "effeminate, and wears his hair long and curled like a fool," and so the father decided to thrash some sense into him. The boy was beaten regularly for the slightest of reasons. In 1730 the conflict between father and son reached a hiatus when the young Frederick tried to flee to England with a friend, Lieutenant Hans von Katte. It ended with his arrest and imprisonment, and the subsequent decapitation of his companion. The King had intended to kill his son as well, but had backed off in the face of international outrage.

Prussian machismo may have been the signature of his father's reign, but Frederick II turned it into a cult. The only true glamour figure in the Hohenzollern family tree was a military genius, one of the most dazzling leaders in European history, lauded as the greatest German who ever lived. Lord Acton said he was "the most consummate practical genius that ever inherited a modern throne." Frederick's wars and battles are textbook classics of historic warfare. He raised Prussia from a second-rate German state into one of the greatest powers in Europe, but his methods were founded on a complete and ruthless disregard for human life.

Frederick's psychological profile reveals personality traits partly inherited and partly a result of his upbringing. Unlike his father, he did not suffer from progressive insanity, but his personality was dangerously flawed. His traumatic childhood at the mercy of his mad father undoubtedly left physical and psychological scars. His private life, depending which side of the conflicting evidence one chooses to believe, was either completely sublimated or disgustingly perverted. He played the flute, composed and conversed with philosophers, but by the age of five the young Frederick also knew the entire Prussian drill manual by heart. As soon as his father died he threw himself into a military life of almost ceaseless warmaking.

Everything he did was subjugated to his military needs. To calm his nerves before a battle, he would casually open a vein. When the tide turned against him he fought on with a vial of poison ready for suicide. Once, he was surprised to find one of his best soldiers shackled in irons. When he asked why this was so, he was told that the man had been caught buggering his horse. Frederick ordered: "Fool—don't put him in irons, put him in the infantry." He then apologized to the soldier for taking his horse away from him.

His military ambitions required the mindless obedience of his Prussian officers, which he famously enforced with commonplace cruelty and his inhumane system of forcible recruiting. "Dogs," he railed at his guards when they were hesitant under fire. "Do you want to live forever?" He was incapable of pity. Medical facilities in his army were practically nonexistent. The wounded were expected to find their own way off the battlefield and to hospital and were even denied rations. As only one in five who entered a Prussian military hospital came out alive, men deserted by the thousand rather than risk medical treatment, and hundreds more committed suicide. The King saw no point in spending money on warm uniforms instead of guns, and so hundreds of his men froze to death in winter. During the Seven Years War he reduced the population of Prussia by half a million.

In time, Frederick became more eccentric and miserly. He drank up to forty cups of coffee a day for several weeks in an experiment to see if it was possible to exist without sleep. It took his stomach three years to recover. His palace became a slum as his pampered Italian greyhounds soiled everything and tore his furnishings to ribbons. The most heroic figure in German history died filthy and neglected, dressed in rags, the shirt on his back so rotten that his valet had to dress him in one of his own for the burial.

FREDERICK WILLIAM THE FAT

The royal House of Hohenzollern produced several homosexuals and sadomasochists but few prolific adulterers, with one spectacular exception. When Frederick II died childless in 1786 the Prussian crown passed to his forty-two-year-old nephew Frederick William "the Fat," a libertine who dedicated his life to maintaining his personal harem. It is unlikely that this King of Prussia ever opened a letter during his eleven-year reign, let alone conducted any serious state business, and abroad was regarded as a joke—a very far cry from his warlike and internationally respected predecessor.

Frederick William was married at twenty to his first cousin Elizabeth, a daughter of the odd Brunswick-Wolfenbüttel family. When Elizabeth found out about his coterie of mistresses she retaliated by taking lovers herself. In 1769, after four years of marriage, Frederick William divorced her. Although she was granted a pension, she remained for the rest of her ex-husband's life a virtual prisoner at Kustrin. Within a few months,

Frederick William was remarried, to Princess Frederica of Hesse-Darmstadt. His new wife bore him seven legitimate children, who were in turn vastly outnumbered by an unaudited horde of bastards acquired by his several mistresses.

The King's most enduring concubine, Wilhelmina Encke, began her acquaintance with him as a fourteen-year-old prostitute. Frederick William generously lavished a fortune on her and her family, providing them with purpose-built private palaces. Miss Encke was eventually married to a bibulous courtier named Reitz, but she was to remain the King's mistress for another twenty years. She and her scheming husband came to form the nucleus of a court clique who bought the King's favor by catering for his urges, mostly sexual. One of these hangers-on, a courtier named Bischoffswerder, introduced Frederick to an Italian drug called Diavolini which was taken to stimulate the libido. The King's drug supplier was rewarded with a free hand to run Prussian foreign policy.

Another important influence was an eccentrically garbed religious fanatic called Mayr, a priest who once attempted to demonstrate his faith by swallowing most of the Bible, although instead of achieving a higher level of consciousness he was only able to induce severe constipation and stomach cramps. One day, Mayr was preaching from the pulpit when he decided to liven up the sermon by firing two pistols into the throng of assembled worshipers. Not a moment too soon he was certified insane and dispatched to an asylum.

When the wanton Wilhelmina Encke began to show her age she continued to make herself useful to the King by procuring his mistresses, including a laundry maid and a couple of stage dancers. To her horror, however, the King entered into not one, but two, bigamous marriages with the very mistresses that she had supplied, Julia von Voss and Sophia Dönhoff. These marriages received the approval of Frederick William's unusually accommodating Prussian court priests, who asserted they had found a precedent for such a bigamous arrangement in Martin Luther's blessing of a similar marriage contracted by Prince Philip of Hesse. They also received the unexpected blessing of his legal wife, Queen Frederica, who simply delighted in the distress that her husband's new sleeping arrangements were causing the much loathed Wilhelmina Encke.

By 1797 Frederick William's bloated body was burned out by a lifetime of excess, and the Prussian court became infested with charlatans and quack physicians hoping to make one last quick profit out of his condition. He was told to inhale the breath of two newborn calves, to sleep each night between two children aged between eight and ten, to listen to the sound of wind instruments, but in no circumstances the violin. He tried the lot and died of heart disease aged fifty-three.

FREDERICK WILLIAM IV

Insanity revisited the Prussian royal family in the mid-nineteenth century. Kaiser Wilhelm II's great-uncle Frederick William IV, the only Hohenzollern "soldier king" incapable of riding a horse, succeeded to the throne in 1840 and from early in his reign was evidently mentally disturbed. His idea of a day out with the family was to take his wife, Elizabeth, and their children to watch surgical operations conducted by his friend, Dr. Johann Dieffenbach, a gentleman who had pioneered an operation to cure stammering by severing the patient's tongue muscles.

In the 1850s the King suffered a series of strokes, causing him to become considerably more unstable, and his younger brother Wilhelm was asked to step in as temporary Regent. In 1858 it became apparent that the King's "softening of the brain" was irreversible and he was certified insane. For the next two years the by now extremely shortsighted King spent much of his time wandering around the Sans Souci Palace gardens, colliding with trees.

EMPERORS OF GERMANY

The first Emperor of the newly united Germany, Wilhelm I, was remarkable for his longevity, as indeed were most of the Hohenzollerns. He became such an institution during his ninety-one years that Berlin guidebooks listed the precise time he could be seen at the palace window watching the changing of the guard. His long life was marked by increasing eccentricity and, later in his reign, senile dementia. He ate lobster salad, potted meat and sorbet washed down with strong tea or champagne, always at midnight, virtually every day of his life. When the Emperor's victorious troops paraded through Berlin after the Franco-Prussian War he threw the parade into confusion by vanishing, then suddenly reappearing at the head of his troops and leading them past the saluting dais where he was supposed to be sitting.

The darker sign of the Hohenzollern psyche resurfaced in Wilhelm I and later in his grandson Kaiser Wilhelm II, both of whom showed signs of morbidity. Wilhelm I hung a picture over his bed of his mother laid out for burial. Later, his grandson "Kaiser Bill" would kill a conversation by proudly producing from his wallet a collection of snapshots, not of his children, but of his deceased Hohenzollern relatives dressed in their funeral attire.

Between the two Wilhelms, Germany was ruled briefly by Frederick III. In him Europe had a glimpse of what might have been. Unfortunately he had nothing to say about his much vaunted liberal ideas for modernizing Germany, or anything else for that matter, because he came to the throne with cancer of the larynx and was dead within four months.

To his contemporaries, Frederick's son Kaiser Wilhelm II was a warmongering Prussian monster, the very embodiment of the evil ambitions of his country. History, however, reveals the Kaiser to have been a vain, ineffective megalomaniac who was completely out of touch with reality. There can have been few sovereigns as bizarrely egocentric as the Kaiser, or with such amusing results. Taking serious risks with historical accuracy, he imagined himself to be the latest of a long unbroken line of Hohenzollern warrior leaders, presenting himself to his subjects and the world as the personification of Prussian machismo. He hero-worshiped Frederick the Great and would quote his illustrious ancestor at every opportunity. He even aped Frederick's famous passion for greyhounds by keeping a pack of court dachshunds which fouled the palace. But, whereas Frederick the Great was a genuine leader and a true military genius, the Kaiser was just a maladjusted poseur.

The Kaiser's mother was Queen Victoria's eldest daughter, Vicky. His arrival in 1859 was a gynecological disaster. During a bungled breech birth, baby Wilhelm was crucially starved of oxygen, which left him with permanent brain damage. The most immediate sign of infirmity was a dislocated left arm which failed to develop properly and which he never recovered the full use of. He also had a slightly lame left leg and crooked spine, and later in life he experienced partial deafness and regular shooting pains down the left-hand side of his head. His grandmother Queen Victoria declared that the malformed limb was a bad omen, a branding by the devil.

With Wilhelm's withered arm came an emperor-sized chip on his shoulder. He spent a lifetime trying to compensate for his physical disability and his feelings of personal inadequacy. He endured horrific orthopedic cures during his boyhood, including electric-shock treatment. At the age of four he was strapped into a macabre contraption comprising leather belts and steel bolts in an attempt to realign his spine. Inevitably these childhood experiences left an unfortunate and permanent mark on his personality. In later years he let it be known that he always slept with a cocked, loaded pistol in a bedside drawer, just to show how tough he was. He always made a point of sitting on a hard chair even if there was a soft one available. He deliberately wore the stones on his many diamond and sapphire rings facing inward so that they hurt people when they shook his hand. The Kaiser was also pathologically narcissistic. He preened, strutted and swaggered, handing out photographs of himself to his friends, always taking care not to show the stunted little arm which barely reached his left jacket pocket. His swept-up mustache was back-combed and pomaded every day by a court barber. He wore so many medals that his chest was described as a declaration of war.

Wilhelm's wife was Princess Auguste Viktoria of Schleswig-Holstein-Sonderburg-Augustenburg. The Kaiser called her Dona to save time; Bismarck preferred to call her "the cow from Holstein." The Empress was a deeply religious woman of the fiercely evangelical variety, and her handpicked ladies-in-waiting were known as the "Hellelujah Aunts." In appearance, the Empress was drab and unfashionable, defying the best efforts of the finest dressmakers in Germany to make her look regal. She was also quite slow on the uptake, a fact that she advertised with a glassy-eyed expression which never left her. In 1889 the Kaiser and his wife paid a state visit to Constantinople, where they found the Sultan eager to treat them on a lavish scale. When the Empress visited the harem, she was introduced to the chief eunuch, the Kislar Aga. It was explained to the Empress that the Kislar Aga's position made him one of the most important people in Turkey. The Empress nodded intently, then asked him if his father had also been a eunuch.

The Kaiser endured the ultimate in royal mother-in-law-from-hell experience. The half-mad Dowager Adelaide, wife of the late Duke Frederick of Schleswig-Holstein, had an obsession with personal hygiene. She evolved a system of washing that involved dividing her body into twenty-four washable sections, or "hemispheres." Each section required an individual but complete set of bowl, pitcher, soap dish, soap and towel. This eccentric routine tended to have a ruinous effect on the domestic arrangements of her hosts and the patience of her son-in-law. Slightly more embarrassing was the predatory old Dowager's imprudent behavior with young men. At two state dinners she made sudden assaults upon her male neighbors at table. When she was strategically positioned out of harm's way between her daughter and a lady-in-waiting she became violent and abusive.

If there was one thing that nineteenth-century monarchs loved, it was dressing up. For the Kaiser and his cousins abroad there was nothing quite as exciting as slipping into somebody else's army uniform. Whenever a Spanish king visited England, for example, the guest would invariably arrive dressed as a British general, and he would be greeted by a British king dressed as a Spanish admiral. The Kaiser's cousin King George V was the arch royal cross-dresser. King George always let it be known that he hated Germans and was very upset by suggestions that he too was transparently German, but nothing could stop him from posing for the camera dressed up in a Prussian general's uniform.

From Frederick William I onward the Hohenzollerns were military-uniform fetishists, but there was none more fanatical than Kaiser Wilhelm II. The Kaiser had more uniforms than Liberace had stage costumes, over 400 of them, stashed away in his mahogany wardrobes, although not one single dressing gown (dressing gowns were for wimps: apparently his grandfather Wilhelm I had once refused a silk robe, growling "Hohenzollerns wear no dressing gowns"). In the first seventeen years of his reign the Kaiser redesigned the uniforms of his German army officers thirty-seven times. He had a squad of tailors in his palace on permanent standby. There were uniforms for every occasion: uniforms for attending galas, uniforms to greet every one of his regiments, uniforms with which to greet other uniforms, uniforms for eating out, "informal" uniforms for staying in. It was joked that he had an admiral's uniform that he only ever wore to see performances of *The Flying Dutchman*. When he attended military parades there was little danger of mistaking the Kaiser among all the other brightly uniformed Prussian automatons: he was the only one wearing a solid gold helmet.

Kaiser Wilhelm II had a fetish for women's arms. His seduction technique involved engaging a woman in conversation, slowly peeling off her long gloves, then passionately kissing her arms from fingertips to elbow. Women who cooperated with the Kaiser's eccentric foreplay strategy were richly rewarded with gifts of jewelry. Not all of them kept silent about their close encounters of the mustachioed kind, however, because the Kaiser's little foible was widely known and laughed about.

Wilhelm did in fact share just one characteristic with his hero, Frederick the Great, although it wasn't one that he cared to acknowledge. Frederick surrounded himself with men and wrote semierotic love letters to his friend Voltaire. An English ambassador in Prussia wrote home: "No female is allowed to approach this court—males wash the linen, nurse the children, make and unmake the beds." Voltaire claimed that in his later years Frederick had homosexual affairs with his soldiers. His first male lover may have been his close friend, the army lieutenant Hans von Katte.

In the Kaiser's militarily dominated, ultra-chauvinist Second Reich, a Prussian soldier's life was built around male bonding and the Spartan ideal of soldierly companionship. Women were generally considered to be useful for breeding, cooking and polishing a chap's spurs: for real friendship, one looked to one's fellow officers. These were not necessarily homosexual friendships, but the culture was undeniably homoerotic. Wilhelm had grown up to be very much a part of this masculine society. However, he was probably looking for something more than a few steins of lager and the smell of new lederhosen while hanging out with the boys from the Gardes du Corps.

The Bulgarian Czar Ferdinand was one of the first royals abroad to discover, to his annoyance, that the Kaiser had a habit of slapping men on the bottom. Many a young officer had his bottom patted or his cheeks tweaked by the Kaiser. Wilhelm formed his own quasi-secret society, known as the White Stag Dining Club: to gain admission everyone had to kneel over a chair, tell a blue joke, then have his bottom smacked by the Kaiser with the flat of his sword.

Berlin was rocked by a series of homosexual scandals, collectively known as "the Eulenburg Affair," which exposed a large homosexual network involving men who were friends, relatives or employees of the Kaiser. Sodomy was still a serious criminal offense in Germany and carried a long prison sentence. The Military Commander of Berlin, Count Kuno von Moltke, was revealed as the homosexual lover of Wilhelm's best friend, a young diplomat called Prince "Phili" Eulenburg. Wilhelm and the Prince were inseparable. Eulenburg was also blackmailed by the proprietor of a Viennese bathing establishment—one which incidentally was also frequented by the Austrian Emperor Franz Josef's homosexual younger brother Ludwig. Inconveniently, another of the Kaiser's military chiefs, Count von Huelsen-Haeseler, dropped dead in the Kaiser's presence, dressed in a tutu in the middle of a drag act.

Meanwhile, the Potsdam garrison was hit by several court-martials for sodomy and a number of suicides. In court, the regimental tight white breeches and thigh-length boots were noted to be particularly provocative. Another close friend of the Kaiser was the incredibly rich industrialist Alfred von Krupp, whose reputation was also destroyed by a vice scandal. Italian police had raided his Capri holiday home and found Krupp and a gang of his German friends sodomizing a string of young boys. Krupp also stood accused of importing a selection of young Italian waiters to the Hotel Bristol in Berlin for the purpose of staging homosexual orgies. The evidence was damning and over-whelming, and Krupp committed—although some believe faked—suicide. There were unconfirmed sightings of him years later in the United States, the Far East and in South America.

So suspicion inevitably fell on the Kaiser himself, but he was never directly implicated. He personally scanned the papers and threatened to blow out the brains of any editor who dared make too much of his association with homosexuals. Whenever any of the Kaiser's friends got into trouble he quickly dropped them, once issuing a statement that his former friends, includ-ing his dearest friend Eulenburg, were "perverts" and that an example should be made of all of them.

The Kaiser sincerely believed that he was guided by God, his speeches always invoking the Almighty's wrath for this or that. He was one of the last monarchs to claim that he ruled by Divine Right, a concept abandoned by his royal cousins in England more than 200 years earlier. "We Hohenzollerns," he proclaimed in one of his more excitable moments, "are the bailiffs of God." The Kaiser overstepped the borderline between the usual delusions of the royal self-obsessed and genuine men-tal illness. During his lifetime he was known to be emotionally unstable and to have suffered from severe personality problems. Frequent gibes were made throughout World War I about the Kaiser's disturbed state of mind, but there was an ironic truth be-hind the obviously crude anti-German propaganda.

In Berlin the Kaiser had thirty-two huge statues erected, each depicting one of his illustrious Brandenburg ancestors. One of the glorious ancestors immortalized in white marble was Otto the Idle, a man who never actually set foot in the land he ruled and once even tried to sell it. Unsurprisingly,

Wilhelm's Avenue of Victory was openly derided by Berliners. For most of the time, the pantomime Emperor was oblivious to the sneers which accompanied his bombastic posturing because he lived in a bubble of perpetual adulation, cocooned by groveling courtiers and generals. Those nearest to Wilhelm knew that it was wiser to bow and kiss his gloved hand than to sneer, because the Kaiser was insanely sensitive to criticism. When two small boys were overheard saying that their father had called the Kaiser a "windbag," Wilhelm had the father arrested and imprisoned for two years.

In the art of statesmanship, the Kaiser was a disaster without equal. Abroad he was prone to wild, aggressive outbursts about militarism and German world domination; his public speeches at home were similarly tactless. He once assured a group of striking workers at the Krupp Works that if they had anything whatsoever to do with the Social Democratic Party he would have them all shot. This speech was wildly applauded by his groveling entourage.

Unlike his idol, Frederick the Great, this Hohenzollern warrior king was a coward. He wasn't personally responsible for starting the conflict in 1914, and the initial outbreak of hostilities left him paralyzed with fear. Throughout World War I his friends observed that the Kaiser appeared to be perpetually on the brink of a nervous breakdown. When it started to go wrong he became so panic-stricken that his doctors feared for his sanity.

The Kaiser passed on some of his more disturbing personality traits to his children. He had six sons and one daughter, the very spoiled and very odd Princess Victoria Louise. Wilhelm bought her a piglet, freshly scrubbed with a blue bow tied in its tail. The Princess grew fond of her pet. Her governess, in the certain knowledge that it could only end in tears, dreaded the inevitable beckoning of pork heaven. When the pet grew up, however, the Princess simply sold it to a butcher, pocketed the money, then sat down to enjoy a sausage supper.

The eldest son and heir, Crown Prince William, was blessed with even fewer social skills than his father. When the Kaiser and William were shooting game together in England, the Prince heard one of their English hosts yell out, "For God's sake, don't shoot the Kaiser—his son is worse yet!" In 1918 when Wilhelm was forced to abdicate and flee to Holland, everyone insisted that his son renounce his rights to succession at the same time. The Crown Prince was eventually allowed to return to Germany in 1923, where he enjoyed a few years of fast living before signing up for the Nazi Party in 1932. In the years that followed, he and two of his brothers lent support to the Nazis by their presence at rallies. Two of Crown Prince William's sons also joined the Nazi party.

The German royal family had a lot more in common with the Nazis than their patriarch would care to admit. The ex-Kaiser's position on the subject of Hitler was ambivalent. Wilhelm was always quick to publicly condemn the rise of Nazism, but he was also quick to send Hitler a congratulatory telegram when he occupied Paris—a gaffe that ruined twenty-one years of hitherto dignified silence in exile.

The German aristocracy played a very important role in the early rise of the Nazi party—many German nobles made their contempt of Hitler clear only when it was politically correct to do so. In the early 1930s the former grandees of the Second Reich were willing to do anything Hitler told them provided it would stop the tide of socialism. The Kaiser's pro-

fessed personal dislike of Hitler had more to do with class snobbery and his Hohenzollern dislike for democrats. There was
very little in the Nazi manifesto that he could have personally
objected to—the distinction between Nazi racial theories and
the German monarchy's obsession with royal purity was a very
fine one. The notion of the "Aryan race" was first floated during the reign of the Kaiser's great-uncle, and it was in imperial
Germany that the more truculent form of nationalism, or
"blood and soil," first took root. The Kaiser was also a rabid
anti-Semite, although he was happy to associate with very
wealthy Jews. He had a statue of Heine pulled down because
he was a Jewish socialist. In 1918 the Kaiser slunk off to retirement at Doorn, blaming World War I on a conspiracy of "international Jewry." His home became a pilgrimage for Nazi
officers who were stationed in Holland.

In 1944 the men who unsuccessfully plotted against Hitler's
life considered restoring the Hohenzollerns as constitutional
monarchs, a plan that was dropped when they realized with
some embarrassment that at least half the German royal family
were members of the Nazi party. In 1951 when the former
Crown Prince William became the last of God's Bailiffs to be
buried in the family vault at Hohenzollern Castle, he did so
wearing the uniform of a Death's Head Hussar.

PETER THE CREATIVE MONSTER

The Russian title "czar" was the Slavic form of Caesar. This
was not inappropriate given that most of the leading members
of the House of Romanov—as did many of the rulers of ancient Rome—suffered from gross personality disorders, and

THE ROYAL HOUSE OF ROMANOV

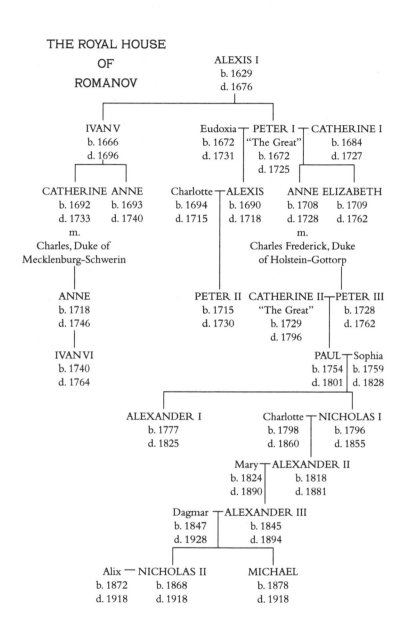

ALEXIS I
b. 1629
d. 1676

IVAN V
b. 1666
d. 1696

Eudoxia ⊤ PETER I ⊤ CATHERINE I
b. 1672 | "The Great" | b. 1684
d. 1731 | b. 1672 | d. 1727
| d. 1725 |

CATHERINE ANNE
b. 1692   b. 1693
d. 1733   d. 1740
m.
Charles, Duke of
Mecklenburg-Schwerin

Charlotte ⊤ ALEXIS   ANNE   ELIZABETH
b. 1694 | b. 1690   b. 1708   b. 1709
d. 1715 | d. 1718   d. 1728   d. 1762
| m.
Charles Frederick, Duke
of Holstein-Gottorp

ANNE
b. 1718
d. 1746

PETER II   CATHERINE II ⊤ PETER III
b. 1715   "The Great" | b. 1728
d. 1730   b. 1729 | d. 1762
  d. 1796 |

IVAN VI
b. 1740
d. 1764

PAUL ⊤ Sophia
b. 1754 | b. 1759
d. 1801 | d. 1828

ALEXANDER I
b. 1777
d. 1825

Charlotte ⊤ NICHOLAS I
b. 1798 | b. 1796
d. 1860 | d. 1855

Mary ⊤ ALEXANDER II
b. 1824 | b. 1818
d. 1890 | d. 1881

Dagmar ⊤ ALEXANDER III
b. 1847 | b. 1845
d. 1928 | d. 1894

Alix — NICHOLAS II   MICHAEL
b. 1872   b. 1868   b. 1878
d. 1918   d. 1918   d. 1918

many more were mentally unbalanced. Even some of the key female Romanovs were degenerate megalomaniacs who used their power to give free rein to their fantastical whims and took pleasure in humiliating the defenseless people around them.

Considered the most heroic of all the Romanovs, Peter the Great was huge both in stature and accomplishment. He was regarded by his contemporaries as the most talented man of his age and he is often described as Russia's first modern man. His sweeping policies, and the mental state that helped to create them, shaped Russia's destiny. He applied his incredible energy to reforming his government and state and turning it into a leading European power, but for much of his reign he was evidently mentally unbalanced. His name was a byword for enlightenment, but the methods he chose to educate his fellow Russians would have made Stalin queasy. Some of his more brutal behavior was that of a violent drunk, and the Czar was drunk for most of the time; in fact he only ever rested when he had a hangover. But Peter didn't need alcohol to be vicious. Like so many leading members of his royal house, he was a paranoid sadist.

His father, Alexis Mikhailovich, was the second Russian ruler from the House of Romanov. Regarded as one of the more laid-back and tolerant czars, Alexis once had 7,000 people tortured and executed after a popular uprising. The young Peter, his fourteenth legitimate child, was unlike any of the Czar's other offspring because he was healthy and strong and stood out in a nursery full of congenitally ugly and malformed Romanov children. Before Alexis died, he proclaimed his eldest living son, Theodore, as his successor, but the puny heir died aged twenty. Peter's real father was probably a close friend of Czar Alexis. Many years later, Peter confronted the man he suspected of being his true father and offered to strangle him if he didn't own up to sleeping with his mother. "I don't know what to say to you," the terrified man stammered, "except I was not the only one."

Czar Peter had amazing physical strength and stamina, although his chronic alcoholism had a disastrous effect upon both his personality and his health. According to most contemporary reports, he was a giant—probably six feet five inches tall—and could bend coins by twisting them in his fingers. He was swarthy and sunburned, cared little for his appearance, was generally unwashed and wore filthy clothes. On the Czar's visit to Prussia in 1717, he and his verminous entourage were described by a German baron as like "baptized bears." They offended their hosts with an open display of bad behavior, including the virtual destruction of a palace at Mont Bijou which had been provided for him by the Prussian royal family.

In Hanover he dined with King George I's mother, the Electress Sophia, a flabby, toothless crone who had replaced all her missing teeth with squares of wax. She was repelled by his disgusting table habits, but found redeeming qualities under the layer of imperial dirt. She noted that the fact "that he has not been taught to eat in a tidy manner is obvious," but she was "much taken with his natural and easy manner." The Electress also commented on Peter's ignorance of whalebone corsets: the Czar was confused by what he believed to be German women's "damnably hard ribs."

In London, Peter met King William III and was put up briefly in a house in Buckingham Street. When the King walked into the room he was overcome by the stench that accompanied Peter and a couple of servants. When the Czar left, he presented King William III with a huge uncut diamond wrapped in a scrap of dirty paper. When the Czar had had enough of London he and friends moved to Deptford and lodged at the home of Sir John Evelyn. They tore up paintings and furnishings, smeared vomit and excrement on the floors and walls, smashed expensive parquet floors and used paintings as target practice with their guns. Sir John later presented the British government with a bill for £350 for damage to his property.

The Czar was given to unprovoked bouts of violence and would often thrash his own courtiers with a cudgel for fun. These beatings became such a regular part of court routine that to take a thrashing from the Czar was looked upon as a mark of favor. He once had a peasant tortured because the poor man was unaware that the Czar now also bore the title "Emperor," although the title was not generally acknowledged in his lifetime. He took pleasure in personally beheading dissidents with his ax, and the road to the Kremlin was regularly strewn with the decapitated corpses of Peter's victims left to rot in the snow for months. The heads were placed on spikes and became food for crows.

In the Czar's most violent drunken binges he suffered from alcohol-induced hallucinations and paranoia. He convinced himself that the whole of Russia was populated with traitors, and used the slightest suspicion as an excuse for a witch-hunt. Shortly before he set out on the first of his famous missions to Western Europe, Peter's spies informed him of a plot against his life. He had the ringleaders arrested and tortured. To make sure the Russian people behaved themselves while he was away, he arranged a little exhibition to concentrate their hearts and minds. The Czar disinterred the remains of a famous dissident,

Ivan Miloslavsky, who had been executed twelve years earlier. Miloslavsky's decomposed corpse was dragged by pigs to the place of execution, hacked into small segments, and placed underneath the scaffold in an open coffin. On the platform above, the plot ringleaders were slowly dismembered so that their fresh blood dripped down on to the remains of the late Miloslavsky. The severed body parts were neatly arranged, and their heads fixed on spikes. The Czar left orders that no one was to remove this grisly display, which lay putrefying until his return.

In 1713, Peter declared that St. Petersburg was now the new capital of Russia. In order to populate it he simply emptied Moscow of thousands of families and forced them to move to St. Petersburg on pain of death. Between 100,000 and 200,000 people died in the process. The city itself was built on the corpses of hundreds of thousands of Russians. In the merciless extremes of the Russian winter, he forced laborers to work without proper tools, often waist deep in water. Although conditions were impossible, discipline was shockingly severe. The Czar ran around the building sites, personally beating workers with his cudgel. Any man caught slacking had his nostrils flayed. He killed more people in the name of civic planning than he did by his almost continuous warfare.

The Czar mixed vodka, wine, beer and mead and swilled them simultaneously. When he traveled to Western Europe in 1697 he was more often than not dead drunk. In a day and a half at Antwerp he and a handful of friends consumed 269 bottles of wine. His trip to France in 1717 was considered by Parisians to be the best free freak show they had ever seen. The visit cost France £150 a day to keep him—one itemized bill was for the women called in to undress and clean up the Czar when he got drunk at a reception and urinated in his pants on the way home.

He created a drinking club, "The Vastly Extravagant Supremely Absurd, Omni-Intoxicated Synod of Fools and Jesters." The name was a dig at the more reactionary features of the Russian Church, but was mainly an excuse for orgiastic drinking sessions which lasted for days on end. At the head of this company was his former tutor, an elderly and senile dipsomaniac named Nikita Zotov. At these quasi-ceremonial binges Peter poured vodka down the throats of his cronies with a funnel, while Zotov, seated on a high ceremonial chair, was sick on the heads down below. The Czar liked to get other people drunk and watch them make fools of themselves while showing off his own legendary ability to drink. He would force everyone who dined with him to drink from bucketfuls of vodka, and anyone who tried to duck out was forced to drink even more. It was a prospect that terrorized many of his guests, but the Czar had sentries posted at the doors of the banquet hall to stop them from leaving until he had been entertained.

Peter the Great was a keen amateur surgeon and anatomist, but his morbid fascination for the macabre far exceeded his interest in medical science. During a trip to Holland, just after a heavy meal, the Czar watched with fascination the anatomical dissection of a human cadaver. When two of his nauseous attendants made it clear that they didn't share his enthusiasm for human intestines, Peter forced them to bite into the flesh of the corpse. Although the Czar was an incompetent surgeon, no one ever dared to disappoint him when he volunteered to wield the knife. When the Czarina Martha Apraxina, widow of his half-brother Theodore III, died, Peter personally opened up her corpse to find out if the rumor that she was still a virgin at the age of forty-nine was true. He once removed twenty pounds of water from the dropsical wife of a rich Russian merchant named Borst. The Czar was extremely proud of his handiwork, but was furious when the woman selfishly died shortly afterward. He ordered an autopsy to prove that he hadn't been responsible for the death—naturally the inquest found that the Czar was entirely blameless.

Peter once saw a bad tooth being pulled, and was suddenly consumed with ambition to turn his hand to amateur dentistry. Overnight, the Czar's retinue of 250 courtiers became unwilling accomplices to his new hobby. He carried out spot dental checks on anyone who happened to be passing—if any tooth looked suspect he whipped it out. Unfortunately, as he was quite unaware of his own strength and sometimes got carried away, he accidentally removed gums also. Peter kept the teeth he'd drawn from his courtiers in a little bag. One day a courtier appealed to him for help: his wife had a terrible toothache, he said, but she was so scared of having a tooth pulled she would pretend nothing was wrong whenever a dentist approached her. The Czar obliged and, ignoring the screams and protests of the woman, pulled the tooth and popped it in his bag. Only later did it emerge that the woman had never had a toothache in the first place: her husband just wanted to teach her a lesson.

Peter built a Museum of Curiosities to satisfy his fascination with freaks of nature. His collection included a man without genitals, a child with two heads, a five-footed sheep, a deformed fetus, the organs of a hermaphrodite, "the hand of a man who died by excessive drinking with all its blood stagnated in the veins" and the corpses of Siamese twins. Each specimen was individually pickled in an alcohol-filled jar. The museum caretaker, a badly deformed dwarf, could look forward to the day when he too would be pickled. One of Peter's prize exhibits was a pickled phallus, donated by the Prussian King Frederick William. This item had caught the Czar's eye on his trip to Berlin and the Prussian King was only too delighted to get rid of it. Peter thought it would be a good jape to persuade his wife, Catherine, to kiss it: she accepted his invitation, but only after he made his offer more attractive by offering to cut off her head if she declined.

The sight of blood whetted Peter the Great's appetite. The Czar would torture people with his own hands and then immediately sit down to enjoy a hearty meal. He loved watching torture sessions and would shout and cheer and urge the torturer on. He was even capable of knouting his own son to death without any sign of remorse.

The Czar had become increasingly paranoid, until he became convinced that even his heir Alexis was a traitor. The Czarevitch had inherited none of his father's talents or ambitions and turned out to be a feeble, shiftless youth who lived in dread fear of his drunken, erratic father. When Alexis was once asked to draw up some simple plans, he shot himself in the hand rather than expose himself to his father's criticism.

When it was time to find a bride for Alexis, the fiancée chosen for him was Charlotte of Brunswick, a skinny sixteen-year-old with a smallpox-raddled complexion. Alexis disliked the idea of marriage in general and his new wife in particular. Shortly after his wife gave birth, he moved his new mistress, a Finnish floor scrubber named Euphrosyne, into their home. When

Alexis discovered that his wife was pregnant a second time he kicked her in the stomach. Charlotte, just twenty-one years old, survived the beating just long enough to give him a son, Peter. The Czar ordered an autopsy on his daughter-in-law and attended it in person, studying her in detail. Charlotte was quickly forgotten and Alexis resumed relations with his mistress.

In 1718 Peter gave his feckless son an ultimatum: mend your ways or you will be disinherited. The Czarevitch took fright and fled abroad. Peter interpreted his son's flight into the custody of a foreign power as an act of treason, and he had Alexis arrested and tortured. Peter supervised the torture and even joined in. Long after the inevitable confession, the racking and knouting continued, until Alexis, fatally weakened by the time-honored practice of bloodletting, finally expired.

By his early thirties the ravages of alcoholism and gluttony had rendered the Czar a physical wreck. The nervous tic he suffered in his youth had developed into a violent spasm which convulsed his whole face, and he began to suffer from epileptic fits and blackouts. In the final years of his life, his early fifties, he refused to retire to bed alone in case he had a seizure and died in his sleep: if a woman wasn't available a male servant would do. The Czar's doctors begged him to take spa waters to repair some of the damage done to his body. He drank the water but always topped it up with alcohol to improve the flavor.

Any one of a variety of health problems could have explained the Czar's final slide into mental derangement. It was preceded by an unexplained and severe illness, possibly encephalitis. His convulsive fits could easily have been delirium tremens or the effect of tertiary syphilis, which can lead to dementia or rapid decay of physical and mental ability. His death from cirrhosis of the liver in 1725 was an inevitable consequence of prolonged alcohol abuse.

EMPRESS CATHERINE I

Curiously for a family littered with lunatics, murderers and emotional cripples, the Romanovs considered Peter the Great's wife, the Empress Catherine I, to be the very biggest skeleton in their wardrobe, because of her non-royal birth. Over a hundred years after her death, the imperial secret police were still under orders to keep the details of her background a state secret.

The Empress Catherine's remarkable rise began from the very bottom rung of Russia's social ladder. She was born Martha Skavronski, the daughter of a Lithuanian slave and part-time gravedigger. Her first husband, Johann, had simply vanished, believed either dead or sent to Siberia to die. Peter met her when she became a camp follower of his armies, but not before she had slept with most of his friends and he had heard them swap notes about her sexual expertise. Catherine was a common laundry woman by trade but she was built like a hod carrier. She was described as having "a little stumpy body, very brown." When she became Peter's mistress, she coated her face with white and pink lead to hide her swarthy complexion and her purple nose, dyed her hair and her teeth black to suit the fashion of the day, and changed her name to the more upmarket Catherine. When he finally married her in 1712, after she had been his mistress for seven years, their illegitimate daughters stood as maids of honor. The Czar boasted to a confused English ambassador that the new marriage was bound to be fruitful, since she'd already given him five children. They had twelve children in all.

Peter the Great had passed a law allowing czars to nominate their successor and when he died in 1725 he was succeeded by his widow, whom he had crowned Empress the preceding year. Next to her husband, the Empress was one of the greatest sots ever to occupy a European throne. In the words of the biographer Henri Troyat, "Catherine was not one to be frightened by a bucket of vodka." In fact, one of the things that had made her attractive to the dipsomaniac Czar in the first place was her ability to drink. The Empress was already a habitual drunk while Peter was alive, but with his death she became many times worse. Her reign became one long destructive round of alcohol abuse. In two years she spent about 700,000 rubles on Hungarian wine alone, and another 16,000 on schnapps. She spent her nights wandering around the palace gardens in an alcoholic haze and would go to bed at dawn. To accommodate her erratic lifestyle, military parades were held in the middle of the night, and her cooks, musicians and even her guests were on twenty-four-hour standby in case she decided to entertain.

The Empress became considerably more obese, her vast blotchy arms as thick as her thighs. Aged beyond her years and befuddled with drink, Catherine shuffled listlessly through her royal engagements. Although she was a raddled old alcoholic with bloodshot eyes, wild and matted hair and clothes soiled with urine stains, she was still accorded the respect and flattery due to a Russian empress, and was fêted and indulged by her fearful subjects wherever she went. She once survived an assassination attempt too drunk to realize that anything had happened: while reviewing a guards regiment a bullet flew past her and struck an innocent bystander dead. The Empress moved on without flinching.

When Catherine died aged forty-three, her body wrecked by twenty years of hard drinking, venereal disease and relentless childbearing, she was succeeded by her late husband's hapless eleven-year-old grandson Czar Peter II. He had a weak constitution and suffered from frequent illnesses. He died of smallpox on what should have been his wedding day. A group of Russia's noblemen offered the Crown to Peter the Great's niece Anne, with the provision that she should move the capital back to Moscow and accept governance of a Grand Council. They thought that they had chosen a quiet, tractable girl who wouldn't give them any trouble. It was a ghastly mistake.

EMPRESS ANNE

Empress Anne was certifiably insane. Her reign marked one of the darkest chapters in Russian history and, according to the nineteenth-century historian Kliuchevskii, "the darkest stain was the Empress herself." Anne's father, Ivan V, had been Czar in name only because he was mentally infirm—what the Russians called a "sad head." Her mother, the Czarina Praskovya, was mad. She filled her palace with dwarfs, jesters and people who were either mentally ill or suffering from some sort of terrible physical disability or deformity—her own private human freak show.

At the age of eighteen Anne was widowed. Her husband, selected for her by Peter the Great, was Frederick the Duke of Courland, a nephew of the King of Prussia. They were both seventeen years old when they met. Their marriage ceremony, orchestrated by the Czar, was a typically extravagant affair, a marathon drinking session punctuated only by toasts, gun salutes and more toasts. At the height of the festivities two enormous pies were carried in and placed before the couple. Suddenly the crusts broke open and a couple of dwarfs, one male, one female, leapt out and danced around the table. Six weeks later the groom was dead from alcoholic poisoning.

Anne never remarried but she took dozens of lovers, never pausing to worry about the social status, or for that matter the sex, of the people she slept with. She allowed one of her less reputable male lovers to turn one of her spare palaces into a temporary brothel. The Empress surrounded herself with a coterie of young girls. She wrote to one of her Governors ordering him to find her tall, exotic-looking "Persian, Georgian or Lesghian girls" who "must be clean, good, and not stupid." When one of her favorite long-serving girlfriends fell ill she ordered Saltykov to find a look-alike: "I believe she will soon die," explained the Empress, "and I want someone to re-place her." She had a passionate lesbian affair with the young daughter of an important Lithuanian official, Mademoiselle Oginska. Anne was so open about this relationship that the wife of an English ambassador was able to remark that the Empress seemed to spend most of her time in bed with her girl-friend.

Her most permanent heterosexual affair was with the brutal and much hated Count Biron. He was already married and Anne insisted on having his wife hang around the palace playing gooseberry while Biron shared the Empress's bed. Biron was her regular lover for the next twenty years, and he used his influence to become one of the richest and most powerful men in Russia. Within a year of Anne's death, the Russian Supreme Privy Council ensured that Biron and his family joined the thousands of peasants Anne had sent packing to Siberia.

While she blew the state's money on luxuries and amusements, Russia starved. She used her power throughout her eleven-year reign to humiliate and oppress. Tens of thousands of her subjects were exiled to Siberia. Thousands more were executed or starved to death, and she had tongues pulled out to prevent her victims from pleading their innocence.

Routine oppression, torture and starvation of the Russian people was hardly a feature unique to Anne's reign, but this Empress also specialized in persecuting her own courtiers. The story about how she had her chef hanged because he cooked pancakes in rancid butter is probably apocryphal, but there were many such anecdotes concerning her sick practical jokes and her lethal mood swings. She once surprised the eminent poet Tredyakovski, who had just given her a private reading of his latest work, with a punch in the mouth. She commanded one of her ladies-in-waiting to sing to her all night: when the woman collapsed with exhaustion Anne sent her to work in the laundry. The Empress was very particular about her laundry. Strictly confidential and curious instructions were passed on concerning the washing of the Empress's smalls. Her dirty underwear was kept under lock and key, and special washerwomen were hired and carefully vetted—no unauthorized person was allowed in the laundry while her linen was being washed.

Her cruelest practical jokes were saved for some of the Russian Empire's leading noblemen and -women. She had two overweight noblewomen force-fed huge amounts of pastries until they almost choked to death on their own vomit. The Russian nobleman Prince Nikita Volkonskii was appointed official keeper of her favorite dog and made to feed it with jugs of cream at appointed hours, while his wife was put in full-time charge of the Empress's white rabbit. He and another prince,

Aleksei Apraskin, were employed as court jesters and made to squat in the corner for hours on end, cackling like hens. Although most of the people she degraded in this manner were intelligent, well-read and cultured men, few dared to resist her wishes. When Prince Balakirev found her games too much and refused to play, he was taken outside and whipped.

Her most infamous and elaborate practical joke was reserved for Prince Michael Golitsyn, a nobleman who incurred the Empress's displeasure by marrying an Italian Catholic. In 1740 it was decided that Golitsyn, by now a widower and in his forties, should marry again, but this time to the woman of the Empress's choice—an ugly old maid. The wedding, the Empress announced, would be the greatest spectacle that Russia had ever seen. Golitsyn and his bride were led through the streets by a procession of goats, pigs, dogs, cows and camels. The court poet read an ode composed for the occasion entitled "Greetings to the Bridal Pair of Fools." The couple were then escorted to their home for the night—a palace specially constructed, at a cost of 30,000 rubles, and made entirely of ice. The Empress accompanied them inside and had them undressed and laid out on their ice bed, where they then spent the night. Russian history books record that the next morning the couple emerged very cold and very embarrassed but still alive.

A few days before she died, Empress Anne, unmarried and childless, proclaimed that the infant son of her German niece, Anna Leopoldnova, should succeed her as Ivan VI. Her twenty-two-year-old niece was elected Regent for the child-Czar. Anna Leopoldnova used her unexpected promotion as a position from which to sate her unconventional sexual appetites. When she became Regent she was pregnant by her husband, Prince Anthony, Duke of Brunswick-Wolfenbüttel. Throughout her pregnancy, Anna had a passionate affair with her favorite lady-in-waiting, Julie Mengden. The couple spent days on end locked in her private apartments, or wandering around the court together wearing only their underclothes. After Anna's child was born she turned her sexual attentions on the Saxon Ambassador, Count Maurice Lynor. During the last weeks of her brief reign she became obsessed with marrying her male and female partners, Lynor and Mengden, to each other.

The wedding never took place: a palace coup brought the brief Regency to a sudden end in November 1741. Anna was exiled to Germany and most of her German relations thrown into Russian jails. The infant Czar Ivan was left to rot in a prison cell for nearly a quarter of a century. Poor Ivan, by then a complete physical and mental wreck who had only ever known the bare walls of his cell, was finally released from his misery when he was murdered by his jailers on the orders of Catherine the Great.

EMPRESS ELIZABETH

Empress Elizabeth, although born out of wedlock, was the last surviving child of Peter the Great. She stepped out of a palace coup at the age of thirty-two and began one of the most scandalous reigns in Russian history. When she died in 1762, few of the thousands of respectful subjects who filed in silent awe past the imperial coffin were aware that they were paying tribute to an immoral old hag who had worn herself out by a life of sex, alcohol and general debauchery. Elizabeth's astonishing sex life has been the subject of great speculation, but 300 is the round figure usually put on the number of lovers she took during her twenty-one years as Empress. She is also believed to have borne eight illegitimate children, although there is not enough evidence to put a precise number on either activity.

Elizabeth was to have been married to Charles Augustus of Holstein-Gottorp, a German prince who died prematurely when he was struck down by smallpox. Soon after his death she began a series of squalid and very public affairs. Although Elizabeth may have gone through a secret morganatic marriage to one of her lovers, Alexei Razumovski, officially she remained unmarried all her life. She would often get blind drunk and too impatient for sex to bother to even undress. Her ladies-in-waiting would cut the clothes off her with scissors and carry her to bed, where the next lover was waiting. Servants, footmen, court officials, coachmen, ambassadors, guards officers, kitchen staff—one after another they climbed into her bed. She kept irregular hours, dining at supper time and retiring to bed at sunrise. Elizabeth terrorized her court officials and ladies-in-waiting; on the rare occasions when she couldn't find a man to share the imperial bed, her ladies were expected to sit up all night and tell her stories or tickle her feet.

Like all of the Romanovs, the Empress survived by inspiring a mixture of dread and veneration. She abolished capital punishment but had tongues cut out and their owners banished to Siberia instead. In the mid-eighteenth century, most Russians given the choice between Siberia and death would have chosen the latter.

Elizabeth's awesome clothing and jewelry collections went some way toward taking Russia to the brink of bankruptcy. When she dressed to impress it was said that she looked like a Holy Shrine. For twenty-odd years she never wore the same outfit twice. Her residence was crammed to the ceiling with incredibly expensive dresses. In a Moscow fire in 1744, Elizabeth lost 4,000 of them, along with countless priceless Romanov family gems. When she died she left 15,000 dresses hanging in her cupboards, 5,000 pairs of shoes, two trunks filled with stockings, and massive debts. It wasn't as though she was stuck for choice, but she also liked to wear tight-fitting men's clothes because they showed off her legs, of which she was inordinately proud. Every Tuesday evening she held balls, known as her "metamorphoses," at which everyone was ordered to cross-dress. Everybody hated her for it, especially the male courtiers, but no one dared complain.

The Empress was extremely vain and would not tolerate competition. No one else at court was allowed to wear her favorite color, pink. She was naturally fair-haired, but had her hair dyed black to conform with the fashion of the day. When the fashion changed and she wanted to revert to blond, she found she couldn't remove the dye from her hair and in a fit of temper shaved it all off. Naturally, all of her ladies-in-waiting were also obliged to have their heads shaved.

Although she was regarded as a beauty when she first came to the throne, her gluttony and her addiction to strong alcohol quickly destroyed her looks. Elizabeth dreaded the approach of old age. She commissioned absurdly flattering portraits of herself which showed her looking decades younger, and had copies of them sent abroad. Before every engagement, her maids would slave for hours on her hair and makeup, burying her puffy, bloated features under an ever-thickening wall of cosmetics. Often she would despair at the end result and elect to stay in bed.

Swollen with fat, barely able to breathe, she ignored her doctors' warnings and drank and gorged herself to an early grave. By the age of forty-seven she was burned out, a miserable, bloated lush tortured by delirium tremens. At fifty, her health was completely shot, but her sex drive was undiminished. By this time the men wouldn't come to her: her legs were so swollen she had to be carried to her lovers' apartments on a litter.

PETER THE PARADOMANIAC

When Empress Elizabeth died in 1762 the imperial crown passed to her nephew Peter III. His reign was as spectacularly crazy as it was brief. The new Czar had just two interests and they consumed most of his waking hours. The first was the Romanov weakness for strong alcohol; the second, inherited from his father, the Duke of Holstein-Gottorp Karl Friedrich, was an obsession with military field-drill trivia.

While the dipsomaniac Duke spent all day drilling his soldiers and generally ignoring his son, Peter was raised by a bunch of German household-guard officers. The first book he learned to read was a manual of arms. The end product of this inadequate education was an emotionally stunted paradomaniac. In his teens, Peter became unusually devoted to his regiments of toy soldiers. When he grew tired of his toys he inflicted his hobby on his wife and servants. He spent his honeymoon drilling his footmen and making them change uniforms up to twenty times a day, and wasted long hours instructing his wife from an arms manual. Occasionally he made her spend all night on sentry duty, standing guard at their bedroom door. One day his wife came into her bedroom and found a dismembered rat hanging over the bed. Peter explained that the rat was guilty according to military law of eating two of his toy soldiers.

On the demise of the Empress Elizabeth, Peter became Czar, just before his thirty-fourth birthday. He made no effort to conceal his delight, and within a couple of hours of his aunt's death threw a party just three rooms away from the bedroom where her body was laid out. Guests were instructed to wear something bright and colorful. The festivities went on for six weeks around Elizabeth's corpse while it lay in state.

At last, as Commander-in-Chief, Czar Peter had some real troops to play with. For a while he was content merely to review his troops ten times a day, but even for Peter the entertainment value of this began to pall. What was needed was a good war, but Peter had no one to fight. He decided to create the illusion of being permanently at war by ordering nonstop salvos of gunfire, and St. Petersburg rocked to the sound of cannon fire from dawn to dusk. One day he ordered that 1,000 cannons be fired simultaneously, but canceled the order when it was carefully explained to him that the city might collapse.

In an astonishingly short time, Czar Peter had managed to wreck Russia's image abroad, alienate his allies, and make enemies of everyone around him, including his own wife. In 1762, just six months after his accession, his reign was suddenly terminated by yet another palace coup d'état, instigated by his wife, Catherine, and organized by the palace guards. A few weeks later he died in custody, apparently as the result of a drunken brawl with another prisoner. The official announcement was made, in the inimitable Russian fashion, that the ex-Czar had died of an acute attack of colic during one of his frequent bouts of hemorrhoids.

CATHERINE'S APPETITES

Catherine the Great succeeded her husband in 1762. She began a thirty-four-year reign for which she is remembered as one of the most extraordinary Romanov leaders of all. In fact her real name wasn't Catherine; she didn't have a drop of Romanov blood in her veins; nor was she even Russian.

Like the Empress Elizabeth, Catherine II was known for her improbable sex life, yet she married aged sixteen without even a rudimentary grasp of the facts of life. Fortunately for Catherine, her immature and drunken husband was not only similarly ignorant but incapable. After eight years of unconsummated marriage she discovered sex for the first time with the husband of one of her ladies-in-waiting, Serge Saltykov.

As a young woman, Catherine was an obsessive horse rider and would spend up to thirteen hours a day in the saddle. Her love of riding gave rise to the popular myth about her allegedly unhealthy equine-related lusts. Although she was not a big hunting enthusiast she liked to take part in the chase—the faster the better. Her riding activities attracted criticism from the Russian court because she preferred to ride like a man—ladies were always instructed to sit sidesaddle because sitting astride the horse was believed to be the cause of gynecological problems.

Given the number of men she slept with and the uncertainties of eighteenth-century contraception, it is strange that during her husband's lifetime she gave birth to only three children by three different men—none of them her husband. Catherine managed to convince him that the first child was his and somehow kept the births of the next two a secret from him. She was able to carry off this deception only by the skin of her teeth. When the arrival of her third child was imminent, Peter was inconveniently close at hand, and Catherine hatched a desperate plan with her valet to distract him. Guessing that her childish husband wouldn't resist the prospect of watching a good fire, she instructed the valet to torch one of the servants' quarters. The plan worked better than expected because the fire spread and destroyed a large part of the palace. Meanwhile, Catherine's valet delivered her baby boy, cut the umbilical cord and whisked it away before Peter returned.

Catherine had a small recess built behind her bed where she could receive her lovers in secret. When anyone asked her about the curtain she would explain that it hid a commode. After the death of her husband she no longer felt obliged to make excuses for her sex life and the secret alcove fell into disuse. Next to Catherine's main bedroom were two smaller rooms, each with the walls covered with exquisite gilt-framed miniatures. In one room these frames held pictures of erotica; in the other, portraits of the men she had seduced.

The selection procedure for her lovers was thorough because of her dread of syphilis. Once a new boyfriend had been nominated, he would be summoned to the court and subjected to a general physical examination by Catherine's English physician, Rogerson. He could then expect to be introduced to Catherine's intimate and trusted friend Countess Bruce, whose job it was to screen the young man before he reached the Empress's bed. Initially this would usually involve a formal interview to ascertain the candidate's IQ. Catherine didn't want her lovers to be too intellectually challenged, but this particular rule could be waived if there were other mitigating circumstances. When the dashing, handsome and exceptionally well-endowed twenty-four-year-old Russian hussar named Rimsky Korsakov arrived on the scene, the Empress was immediately smitten, drooling that he was "a masterpiece of nature." He was installed in his new apartment and a librarian was instructed to acquire a body of reading material for him. When Rimsky Korsakov was asked which books he would most like, he replied, "Oh, you know, big volumes at the bottom and little ones on top like the Empress has."

According to procedure, the Countess Bruce would then subject the candidate to an intimate examination of his physical capabilities, which could involve anything up to and including full sexual intercourse with the examiner. On one occasion the Countess courted disaster when she fell in love with a candidate and asked him back for a second, third and fourth interview. Finally, the young man would be thoroughly briefed about Catherine's particular sexual requirements. Once the candidate had received instruction on the etiquette of sleeping with an empress, a detailed report would be submitted to Catherine. If the young man met with her approval he would be taken to his new apartment, where he would find his customary first gift— a box containing 100,000 rubles. That evening, he would be "presented" to court on the Empress's arm. At precisely ten o'clock they retired to the Empress's bedroom.

Catherine's lovers were expected to be on call to service her sexual needs round the clock. By night they were tireless athletes; by day they were dressed up and paraded at the Empress's side. Life was tough on top, because Catherine allowed only occasional failure in the execution of duty. Her lovers often became paranoid about not being able to perform on command, and naturally the fear of failure would make it even more likely. When one of her lovers fell ill he dosed himself with a cocktail of aphrodisiacs to try to keep the side up and made himself violently sick. Catherine was, however, as generous in her rewards for good performance as she was ruthless with failure or infidelity. Once a lover had been sacked he would normally receive a generous settlement and discreetly vacate his apartment while a replacement was found.

Gregory Orlov, who helped her seize power, was her lover on and off for thirteen years and gave her three sons. He was made a prince and became extremely rich. In 1772 she found out that he was sleeping with his thirteen-year-old cousin. Orlov was pensioned off and he eventually died insane. Another lover, the twenty-six-year-old Ukrainian Peter Zavadovsky, serviced Catherine for a few months and then was relieved of his duties with a pension of 50,000 rubles and an estate of 9,000 Ukrainian peasants. Although she was acclaimed for her liberal views, she gave away serfs by the thousand, and the land that they lived on, to the men who shared her bed. Zavadovsky's immediate replacement, Simon Zorich, for example, received a gift of 1,800 peasants for his "trial run."

Catherine the Great's lovers were generally large in stature. The nearest she ever came to a monogamous relationship was with Gregory Potemkin, a giant, hirsute, one-eyed Russian known as "Cyclops"—he had lost one eye in an argument over a game of billiards and he had a squint in the other. Catherine was attracted, if not by his looks, by his fiery temperament and his awesome libido. His sexual appetite was said to be even more ferocious than hers. In her letters, Catherine often referred to Potemkin as her husband. It was rumored that they contracted a morganatic marriage. According to some accounts, a wedding ceremony took place in 1774 before a few witnesses sworn to secrecy. Their relationship finally ended when the cyclops, aged forty-three, married his fifteen-year-old first cousin, Catherine Zinoviev. Potemkin continued to be the Empress's confidant long after the mutual physical attraction had passed, and in later years it was usually Potemkin who did the hiring and firing of Catherine's lovers because he knew her requirements more intimately than most.

After Potemkin, the Empress's greatest love was probably the "irreplaceable" Sacha Lanskoy, who died of diphtheria in her arms aged twenty-six. She was so inconsolably grief-stricken that it was several weeks before she took another man to her bed. Then she explained that she needed to resume her sex life for health reasons.

Catherine was predisposed to extreme vanity and a dread of old age. She kept two dwarfs, one to look after her powder and combs, and another to take care of her rouge, hairpins and black stick-on beauty patches, called "mouches." She was notoriously touchy about her hair. When she was a child she suffered from impetigo, and had to have all of it shaved off several times in order to remove the scabs. In later years she lost her hair a few times through illness. When she found out that she was suffering from dandruff she had her hairdresser locked up for three years to prevent him from telling anyone else about it.

As the years passed she refused to admit that she was losing her looks, always sleeping with men who were years younger than her because they made her feel more youthful. Although her first half a dozen official lovers were only slightly younger than she was, the age gap grew less respectable as the Empress grew older, eventually arriving at the point where her activities with men young enough to be her grandchildren became too much for her own family to contemplate without feeling nauseous. She was sixteen years older than Zorich, twenty-five years older than Rimsky Korsakov and Alexander Ermolov, thirty years older than both Sacha Lanskoy and Alexander Dmitriev-Mamonov. This alarming trend reached its unsavory nemesis with the desperate Platon Zubov, who was nearly forty years younger than his famous mistress.

By old age, Catherine's health and looks were wrecked by

hard drinking and burning the candle at both ends. Her hair, although still very long, was completely white, and her face was hidden behind an impenetrable mask of paste. She became so obese that she appeared grotesquely deformed, her massive legs swollen and ulcerated. She was so bloated that the palace stairs had to be replaced with ramps because her legs could no longer support her weight. She was just turned sixty when she took her last official lover, twenty-two-year-old Platon Zubov. By then she was a toothless, bloated, breathless old crone with a heart condition, but she refused to accept that she was anything but physically desirable. Her sex drive went marching on. It took a brave man or a blind man to stomach the climb upstairs to Catherine's bed.

Zubov was neither, but he was ambitious enough to continue pressing the imperial cellulite for the next seven years. The arrogant new lover strutted around the court giving out orders, shamelessly exploiting his new position. His private apartment was crowded with hangers-on who hoped to beg favors from the most important man in Russia. Under Catherine's very nose he tried to seduce a sixteen-year-old grand duchess, Elisabeth Alekseevna, wife of the future Czar Alexander I. It was the first time that one of the Empress's lovers had dared treat her so casually, but she was beyond caring.

In 1796 the old Empress fell off her toilet seat with a massive stroke and died thirty hours later in her sixty-seventh year.

THE TWISTED HEIR

The most spectacularly insane Russian monarch was Czar Paul, whose four-year reign saw Russia into the nineteenth century.

It is tempting to point to Paul as evidence of yet more mental instability in the Romanov line. He was, however, the issue of an illicit affair between his mother, Catherine the Great, who was German, and her first lover, Sergei Saltykov. Catherine successfully passed him off as the son of her witless, sterile husband. Paul, without a single drop of Romanov blood in his veins, was accepted as the legitimate heir.

Czar Paul was small and very ugly, with a disproportionately large head and a saddle nose typical of sufferers from congenital syphilis. The Empress Catherine did nothing to prepare him for rule. He was the archetypal prince without a role, pushed to the sidelines, a grand duke with nothing to do. The twisted heir cultivated a grievance against the mother he believed was keeping him from the throne for three decades, and nursed it into a pathological hatred. It wasn't until a few months after he became Czar at the age of forty-three that it became all too evident that he was dangerously insane—a Russian Caligula.

One of his first acts as Czar was to avenge the man he believed to be his father. Peter III was exhumed from a crypt at the Alexander Nevsky Monastery. By this time Peter had been dead for thirty-four years, a fact that state-of-the-art Russian embalming technology was unable to disguise. The remains were dressed in one of Peter's elaborate military uniforms, robed in ermine, and taken to the throne room at the Winter Palace. The body was seated on the throne and the imperial crown was placed on its skull. Paul's courtiers and officials were then instructed to make obeisance to the "true Czar," the rightful occupant of the throne, usurped by his evil wife, Catherine. There followed a double funeral, as the bodies of Peter III and Catherine were laid side by side so that their remains could mingle.

Czar Paul may not have been Peter III's true son, but he

was infected by his childlike devotion to Prussian militaria. Whereas his mentally infirm predecessor had spent most of his time abusing toy soldiers, Paul preferred the real thing. The entire army, of which he was now Commander-in-Chief, was forced to adopt the antiquated Prussian uniform of his hero, Frederick the Great, right down to the last detail of old-fashioned gaiters and powdered pigtails. It was a massive humiliation for the Russian military, but, as they would soon discover, this was the least of their problems. For no apparent reason, Paul once ordered an entire regiment on a 4,000-kilometer march which took two years to complete and killed hundreds of horses.

Paul became fanatically obsessed with his soldiers' uniforms at the expense of military efficiency. He made them wear costumes that were so tight-fitting they made breathing difficult and fighting practically impossible. Underneath they wore straitjackets to make them stand erect, and on their heads they wore thick, heavy wigs with iron rods inserted to make the hairpiece sit straight. To make his soldiers goose-step perfectly without bending their legs, he strapped steel plates to their knees. The night before a parade his men would labor until dawn to cover their wigs with grease and chalk. They all knew that even a hair out of place could mean arrest, a thrashing, or deportation. His officers grew to fear his unpredictability so much that they got into the habit of saying a final farewell to their wives and families before they went on parade.

As Paul grew older he grew uglier and more paranoid. He was both snub-nosed and bald, but once had a soldier knouted to death for referring to his Imperial Highness as "baldy." He issued a proclamation that the words "baldy" and "snub nose" were banned and anyone heard using these words would receive a similar treatment. At mealtimes he splashed dessert around the room for the fun of watching his servants scrape up after him. Eventually the whole of Russia learned to tremble before him.

The Czar saw subversion everywhere, even in the way his people dressed. In 1797 he made a law that forbade his subjects to wear round hats, top boots, straight pants or shoes with laces—modern dress which had become associated in the Czar's mind with the French Revolution and progressive political ideology. To enforce this regulation, a couple of hundred armed troops were sent on to the streets of St. Petersburg with orders to randomly attack anyone who didn't conform to the Czar's dress code. People were stripped of clothing where they stood: shoes, hats, breeches and waistcoats were ripped to shreds or confiscated. The Czar censored his own family's mail, closed down all private printing presses and deleted from the Russian dictionary the words "citizen," "club," "society" and "revolution." His police spies attended parties and concerts even in private houses. He had every cab driver in St. Petersburg banished because one of them had been found carrying a gun. He passed another law that required everyone to get out of the carriage they were in whenever he passed by. Most of the time people hid when they saw him coming. He imposed a nine o'clock curfew and blockaded all exits to the capital. It became almost impossible to move without being harassed by the Czar's police. St. Petersburg, which under Catherine the Great had become the third most fashionable city in Europe, was now a ghost town. Even his allies realized that it was time for him to go.

By Romanov standards it was a rather dull coup. Paul had

pulled down one of Russia's finest buildings, the New Summer Palace in St. Petersburg, and on the site built a new residence known as Michael Castle, an unsightly thick-walled fortress with battlements, a moat and a drawbridge. He had been living there for only a week when late one evening there was a knock on his bedroom door. In stepped a small group of officers with a proclamation of abdication which they asked him to sign. There was a scuffle, and minutes later Paul lay dead, strangled. The official announcement was that the Czar had died of "an attack of apoplexy"—a euphemism that the average Russian well understood by now. Even though they were supposed to observe a period of official mourning, the Russian people could not contain their joy at being released from the four-year nightmare.

THE LAST CZARS

Paul's great-grandson Czar Alexander III was a drunken and reactionary tyrant who persecuted anyone who didn't speak Russian or subscribe to the Russian Church, including Jews. He died in the Crimea as a consequence of his alcoholism on November 1, 1894, and his remains were carried 1,300 miles back to St. Petersburg. The funeral ceremony, which lasted four hours, was a desperate ordeal for his son Nicholas to endure. The deceased Czar, dead for nearly three weeks, had to be kissed on the lips. His face, reported one of the royal mourners, "looked a dreadful color and the smell was awful." The color of the new Czar Nicholas II's face was more dreadful yet.

One mysterious quality of the House of Romanov was

that, although its foulest leaders had always been reviled by their own people, abroad they inspired great admiration and respect. Their unpopularity at home appeared to be in mathematically inverse proportion to their international status. So it was with Nicholas II. The Czar had the added cachet of lots of good-looking young children and close blood ties with the British royal family. The obvious facial resemblance to his cousin King George V appealed massively to popular sentiment in Britain. Surely someone who had such a nice family and looked so strikingly like our own King George must be a thoroughly decent sort of chap. Why, the Czar was almost British.

The British public were deceived on almost every count. Nicholas was as British as George V only in the sense that they both had Danish mothers and their paternal ancestors were almost exclusively German. Nor could he by any stretch of the imagination be considered an ordinary family man. This was someone for whom peasants would prostrate themselves in the fields as his train went by; a man many Russians still believed went to heaven once a week to talk to God. His image was so feared that in some parts of Russia post office officials were afraid to overstamp the Czar's head. His death, however, transformed him from brutal tyrant to royal martyr.

His reign was a disaster from the first day. At his coronation celebrations several thousand people lost their lives and many thousands more were seriously injured as men, women and children who were waiting for a glimpse of their new Czar were trampled to death. Nicholas was aware of the awful casualties but insisted that the celebrations continue as planned, a decision for which he was bitterly criticized at home and abroad. Security on that day was handled by his uncle the Grand Duke Sergei. Years later, Nicholas's incompetent uncle became the first Romanov casualty of the Socialists when one February afternoon in 1905, as the Grand Duke's carriage passed through the Kremlin gates, a nitroglycerin bomb was lobbed directly into his lap, blasting Sergei so completely to smithereens that bits of him were later found on the roofs of nearby buildings.

Nicholas had a nervous breakdown at the prospect of becoming Czar. He wept, "I know nothing of the business of ruling. I have no idea of even how to talk to ministers." This was not false modesty. Like his cousins the Kaiser and King George V, he was a man of desperately limited abilities, dull, indecisive, and very easily led. Foreign ambassadors came away with the impression that the Czar always agreed with whoever spoke to him last. His German wife dictated most of what he did for the best part of twenty-five years.

Nicholas wrote in his diary on November 1, 1905, "We've made the acquaintance of a man of God, Gigorii, from the Tobolsk Guberniia." Rasputin was only one of many quacks and charlatans whom Nicholas allowed to surround the royal family. The "mad monk" was neither mad nor a monk, but a talented debauchee who had somehow managed to talk his way into the beds of most of the bored noblewomen of St. Petersburg even though he smelled like an open sewer. Unsurprisingly, he was hated by Russia's male aristocrats, who helped encourage a widespread suspicion that the uncouth, hairy mystic was a malign influence on the royal family, especially the Czarina.

Nicholas's wife, Alexandra, was arrogant and extremely unpopular. When she ventured out into public she appeared sullen and aloof. "Russia is not England," she told Queen Victoria. "Here it is not necessary to make efforts to gain popular affection." In a notorious incident in April 1915, Rasputin became roaring drunk in a Moscow bar and boasted loudly and publicly that he was the Czarina's lover. When Rasputin was challenged by the police to prove his identity, he dropped his pants and waved his private parts at them. The Czarina's failure to have Rasputin locked up immediately was seen by everyone as conclusive proof that they were indeed lovers. In truth, Rasputin owed his freedom to the fact that the Czar's family saw him as the only hope to cure their son's illness. Alexis suffered from the "royal disease" hemophilia, a condition that carried such a great stigma that there was little or no mention of it in the Czar's household. Consequently, the nature of the Czarevitch's illness was completely unknown outside the palace and even to the majority of palace insiders.

Rasputin was relatively successful in reducing Alexis's suffering, a feat which was attributed to his supposed mystical powers. The most plausible explanation is that Rasputin was simply taking advantage of a fact about hemophilia that was unknown to doctors until the 1960s—high blood pressure, often caused by tension and emotional stress, can aggravate hemophilia. Conversely, relaxation can reduce or even stem it completely. Rasputin's "mystic" powers were almost certainly nothing more than his ability to put the Czarevitch at ease, thus lowering the boy's blood pressure.

Two of Rasputin's eventual assassins were minor members of the Russian royal family. One, the Czar's dissipated cousin Grand Duke Dmitri Pavlovich, was an army officer who spent considerably more time in the St. Petersburg nightclubs than he did on army maneuvers. The other was Prince Felix Yusupov, the transvestite husband of Nicholas's beautiful niece Irena. The assassination itself, grown in legend over the years, did not go quite to plan. Pavlovich, Yusupov and two coconspirators lured Rasputin to Yusupov's home using the Prince's wife as bait— playing upon Rasputin's known weakness for high-class women, they correctly gambled that he would find the prospect of sleeping with a member of the imperial family irresistible.

While Rasputin sat and waited for the arrival of the Princess Irena, Yusupov set up a gramophone and played the only record they had, "I'm a Yankee Doodle Dandy," over and over. A minor army medic, Dr. Lazovert, meanwhile was given the famous task of lacing cakes and wine with potassium cyanide. The popular version of the story, greatly enhanced by Yusupov himself as the years went by, is that while Rasputin waited he ate enough cakes to kill half a dozen men but because of his superhuman powers was largely unaffected. Lazovert, however, confessed on his deathbed that he had completely lost his nerve and hadn't in fact poisoned anything at all. This was how Rasputin was able to carry on gorging himself with food and drink while his terrified assassins sat around waiting for him to drop dead. Eventually they all lost their nerve and shot him once in the back. He lay motionless for a while, apparently dead, but then dragged himself to his feet and ran out of the house into the courtyard. Two more bullets and a kick to the head finished him off, after which they dumped the corpse in the river. There was easily enough evidence to convict both royals of murder but neither was charged because of the embarrassment it would have brought upon the Romanov family.

When the Bolsheviks took control, the Yusupovs fled to New York and became overnight celebrities, once bizarrely introduced at a society function as "Prince and Princess Rasputin." Although they had no income, they kept up appearances by frittering away the jewelry they had managed to escape with until nothing was left. Felix Yusupov's fictionalized version of Rasputin's murder is the one that persisted for decades. In 1927 he wrote the "definitive" account of Rasputin's death, *Rasputin, His Malignant Influence and His Assassination*, which was, he claimed, to set the record straight, but was more to do with the fact that he was desperately broke. Yusupov retold the story many times and it became more flamboyant in the telling as the years rolled by. When Hollywood made a film of Rasputin's death he successfully sued MGM when the film version suggested that Rasputin had seduced his wife. Irena was awarded £25,000 in damages—worth more than half a million today.

When his country mobilized for war with the Kaiser, the Czar of Holy Russia did what the Romanovs so often did in times of stress: he hit the bottle. Nicholas spent the final two years of his reign high on a cocktail of alcohol and addictive drugs. A Russian ambassador who visited Nicholas in 1916 found him so heavily drugged that he could "not succeed in fixing the Emperor's eyes or attention." People who hadn't seen the Czar in twelve months were shocked by his appearance and found him barely recognizable. Visitors remarked on his slurred speech, dull gaze, dilated pupils, hollow cheeks, vacant smile and his apparent lack of concern about the impending crisis. In St. Petersburg it was rumored that the Czar had suffered a mental breakdown or else was insane.

The Czar's slide into alcohol and drug dependence was partly self-inflicted, and partly accidental. Morphine and other opium-based drugs were used as a painkiller for the most trivial of ailments, including coughs, colds and minor headaches, and were quite casually dispensed by doctors. Heroin, introduced in the second half of the nineteenth century to wean people off opium, was considered nonaddictive. (Between 1897 and 1914, Nicholas's British cousins were regular but innocent users of cocaine and even heroin. Record books from a pharmacy near Balmoral show that the royals and their guests were supplied with cocaine and heroin solutions as well as sleeping pills.) The Czar fell into heavy morphine abuse after taking it originally to overcome constipation. Both he and his wife also used opium and cocaine to cure head colds and stomach complaints. Nicholas recorded in his diary in November 1915: "I woke up with a shocking cold in the left nostril, so that I am thinking of spraying it with cocaine." Nicholas also drank a brew containing "a variety of herb infusions" prepared by a Tibetan herbalist called Dr. Badmaev. This "tea" induced a state of euphoria and contained hallucinogens.

The last ruling Russian Czar may not have had the licentiousness of Alexander I, the drunken debauchery of Catherine or Elizabeth, the cruelty of Peter the Great, or the violent mental instability of Paul or Empress Anne, but while his army remained loyal enough to do his dirty work for him he was capable of being as ruthless a tyrant as any Romanov. "Terror," wrote Nicholas II, "must be met by terror." At the first whiff of subversion he sent his troops out into the Russian countryside to wage war on his countrymen, with the personal order "Don't skimp on the bullets." His soldiers invaded and wiped out entire villages, burning and executing in their wake, leaving the countryside full of wounded, homeless and starving peasants. When the reports of mass carnage filtered back from his so-called Punitive Expeditions he read them with undisguised glee. When the Soviets lined him up against a wall in Ekaterinburg they did to him what the Royal Martyr would have had done to them given half a chance.

Ultimately, Nicholas II proved to be the weakest link in a Romanov-Holstein-Gottorp chain which had spanned 300 years and fifteen rulers. Nicholas was considered by Russia's right-wing hard-liners too inept and too soft to be a really successful despot, even though he was one of the most reactionary and autocratic of all the Czars. But the real lament of the Romanovs was that Nicholas II was not unfortunately quite ruthless enough.

The story of the Czar and his immediate family ends at the bottom of a mine shaft at Ekaterinburg, but there were five or six dozen other Romanovs around at the start of the Russian Revolution, and there were quite a few potential family embarrassments within their number. A colony of the imperial family sprang up in Paris, populated with their semi-legitimate and illegitimate wives and children. The Czar's youngest brother, the Grand Duke Michael, shocked his family by getting engaged to a twice-divorced commoner. Michael and mistress Natalia were eventually married abroad, but not before she had given him a son. Nicholas's cousin the Grand Duke Cyril had committed a cardinal sin by marrying, without the Czar's consent, his first cousin Victoria Melita of Saxe-Coburg, a lady who had earlier upset the family by jilting the Czarina's brother, Alexander of Hesse. The Czar's youngest uncle, the Grand Duke Paul, also married a divorcée, an act that his enraged nephew described as "undisguised selfishness." Nicholas's remaining uncle, the Grand Duke Alexis, spent the rest of his days in Paris nightclubs.

6. HANOVER FAMILY VALUES

BRITAIN WAS SCRAPING the bottom of the genealogical barrel when the elephantine Queen Anne died heirless and the Crown passed into the hands of George Guelph, the son of a minor German duke from Celle. Fifty-seven living people had a better claim by birthright to the British throne, but they were all Catholics and excluded by the Act of Settlement. From that time to the present day, Great Britain's throne has been occupied by a family of badly inbred Germans with a history of mental instability.

George I was born on March 28, 1660, son of Ernest, Elector of Hanover, and Sophia, granddaughter of James I. When King George I landed at Greenwich on September 30, 1714, most people in Britain had never even heard of Hanover, one of a cluster of states in northern Germany known to historians as the Holy Roman Empire. He arrived with a full com-

THE ROYAL HOUSE
OF
HANOVER

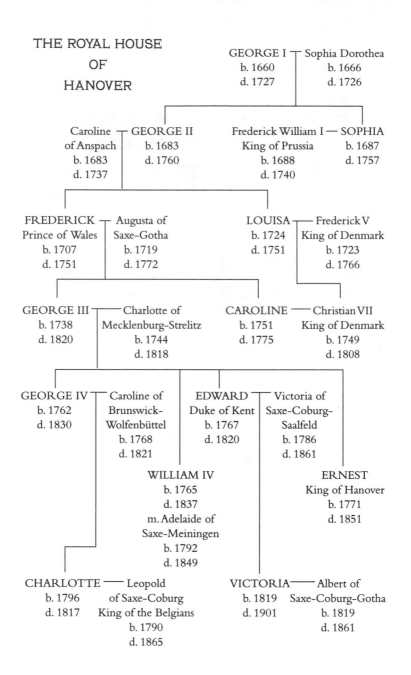

GEORGE I ⊤ Sophia Dorothea
b. 1660 | b. 1666
d. 1727 | d. 1726

Caroline ⊤ GEORGE II
of Anspach | b. 1683
b. 1683 | d. 1760
d. 1737

Frederick William I — SOPHIA
King of Prussia | b. 1687
b. 1688 | d. 1757
d. 1740

FREDERICK ⊤ Augusta of
Prince of Wales | Saxe-Gotha
b. 1707 | b. 1719
d. 1751 | d. 1772

LOUISA ⊤ Frederick V
b. 1724 | King of Denmark
d. 1751 | b. 1723
| d. 1766

GEORGE III ⊤ Charlotte of
b. 1738 | Mecklenburg-Strelitz
d. 1820 | b. 1744
| d. 1818

CAROLINE — Christian VII
b. 1751 | King of Denmark
d. 1775 | b. 1749
| d. 1808

GEORGE IV ⊤ Caroline of
b. 1762 | Brunswick-
d. 1830 | Wolfenbüttel
| b. 1768
| d. 1821

EDWARD ⊤ Victoria of
Duke of Kent | Saxe-Coburg-
b. 1767 | Saalfeld
d. 1820 | b. 1786
| d. 1861

WILLIAM IV
b. 1765
d. 1837
m. Adelaide of
Saxe-Meiningen
b. 1792
d. 1849

ERNEST
King of Hanover
b. 1771
d. 1851

CHARLOTTE — Leopold
b. 1796 | of Saxe-Coburg
d. 1817 | King of the Belgians
| b. 1790
| d. 1865

VICTORIA — Albert of
b. 1819 | Saxe-Coburg-Gotha
d. 1901 | b. 1819
| d. 1861

plement of German cooks, attendants and servants, and a couple of black men, Mohamet and Mustapha, captured during a Turkish campaign. All were determined to profit from the adventure. Thackeray noted, "Take what you can get was the old monarch's maxim. The German women plundered, the German secretaries plundered, the German cooks and attendants plundered, even Mustapha and Mohamet . . . had a share in the booty."

George's arrival marked the point at which the British royal family could be ridiculed by writers and artists with impunity, because the Hanoverians were certainly ridiculous. It was with good reason that the first two Georges were known as Dunce the First and Dunce the Second. The Hanoverians liked their gardening, but their courts were artless and witless. Ever since George I announced, "I hate all boets and bainters," the British royal family reveled in their simple ignorance.

"Farmer" George III loved the theater, as long as the entertainment featured clowns or pantomime, and certainly nothing as cerebral as Shakespeare, which he thought was "bunk." His son William IV, the last English monarch to dismiss a ministry on a whim, was of desperately limited ability. His visits to the West Indies made him, he thought, an expert on slavery. He came home believing that slaves were "the happiest people in the world" and made several impassioned speeches in the House of Lords in support of slavery. His deliberations on "these newfangled principles of liberty" were by and large ignored as few people took him seriously.

Edward VII was too busy chasing women to ever sit down and read a book: in spite of the vast educational resources available to him it is likely that the only Latin he ever knew was "coitus interruptus." At a literary dinner that had been forced on him, he inquired about the identity of a fellow guest and was informed that the gentleman was "an authority on Lamb." The King threw down his knife and fork and bawled in disbelief, "An authority on lamb?"

START OF A DYNASTY

Like most of the male Hanoverians, George I was afflicted by a weakness for adulterous fornication. When he was sixteen he impregnated his sister's under-governess, which was a family embarrassment as the girl was from an influential German royal dynasty, the Heidelbergs. His father, Ernst August, took him aside and told him he could sleep with whoever he liked providing he wasn't careless enough to let half of Europe know about his bastards. The child, said to have been the spitting image of George, was never acknowledged and nothing is known of its fate or that of the mother. George, however, had learned his lesson, because, although a succession of women bore him children in later years, none was ever acknowledged to be his. He took such care to cover his tracks that only one of his bastards can be named with any degree of certainty—Maria Katharine von Meysenburg.

George I was already divorced when he took up his throne and he never remarried. Instead, he slept in rotation with his three concubines. Two of the King's mistresses came with him from Hanover. One, a vast fräulein named Madame Kielmansegge, soon to be created Countess of Darlington, was described as "an ogress" with "two acres of cheeks spread with crimson." She was reputedly a nymphomaniac, and was probably George's half-sister. Lord Chesterfield remarked, "The standard of His Majesty's taste, as exemplified in his mistresses, makes all ladies who aspire to his favor . . . strain and swell themselves, like the frogs in the fable, to rival the bulk and dignity of the ox. Some succeed, and others burst." The other was Melusine von der Schulenberg, which was later anglicized as the Duchess of Kendal. She was as tall and skinny as her rival was fat, and completely bald, having lost her hair through smallpox. Together, Mesdames Kielmansegge and Schulenberg were known as "the Elephant and the Maypole." The King's third regular mistress, the much younger Countess von Platen, stayed behind in Hanover so that George had someone available for sex on his frequent trips home. All three were said to be proof of "the King's strong stomach."

George and his British subjects were conspicuously indifferent to each other. At fifty-four he was too old to absorb any of the new English culture and spent at least half of his time avoiding it by living in Hanover. His preference for Germany meant that Cabinet positions assumed great importance. As the King and his son, George II, quite literally hated each other, he preferred to rely on his ministers when he was abroad rather than leave power in the hands of the son. The King's ministers represented the executive branch of government, while Parliament represented the legislative. George's absences also required the creation of the post of Prime Minister, the majority leader in the House of Commons who acted in the King's stead. Robert Walpole was the first, and he went on to dominate British politics for the next twenty years. When Walpole retired in 1742, he had overseen the foundation of modern constitutional monarchy—an executive Cabinet responsible to Parliament, which was in turn responsible to the electorate.

Thackeray, in *The Four Georges*, noted of George I:

Though a despot in Hanover, he was a moderate ruler in England. His aim was to leave it to itself as much as possible, and to live out of it as much as he could. His heart was in Hanover. He was more than fifty-four years of age when he came amongst us: we took him because we wanted him, because he served our turn; we laughed at his uncouth German ways, and sneered at him. He took our loyalty for what it was worth; laid hands on what money he could; kept us assuredly from Popery and wooden shoes.

King George II was a satirist's dream, lampooned by cartoonists, the paparazzi of the day, with his breeches round his ankles, breaking wind and defecating. Foul-tempered, ludicrously vain and sexually promiscuous, he was in the words of his own eldest son "a miserly martinet with an insatiable sexual appetite." Unlike his parents, George II and his wife went on to achieve something like a solid and lasting relationship, although not in the conventional sense.

The King fancied himself as a sexual athlete and liked to boast about his prowess in bed, usually with other women. He normally had at least two adulterous affairs on the go at the same time. His wife, Queen Caroline, a shrewd and pragmatic woman, handled his compulsive philandery with the skill of a seasoned diplomat. When she found out about his first mistress, Henrietta Howard, she simply offered her rival a job in court. From then on she always selected the King's mistresses for him. George II thought nothing of seeking his wife's advice, or even enlisting her help in picking up other women. When he was away on one of his frequent excursions to Hanover, he regularly consulted his wife about his adulterous affairs in forty- and fifty-page letters; highly personal and intimate correspondence which Queen Caroline perversely liked to share with, among others, Horace Walpole and Lord Hervey.

One of the King's more high-profile affairs began in 1735 when, as a middle-aged man, he took up with a courtesan named Amelia Sophia von Walmoden. She was a niece of one of his father's regular mistresses, Countess von Platen. The King shared his new sleeping partner with at least two other men, a husband he knew about, and a young army officer he had yet to discover. One night he found a ladder leading from the garden into her bedroom and a young man hiding in a bush. When the King confronted his mistress she swore it was a plot to blacken her name. George gave her the benefit of the doubt and the incident was forgotten.

Although the King was apparently incapable of staying faithful to his wife for more than a few hours at a time, it was to the Queen's bed that he always returned. Caroline helped to achieve this largely by carefully selecting mistresses for her husband who were even uglier than she was. However, one of the King's daughters, Princess Anne, hoped he would take even more mistresses so that "Mama might be a little relieved from the ennui of seeing him in her room." Unusually, George II continued to sleep with his wife until her death. In 1737 the fifty-three-year-old Queen Caroline fell seriously ill when she was at the receiving end of a badly bungled attempt to cure a neglected strangulated hernia. After her operation, as she lay in bed surrounded by courtiers, her bowel burst open, showering a torrent of excrement all over the bed and the floor. After an embarrassed silence, one of her courtiers said that she hoped the relief would do Her Majesty some good. The Queen replied that she hoped so too, because that was the last evacuation she would ever have.

As she lay dying of what *Gentleman's Magazine* later confirmed as "a mortification of ye bowels," the Queen selflessly begged her husband to remarry. The King spoiled the moment by declining her offer, adding that he'd rather stick to his mistresses. Upon her death soon afterward, Alexander Pope was moved to write:

> *Here lies wrapt in forty thousand towels*
> *The only proof that Caroline had bowels.*

The year after the Queen's death, George II's favorite courtesan, Sophia von Walmoden, was brought over to England from Hanover and installed on a more permanent basis. The King continued to take mistresses for another twenty-three years, until death came ingloriously on October 25, 1760, when he was seventy-seven. At about 7:30 A.M. his German valet de chambre heard a roar which he judged to be "louder than the royal wind" and found the King slumped on the floor, his face covered with blood. He had died of a heart attack while straining to overcome constipation on the lavatory, slicing his face open on the edge of a cabinet as he fell.

FATHER-SON BONDING

George II's heir, Frederick the Prince of Wales, never made it to the throne. Years earlier, he had caught a chill, which was probably aggravated by an old cricketing injury, and died suddenly and unexpectedly a few weeks afterward on March 20, 1751, aged forty-four. The King's reaction would have been considered unusual coming from anyone other than a Hanoverian. "I have lost my eldest son," George observed, "but I was glad of it."

One of the less endearing features of George II's reign, as was the case with many members of his dynasty, was the infamously bitter and long-running feud between father and eldest son. The deep and personal enmity which existed between the Prince of Wales and both parents ran much deeper than the usual royal family squabbles about money. When they moved to England, Frederick was deliberately left behind in Hanover. At the age of twenty the prince became Heir Apparent and his parents, who hadn't seen him since he was seven, reluctantly summoned him to London and proceeded to openly insult him at every opportunity.

Queen Caroline described her son as "the lowest stinking coward in the world," adding for good measure that he made her want to vomit and that she hoped he would drop down dead with apoplexy. The feeling was entirely mutual: when King George II traveled to Hanover, the Prince of Wales prayed that his father would drown. Even as she lay terminally ill the Queen thought it worth pointing out that at least death would bring the consolation of never having to set eyes on her son again. The Prince, meanwhile, sportingly dispatched relays of messengers to find out whether his mother was dead yet. Perhaps a clue to the King and Queen's aversion to their son may be found in Sir Robert Walpole's vitriolic description of the Prince of Wales. The Prime Minister found Frederick to be "a poor, weak, irresolute, false, lying, dishonest, contemptible wretch, that nobody loves, that nobody believes, that nobody will trust."

Frederick inherited his father's indiscriminate taste in women. By the age of twenty-one he had acquired a regular mistress called Anne Vane, one of his mother's maids of honor and described as a "fat and ill-shaped dwarf." Miss Vane had already made herself useful in royal circles by having multilateral flings with courtiers, one of whom was a close friend of Frederick and almost old enough to be her grandfather. She became pregnant, and bore a son whom the Prince of Wales naively acknowledged as his own. She earned herself a pension of £3,000 a year, a large London house and a full livery of servants. When Frederick's lust for Miss Vane began to wane, he transferred his attentions to her chambermaid. The next mistress, Lady Archibald Hamilton, was appointed as a lady-in-waiting to his new wife, Princess Augusta of Saxe-Gotha. By the time he met Lady Hamilton she was thirty-five but looked considerably older, having already borne ten children.

George III was a blip in the line of compulsive philanderers, the only male member of the ruling House of Hanover to have a relatively chaste private life, although there were widespread rumors about his marriage to a nineteen-year-old Quaker girl before his marriage to Charlotte. But his court was one of the dullest, the meanest and the most uncomfortable in Europe. Everyone, even the old, the seriously infirm and the heavily pregnant, was obliged to stand bolt upright in the King and Queen's presence, sometimes for hours on end. One of his courtiers, Fanny Burney, described the court regime: "You must not cough, sneeze or wince for any reason," she wrote, "though you may privately bite the inside of your cheek for a little relief, taking care meanwhile to do it cautiously as to make no apparent dent outwardly." The rules of etiquette which were ruthlessly observed by both the King and Queen made normal relationships with their children impossible as not even they were allowed to sit down in their presence or speak to their parents unless spoken to first.

REGENCY REVULSION

Although Britain's tacky ruling house had in four generations produced a host of shallow and often absurd debauchees and one celebrated madman, they didn't really hit their stride until the last quarter of the eighteenth century. King George III and Queen Charlotte were prolific. Their thirteen offspring who survived into adulthood included seven dysfunctional sons, described by the Duke of Wellington as "the damnedest millstones that ever hung around a government's neck." Shelley called them the "royal vampires."

George III's eldest son, "Prinny," was quite unlike the other Georges: bright, witty and capable on the one hand; indolent, spoiled and neurotic on the other. He was, said the Duke of Wellington, "the most extraordinary compound of talent, wit, buffoonery, obstinacy and good feelings; in short, a medley of the most opposite qualities, with a great preponderance of good—that I ever saw in any character in my life." As a recklessly extravagant patron of the arts, he left many artifacts to posterity. He had his father's vast book collection donated as the foundation of the British Museum Library, and his building projects inspired the Regency style of architecture. However, the Duke of Wellington's mixed, but generally favorable, opinion of Prinny was not shared by the British public. George's profligacy coincided with a time of massive social distress and misery following the Napoleonic Wars, and tremendous changes wrought by the Industrial Revolution.

In short, George IV was the most detested of all the Hanoverian kings: he was perceived as a vain, overblown, indolent, philandering sot whose corpulent rump brought more shame to the throne than any British monarch before or since. Prinny was loathed by everyone from poets to politicians. The poor hated him because he was a debauched and scandalous spendthrift at a time when they were being starved to death by the war with France and were rioting for bread in the streets. The tax-paying middle classes couldn't stomach him because they were footing the bill for his mistresses and his debauches. Britain's writers and artists despised him because he had carelessly attacked one of their own: although he was massively obese he had the poet Leigh Hunt fined £500 and jailed for two years for suggesting that he was fat.

From then on, Prinny became the object of unprecedented ridicule from the very people who knew how to do it best. He kept the printing industry out of recession single-handedly. Prinny may have cursed his bad luck that he was around at the same time as some of England's most brilliant cartoonists, Gilray, Rowlandson, Cruikshank and Heath, who all made personal fortunes out of ridiculing him. At one point he was reduced to offering Cruikshank £100 if he would stop portraying him as a lecherous old drunk. (The more subtle form of bribery known as the Honours List had not been devised.)

Unlike his great-grandfather George II, an unusually sensitive man who sacked one of the Lords of the Bedchamber when he casually inquired after the King's piles and anal fistulas, George IV was often oblivious to criticism. Most of the time his fortunately thick skin and fantastically overblown ego allowed him to ignore the most stinging of personal attacks, but there were limits to even his royal powers of self-delusion. There were two words guaranteed to reduce him to a quivering royal jelly—"French Revolution." By the 1790s even he began to recognize that his own unpopularity was so great that it could inspire revolt in England, and from then on he lived in perpetual dread that the horrifying events he had heard about in France would be repeated on his side of the Channel.

His fears were well grounded. Throughout his Regency, his subjects bombarded him with death-threat letters. When George became King, the manager of the Theatre Royal at Brighton scrapped the traditional singing of the national anthem in case it started a riot. Wherever George went, he was verbally abused and his carriage pelted with mud. In 1812, starving Londoners took to the streets with cries of "Bread or blood" and his home, Carlton House, had to be protected by troops. By that time, however, he had almost completely abandoned his London residence and was cowering full time in his precursor to Gracelands, the Brighton Pavilion.

Although Prinny had kept his head well below the parapet throughout the war with France, he claimed Napoleon's defeat as a great personal victory. In 1815 he broke cover to invite all of Britain's allies to join him in a great celebration party in London. Yet, as hard as he tried, even the reflected glory of victory at Waterloo didn't rub off on him. Anyone who even associated with George risked unpopularity, as England's greatest national hero, the Duke of Wellington, discovered when he was booed on the streets of London because he had declared his loyalty to the King.

George IV was a scandalously irresponsible spendthrift all of his life. By 1786, while still Prince of Wales, he was a quarter of a million pounds in debt, and within six years the debts had almost doubled. He was once threatened by bailiffs who surrounded the house he had holed himself up in with his mistress, Mrs. Fitzherbert, and gave him twenty-four hours to pay a £2,000 bill. As he'd already pawned most of his own jewelry, he paid off his creditors by pawning Mrs. Fitzherbert's.

The Prince overreached himself with Carlton House, which was a gift from his father on his twenty-first birthday. He decided to make it into one of the finest palaces in Europe, one which would stand comparison with Versailles in its heyday or the Winter Palace in St. Petersburg. His new house became a bottomless pit into which the Prince poured taxpayers' money. Without regard to cost, he hired the best craftsmen in Europe to make lavish alterations, filling it with the most fantastic bric-a-brac. Carlton House existed in a perpetual state of refurbishment: in a single year he spent over £250,000 on new furniture; in another year the bill for new upholstery alone was £49,000. Robert Walpole was invited to see it at firsthand; was staggered by the display of ostentation and afterward wondered aloud how the country was going to pick up the tab: "All the tin mines in Cornwall," he told friends, "would not pay a quarter."

The public who paid through the nose for its upkeep never got to see inside this monument to greed and extravagance because, when George grew tired of it in 1826, he simply had it demolished. All that remains today from this spectacular act of royal vandalism are the columns from the original entrance, which were reused in the portico of the National Gallery overlooking Trafalgar Square.

George IV was conservative and infrequent in his political

involvement, but neither conservative nor infrequent in his personal life. Short of rape, George IV pulled every trick known to man in order to persuade women to go to bed with him. If he couldn't get his own way he would whine, sulk or throw temper tantrums. If no amount of money or tears could buy their sexual favors he would pretend he was terminally ill or would threaten to kill himself. Prinny had a system for recording the number of women he slept with: he would ask for a lock of hair from his lover and then placed it in an envelope and labeled it. When he died his brothers went through his personal belongings and found 7,000 envelopes containing enough hair to stuff a sofa, plus hundreds of women's gloves and reams of love letters.

When George couldn't find an available aristocratic lady friend he would fornicate with his servants. His first recorded sexual experience was the seduction of one of his mother's maids of honor when he was sixteen years old. Twelve months later he seduced an actress, Mary Robinson, who was four years older than him. She turned out to be one of his costlier conquests. Although his affair with her lasted only a few months, the Prince had been so desperate to bed her that she was able to extract a promise from him that in return for sex he would pay her £20,000 as soon as he was twenty-one. Although she gave him a baby daughter, the Prince had no intention of keeping his end of the bargain, until his mistress reminded him that she had a sackload of his love letters which she wouldn't hesitate to use. King George III paid her off with a lump sum of £5,000 and an annual pension of £500.

The women Prinny chose to sleep with were usually very stout and nearly always older than him. The Prince's "usual circle of old tabbies," as his brother Frederick called them, included Lady Augusta Campbell, Lady Melbourne, who probably bore his child, a singer called Elizabeth Billington who was married to a double-bass player in the Drury Lane Orchestra, and Maria Amelia, who was twelve years older than him. He also had an unfortunately conspicuous affair with the Countess von Hardenburg, wife of the Hanoverian officer and statesman Karl August von Hardenburg. The Countess was shipped back to Germany to avoid a court scandal. When he found himself unable to lay his hands on a convenient mistress or even a servant, he frequented London's brothels. He was a regular customer of one that specialized in flagellation and was run by a Mrs. Collett of Tavistock Court, Covent Garden. She ran a successful whipping establishment at those premises for many years before moving to Portland Place.

George IV was a drunk for most of his adult life. Charles Lamb wrote a poem about the Prince of Wales which began:

Not a fatter fish than he
Flounders round the polar sea
See his blubbers at his gills
What a world of drink he swills

George swigged anything he could lay his hands on, including liqueurs of every description, particularly cherry brandy, which he knocked back "in quantities not to be believed." At dinner he would demolish at least three bottles of wine, chased by maraschino punch and Eau de Garouche. He celebrated every special event by drinking himself insensible, and his guests were expected to do the same. He made a spectacle of himself all over London and there were almost daily reports of brawls involving George and his friends. At a party he threw for the politician Charles Fox, George fell flat on his face in the middle of a quadrille and threw up over the floor. In January 1814 he turned up to stand as godfather to the Duke of Rutland's son and drank himself legless from a fifty-gallon cistern of punch. Several times he was seen obviously drunk riding his horse "like a madman" through Hyde Park.

After every marathon drinking spree he would take to his bed for a few days and have a vein opened. His physician, Sir Henry Halford, was sure that the cycle of bingeing and bleeding would kill him, but when Halford told him he had been bled enough George took to opening his veins himself. The cures he took for his appalling hangovers included opium, and laudanum taken in doses of up to a hundred drops at a time. His family warned him repeatedly that he was killing himself, but as soon as he recovered he carried on drinking as hard as ever.

The court diarist Charles Greville described the King's routine in 1829:

He lives a most extraordinary life—never gets up till six in the afternoon. They come to him and open the window curtains at six or seven o'clock in the morning; he breakfasts in bed, does whatever business he can be brought to transact in bed too; he reads every paper quite through, dozes three or four hours, gets up in time for dinner, and goes to bed between ten and eleven. He sleeps very ill and rings his bell forty times in the night; if he wants to know the hour, though a watch hangs close to him, he will have his valet de chambre down rather than turn his head to look at it.

The same thing if he wants a glass of water; he won't stretch out his hand to get it. His valets are nearly destroyed . . . they cannot take off their clothes at night and hardly lie down.

Although he was very sexually experienced, the Prince had a weakness for women who wouldn't immediately climb into bed with him. Maria Fitzherbert was typical of the type he found appealing: big, matronly and looking older than her years. A contemporary description records her as having a long pointed nose and a mouth misshapen by badly fitting false teeth. The Prince was twenty-two when he met her; she was twenty-eight, twice widowed and a Roman Catholic. Maria Fitzherbert flatly refused to get involved in an adulterous relationship. When she rejected his advances, the fat Prince sulked and began to drink even more heavily than usual, but found solace in the bed of Lady Bamfylde, wife of Sir Charles. A courtier commented, "She is fat, old and ugly, but his Royal Highness is not noted for his taste in females."

In spite of the ample distractions available to him, the Prince obsessed about the unattainable Mrs. Fitzherbert. Every time she refused to sleep with him he pretended he was seriously ill. When this failed he asked Mrs. Fitzherbert to agree to marry him. If she didn't, he told her, "My brain will split." His pathetic threat had the desired effect because she accepted his proposal but, as it transpired, only as a ploy to get rid of him. She quickly withdrew her promise and went abroad—the marriage agreement had been elicited under pressure, she informed him by letter, and she felt no obligation to keep her word. This time the Prince put his emotional-blackmail campaign into top gear and regaled her with a series of forty-two-page suicide threats. Fearing for his sanity, she relented.

On December 15, 1785, a young curate called Reverend Burt was spirited out of the Fleet Prison, where he had been imprisoned for debt. A few hours later he found himself officiating at the wedding of the Prince of Wales and Maria Fitzherbert at her house in Park Street, Mayfair. The bride was given away by her uncle, who also acted as a witness, alongside her brother John Smythe. One of the Prince's best friends stood guard at the door. The Reverend Burt was handed £500 and promised promotion to bishop if he kept his mouth shut. Unfortunately it was one of the worst-kept secrets in the history of the British royal family, and within a few days half of London was talking about the secret Park Street wedding. To all but his closest friends, however, the Prince denied a ceremony had taken place. The only close friend who didn't seem to know what was going on was also his closest political ally, the politician Charles James Fox. Fox was duped into standing before Parliament to categorically deny the rumors surrounding his friend's wedding. He never forgave the Prince of Wales for making a fool of him.

Mrs. Fitzherbert's position was now a curious one. In private she milked her new status as the official Princess of Wales, acquiring well over £50,000 worth of jewelry, a livery of servants and a splendidly furnished house in Pall Mall where she entertained on a royal scale. The marriage was canonically valid, whether it was a secret or not: the couple were indeed man and wife. To the Prince, however, the marriage was probably no more than a ruse to get her to share his bed on a more regular basis. He knew that as she was a Catholic the Act of Settlement would never let the marriage stand, and nor would the recently enforced Royal Marriages Act. As far as the royal family and Parliament were concerned, the marriage certificate was a worthless piece of paper.

The relationship endured for twenty-seven years, outlasting his "official" marriage to Princess Caroline of Brunswick-Wolfenbüttel, the separation, and hundreds of other women. It ended when Maria Fitzherbert was fifty-five years old, the King dismissing her as a "cantankerous old woman." The split was mutual: although she had long since got over the shock of what she correctly interpreted as his treacherous and bigamous marriage to Princess Caroline, she was no longer prepared to tolerate his senile philandering. She demanded a formal separation and after a great deal of undignified haggling the Prince agreed to pay her off with a pension of £10,000 a year.

George's next regular belle was Lady Isabella Hertford. She was the daughter of the ninth Viscount Irvine, and as large as a stately home. "The old lady of Manchester Square," as the vast Marchioness was known, attracted more abuse than any of his previous mistresses. One M.P. described her as an "odious character . . . issuing forth from the inmost recesses of the gaming house or brothel and presuming to place itself near the royal ear."

In 1818 an angry mob of Londoners gathered around Lady Hertford's house and threw stones at her windows. If they had been paying attention they would have known that she had by that time long since been replaced in George's affections by Lady Coyningham, a large fifty-two-year-old married woman with four grown-up children. This was to be his final long-term relationship, and she came to be known to Londoners as the "Vice-Queen." As had been the case with Lady Hertford, the cuckolded husband was also required to join in the fun: the

King was often seen quite openly kissing and groping his new mistress on the sofa while her sad spouse, Lord Coyningham, sat beside them playing gooseberry.

The Prince's hangers-on, the royal rat pack, comprised some of the most hardened reprobates in London. One of the more regular members of this gang was his own brother, Frederick the Duke of York, who divided his time equally between prostitutes and the bottle. Other members included the Earl of Clermont, "remarkable for only his profligacy"; the actor John Kemble, who swallowed wine by "pailfuls"; Richard Cosway, a famous miniaturist who augmented his income from the easel and paint palate by running a brothel from his home; and Sir John Lade and his prostitute wife, the lewd Lady Letitia.

Two of the Prince's most constant drinking companions were considerably older than he was. Both had made their names as upper-class drunks when George was still in his cot. One, a titled wino known as the "Dirty Duke" of Norfolk, was considered to be quite literally one of the filthiest men in the kingdom. His reputation for never bathing went before him, especially when he stood upwind. When his servants could no longer bear his personal stench they would wait until he had passed out in a drunken stupor, then wash him while he was still unconscious. Norfolk complained one day to a friend, Dudley North, that he suffered from rheumatism and had tried everything to relieve the pain without effect. "Did you ever try a clean shirt?" suggested North. In old age the Duke's astonishing capacity for alcohol rendered him so obese that he was unable to get through a standard door frame. The venal Duke of Queensbury—"old Q" or "degenerate Douglas" to his friends—was a tiny man, thirty-eight years older than the Prince. He was particularly reviled at Windsor for getting permanently drunk on George III's champagne throughout the Regency crisis when the old King lay terminally ill.

The Prince's most frequent guests at Carlton House were the Barrymore family, notorious for their wild lifestyles and colorful nicknames. The young seventh Earl of Barrymore blew an inheritance of £20,000 a year on alcohol, and was known as "Hellgate." His brother Augustus was a clergyman, also a compulsive gambler perpetually on the verge of being thrown into debtors prison, and was therefore known as "Newgate." The youngest Barrymore brother had a clubfoot and was known as "Cripplegate." The family picture was completed by their little sister, who for reasons unconnected with the sale of fish was known as "Billingsgate."

Decades of bibulous excess left George IV trapped inside a bloated, broken body which was in an alarmingly advanced state of physical degeneration. He spent a fortune on oils, ointments, creams, pastes, rosewater, eau de cologne, vanilla and oil of jasmine to try to hide the damage. His hair was colored with vegetable dye; his halitosis disguised with myrrh; his hands whitened with enamel. He wore so much makeup that his skin looked permanently glazed. The young Princess Victoria almost threw up when she was required to kiss her oily uncle on the cheek and found it thick with greasepaint.

He had high blood pressure and often had himself bled before he appeared in public to make his florid, broken-veined complexion appear a lighter shade of purple. He also suffered from unsightly swollen glands in his throat, a problem that upset him considerably. He went to great lengths to hide his affliction and thus accidentally started a fashion for high neckcloths. His bloated body was crammed into corsets and stays; his pendulous gut drawn in by a great belt. When he opened Waterloo

Bridge to celebrate the second anniversary of Napoleon's defeat, George made a rare appearance without his gravity-defying girdle and his stomach swung around his knees. William Cobbett observed the "uncommonly huge mass" and speculated that George weighed "perhaps a quarter of a ton."

For the last eight years of his life, George IV suffered from arteriosclerosis, which could have finished him off at any moment, cirrhosis of the liver and dropsy. In his final months he suffered terribly, swollen with booze and gout like a poisoned dog, unable to walk or sleep or even to lie down because of respiratory problems. Although he drugged himself daily with a potentially lethal cocktail of opium, hemlock, brandy and eau de cologne, he was in so much pain that the guards outside Windsor Castle could hear his screams.

When George IV died, his already bloated hulk was so poorly embalmed that it became even more swollen and threatened to burst through the lead lining in his coffin, until someone drilled a hole in it to let out some of the putrid air. An eyewitness, Mrs. Arbuthnot, recorded that his funeral had been in many ways like his reign—altogether an unpleasant experience. The press, who had consistently condemned him throughout his life, abandoned the usual obsequiously crafted posthumous tributes that they were obliged to bestow on even the most ghastly of royals. "There never was an individual," *The Times* noted, "less regretted by his fellow-creatures than this deceased king."

THE GRAND OLD DUKE OF YORK

George III's second eldest son, Frederick the Duke of York, was one year younger than the Prince of Wales and the first of the royal Dukes to die, at the age of sixty-three, officially from dropsy. This was the brother immortalized in the nursery rhyme as "The Grand Old Duke of York," a piece of doggerel that summed up his contemporaries' faith in his competence as Commander-in-Chief of the British army. He was very tall, bald and—although he had skinny, underdeveloped arms and legs—had an enormous gut, perfectly counterbalanced by a huge backside. "One was always afraid that he would tumble over backward," observed Baron Stockmar. As one of the Prince of Wales's regular cronies, he took his wastrel older brother as a role model and settled down to an existence of general debauchery.

Frederick's was not the most normal of childhoods, even for a member of the British royal family, as he became a bishop at six months old. As soon as he was able to hold a glass he decided that drinking himself to death was an obviously more attractive lifestyle than anything the Church could offer. The Duke had two "wives," an official one he hardly ever saw and an unofficial one he lived with in Gloucester Place, London. His real wife was the Prussian Princess Frederica, a strange woman badly marked by smallpox. She was an insomniac and spent most nights in her smelly garden grotto where she kept forty dogs, and several kangaroos, monkeys and parrots. In thirty years of wedlock the Duke and Duchess spent barely more than a couple of nights under the same roof.

When the Duke of York was forty he set up home with a Mrs. Clarke, the daughter of a London stonemason. She was an exceptionally corrupt woman who had made her reputation in the beds of some of London's wealthiest socialites. She destroyed what little was left of the Duke's reputation by selling army commissions while he was Commander-in-Chief. He was charged in the House of Commons with "personal corruption and connivance," but by a vote of 278 to 196 was found not guilty. It was a hollow victory and he was forced to resign his army post in disgrace. Even more embarrassment was heaped on the royal family by the explicit evidence given during the trial. At one point the entire House of Commons sat laughing as excerpts of his love letters to Mrs. Clarke were read aloud, details of which became widely available in the popular press.

ROYAL RAPIST

The king's fifth son, Ernest the Duke of Cumberland, was an extraordinarily sinister figure. He was disliked by his father, feared by his own mother and sisters and shunned even by his debauched brothers. His sister-in-law Princess Caroline of Brunswick simply described him as "very odious." If there had been a popularity poll between Cumberland and Napoleon in Britain in 1810, it would have been too close to call. In appearance he was quite different from the other members of his dynasty. Whereas most of the Hanoverians were short and portly, Cumberland was very Prussian-looking—tall, lean, his face alarmingly disfigured by a deep saber cut above his right eye. His looks did much to encourage the popular view that he was some sort of royal monster—many people were even convinced that he was somehow involved in the deaths of his niece Princess Charlotte, who died in childbirth, and her baby. The Georgian press was happy to Satanize him at every opportunity.

In the early 1800s the Duke of Cumberland was embroiled in two sensational royal scandals. The Prince of Wales often warned his sisters against being alone in a room with Cumberland, with good reason, as the Duke was widely suspected of having incestuously raped and impregnated their young sister Sophia. In August 1800, when the unmarried Princess Sophia was twenty-two years old, she secretly gave birth to a baby at Weybridge. Everyone in the family knew about the pregnancy except King George III. Throughout her pregnancy he was told that she was bloated with dropsy, but at Weybridge had taken a mysterious cure comprising a roast-beef diet. The King thought it was "an odd business" but accepted the explanation. He had not, at that time, taken leave of his senses, but he did have eleven other children to keep tabs on and by this time his vision was seriously impaired.

The royal rape story originated with the court diarist Charles Greville, a man usually considered by historians to be a reliable source. He reported that he had seen letters, written by the Princess to an equerry, which stated that her brother the Duke of Cumberland had sexually abused her. Although the Palace never officially acknowledged that the child existed, the approved version was that the real father of the child was the equerry himself, General Thomas Garth.

Garth was an unlikely scapegoat, to put it mildly. This man with whom Princess Sophia was supposed to have had an affair was ugly, dwarfish, his face badly disfigured by a large purple birthmark, and thirty-three years older than her. General Garth retained his prestigious job in the royal household and was still there when he died, aged eighty-five. His continued service, it was noted, was an odd way to treat an alleged rapist. The Prince of Wales and Edward the Duke of Kent were privately convinced that Cumberland was the child's father, and that the loyal Garth had been nominated to take the blame.

Cumberland had his second brush with serious scandal in 1810. In the early hours of May 31, shortly after the Duke returned home to his apartments at St. James's Palace, his servants were disturbed by loud swearing and scuffling from Cumberland's chambers. After a while the Duke was heard to cry out, "Neale, Neale, I am murdered." His page Neale ran to the Duke's quarters, to find his royal master standing in the middle of the room, covered in blood, and with a sword at his feet. The Duke informed him that he had been attacked and, although he had himself been seriously wounded, had forced the assailant to flee. The Duke sent for the physician Sir Henry Halford, who examined him. The official inquiry would be told later that Cumberland had a gaping head wound which exposed his brain, but Halford found only superficial cuts to both hands. Two hours later, Cumberland instructed Neale to fetch his Corsican valet, Joseph Sellis, from his room. The tiny Sellis was discovered propped upright in his blood-soaked bed, his throat cut from ear to ear. The wound was so deep that his head was almost completely severed from his neck. At the other end of the room, much too far away for Sellis to have dropped it, lay a razor.

At the formal inquiry into Sellis's death, Cumberland claimed that the valet had attempted to murder him in his sleep. According to the Duke, he had fought off his assailant, who then fled and decided to take his own life rather than submit to arrest. Although no motive was ever offered for the original murder attempt by Sellis on his master, this was the version of events accepted at the inquest, and a verdict of suicide was brought against Sellis.

The verdict caused a sensation. According to the overwhelming tide of popular opinion, the jury had been duped and the sinister Duke had literally got away with murder. Most contemporaries believed that he had butchered his valet to prevent a blackmail attempt: he had slit his manservant's throat with a razor while he was asleep, cut himself with his sword to make it look as though he had been in a struggle, then returned to his own room. One popular motive theory was that Sellis was blackmailing Cumberland because the Duke had made a homosexual pass at him. Another was that Cumberland had been caught in bed with the butler's wife. The most fancied rumor was that Cumberland had raped Sellis's daughter, who committed suicide when she found out she was pregnant.

After the trial, Cumberland became more hated than ever. He was openly booed on the streets of London. On one of his rare public excursions he was dragged from his horse and lynched and was lucky to escape with his life. At the age of forty-six the Duke married a twice-widowed German Princess, Frederica of Mecklenburg-Strelitz. It was quite a match, as she was a lady with a singularly checkered past. At best Frederica was a politically insensitive choice of wife because she had already jilted Cumberland's younger brother Adolphus. Slightly more worrying were the allegations that she had murdered her two previous husbands. The King and Queen refused to receive the new daughter-in-law and she was banned from the British court.

Cumberland continued to inspire hatred for the rest of his days. At the age of sixty-six his brother King William IV died, thus separating the joint rule of Britain and Hanover because German Salic law prevented his niece Victoria from ascending the throne of their ancestral homeland. Cumberland was invited to become King of Hanover, an offer that he gratefully accepted. He asked the Duke of Wellington's advice on how long he should spend putting his affairs in order in England before taking up his new job. "Go now," Wellington told him, "before you are pelted out."

SCRAMBLE FOR AN HEIR

In 1817 the death of the Prince Regent's daughter, Princess Charlotte, in childbirth had precipitated a major crisis for the British royal family. Although King George III had fathered fifteen children, he did not have one legitimate grandchild. The Prince Regent was fifty-five years old, impotent, and long since separated from his wife. His six younger brothers had between them produced only a string of bastards. The King's five surviving daughters were all middle-aged and childless spinsters. The House of Hanover faced imminent extinction.

In a belated attempt to secure the succession, one by one the Prince Regent's dissipated and decrepit brothers dumped their assortment of long-standing girlfriends and scrambled to become the first to produce a legitimate heir. Suddenly, ugly princesses from some of the more minor German principalities and Duchies that previously the Dukes wouldn't have touched with a royal mace became highly eligible. Even in the context of royal marriages, it was a desperate situation all round.

Adolphus, the Duke of Cambridge, was the youngest of the seven sons. He was on the face of it an unlikely family man, as for most of his life he had shown little interest in women and wore a blond wig. When the glittering prospects suddenly created by the timely death of his niece dangled before him, he put his bachelor days behind him and proposed within a week of the funeral to a woman he had never met before. At best Adolphus was highly eccentric; the Duke of Wellington, more bluntly, described him as "as mad as Bedlam" (more bad news, incidentally, for the British royal family gene pool, as Adolphus's granddaughter became Queen Mary, wife of George V).

The Duke had a habit of talking in an excitable, unfathomable, high-pitched babble, and often startled churchgoers by shouting out loud in his heavy German accent during sermons. He was also eccentric in appearance, his most notable feature, apart from his wig, being his strange little beard, known as a Newport Fringe. His new wife, Princess Augusta of Hesse-Cassell, was a severe, beetle-browed, masculine woman with a very limited grasp of English. Conversation with either of them was strained, and consequently it was possible for visitors to the Cambridge household to leave without having understood a single word that either of their hosts had said.

THE SAILOR KING

As George IV died heirless, the Crown passed sideways to his idiot brother the Duke of Clarence, who ruled as William IV for seven years. The present royal family should have remembered that "William" was certainly an unfortunate name the last time it was used by a British monarch.

George IV's greatest gift to the Hanoverian dynasty was that he lowered popular expectations of the monarchy so much that he made even a bleary-eyed buffoon like his younger brother look acceptable. William IV was easily as big a disaster as his brother: he was a boorish, hard-gambling roué with a great talent for suicidal drinking and running up debt, a lifestyle which led inexorably to death by cirrhosis of the liver.

King George III sent the young Duke of Clarence to sea at the age of thirteen with little or no formal education, ostensibly to boost public pride in the British navy. Although the Duke captained two ships and spent more than half a century at sea, including the entire duration of the Napoleonic Wars, the "Sailor King," as he later came to be known, was able to avoid active service. This was not his fault: it was deliberate Admiralty policy as he was considered a blundering idiot and too great a liability to be let loose on a ship in battle. Eventually, nepotism enriched him with the position of Admiral, but only after Napoleon had long since ceased to be a problem and there was little likelihood that the King's son would be called upon to do anything dangerous.

As a philanderer he was more than a match for any male member of the British royal family. He raped one of his mother's maids of honor when he was fourteen years old and never looked back. His father, who had packed him off to sea with the advice "I strongly recommend the habitual reading of the Holy Scriptures," could not have foreseen that his son would become a minor expert on the brothels of the British colonies. During his visits to the West Indies, the local whorehouses gave him a taste for native black women and several more doses of venereal disease. The young Duke found Jamaica to be "a very gay and lively place full of women, and those of the most obliging kind." A fellow naval officer, William's friend Horatio Nelson, wrote home to his fiancée, "Only William's departure from the capital of Antigua had protected the ladies of St. John's from total collapse."

The Duke also showed early promise as an astonishingly

heavy drinker, and his contemporaries were amazed by his seemingly endless capacity for sex and alcohol. In a brothel in Bridgetown, Barbados, in 1786 he and a group of his drunken cronies caused £700 worth of damage, and were confronted by the formidable madame Rachel Pringle, who demanded recompense in full. The Duke's ship then moved on to Halifax, Nova Scotia. His shipmates noted that before very long he was familiar with every brothel in the entire province. In Germany he copulated with the streetwalkers of Hanover "against a wall or in the middle of the parade." He wrote to the Prince of Wales complaining how much he had learned to hate German prostitutes, and how he looked forward to coming home to London and "at least to such as would not clap or pox me every time I fucked."

When he was in his mid-twenties the Duke of Clarence bought himself a house near the Thames in Richmond and in between his maritime duties settled down to live with a London prostitute. This arrangement came to an abrupt end when William had a backstage encounter with an Irish actress. Dorothea Jordan, although neither highly talented nor a great beauty, was a vivacious girl, and by 1790 she was celebrated as one of the most popular comic actresses of the London stage. William first saw her in a farce called *The Spoil'd Child*. She was five years older than William, and already had four illegitimate children by two previous lovers. At the time she was still living with one of them, a lawyer and prospective member of Parliament named Richard Ford, by whom she had two daughters. At first she had no intention of leaving Ford, and in fact hoped that the appearance of the starry-eyed royal suitor would make Ford jealous and spur him into making an honest woman of her. When the awaited proposal of marriage failed to materialize, she decided that a prince was a prince after all—even one nicknamed "pineapple head" because of his oddly shaped dome and florid complexion.

Much to the amusement of London society, the charming couple set up home, first at Petersham Lodge, and then from 1797 at the red-bricked Bushey House, near Hampton Court Palace. They lived together as man and wife for the next twenty years, and raised a family of ten illegitimate children, five sons and five daughters. Although the arrangement was frequently ridiculed in the London press, the royal Duke and his mistress were more or less left alone to get on with it. So long as Prinny was alive, he presented such a massive and easy target for the satirists and republicans of the day that the Duke of Clarence went largely unnoticed and was able to live in Bushey Park with his actress friend and their ten bouncing bastards in relative anonymity.

Mrs. Jordan did not relinquish her career and continued to tread the boards in between childbirths. There was a more practical reason for her continued work than her love of greasepaint. In the words of a popular ditty of the day, people wondered whether the Duke of Clarence was keeping a mistress or the mistress was keeping him. In fact the Duke was a hopeless spendthrift who failed dismally to live within his means, and he wasn't too proud to top up his annual allowance with the earnings of his working mistress.

By the time he was in his mid-forties the Duke's profligate spending had left him more or less broke, so he demanded a 60 percent increase on the £18,000 annuity he received from Parliament. He was curtly advised that this and any similar requests would be ignored until he found himself a wife, and only a genuine royal bride who would pass the test of the Royal Marriages Act. After two decades, Dorothea Jordan was dumped. According to a popular story of the day, when William tried to reduce the annual pittance he had promised her to buy her off, she handed him a piece of paper which at the time was attached to all playbills. The note read, "No money refunded after the rising of the curtain."

The florid and bejowled Duke was so deeply unattractive to the opposite sex that half the titled women in Europe fled from his proposals. Over a period of several months, he made a fool of himself with indiscriminate offers of marriage to the likes of Princess Anne of Denmark, the eldest daughter of the Elector of Hesse-Cassel, the Czar's sister the Duchess of Oldenburg, and several homegrown titled ladies, including Miss Catherine Tilney-Long, the Dowager Lady Elphinstone, the Dowager Lady Downshire, Miss Margaret Mercer Elphinstone and Lady Berkeley, all of them repelled by his odd appearance, his bad manners and his foul language. He did in fact make one successful proposal to a wealthy English heiress called Miss Wyckham, but she was deemed unacceptable by the Prince Regent on the grounds that she was "half-mad."

After being rejected by eighteen different women, he finally found one who said "*Ja.*" The tiny Princess Adelaide, eldest daughter of the Duke of Saxe-Meiningen, had fair hair and pale skin showing signs of scurvy, and was described by a contemporary as "frightful . . . very ugly with a horrid complexion." She was younger than William's eldest child. The German Princess arrived in England in July 1818, without ever having met the obese middle-aged man she was to marry, and found herself pitched into a bizarre and unprecedented dual wedding ceremony. William and his younger brother Edward the Duke of Kent, who had similarly ditched his mistress to cash in on a royally approved marriage, had decided on a double wedding at Kew Palace to save time and money. The chief witness to this weird and indecently hasty arrangement, Queen Charlotte, was near to death and barely conscious. As neither bride knew a word of English the service was printed in German, subtitled with English phonetics.

William IV was a witless debauchee, but mysteriously never quite generated the level of embarrassment achieved by his Hanoverian predecessors. He was welcomed with open arms by a British public repulsed by the fourth George. Upon the death of the unimpressive William, the *Spectator* eulogized: "His late Majesty, though at times a jovial and, for a king, an honest man, was a weak, ignorant, commonplace sort of person." His former long-standing mistress, Dorothea Jordan, died in France, alone and in obscurity. A biography of King William IV published toward the end of Queen Victoria's reign did not acknowledge her existence.

THE BEAST

Quite the most sinister of all King George III's sons was Queen Victoria's father, the sadistic Edward Duke of Kent, who was, according to the court diarist Charles Greville, "the greatest rascal that ever went unhung." Edward was the strongest and most physically imposing of George III's sons and made a career as a soldier, often boasting that he would outlive all his brothers because he lived a tough army life while they were all wasted by debauchery. He may have been less dissipated than his brothers in some respects but he had other vices to compensate.

The Duke was a vicious bully who believed that the only way to lick a soldier into shape was to flog him into submission. The added bonus for the Duke was that he was sexually aroused by the sight of men being whipped, which unfortunately also made him wet his trousers. Consequently, he quickly made his mark as a brutal and tyrannical disciplinarian who would thrash his soldiers at the drop of a hat, and the number of floggings in the Duke's regiment went up roughly in line with his laundry bill.

The Duke was sent to Gibraltar as Colonel of the Royal Fusiliers. It was there that he first earned his nickname, "the Beast," and his reputation as the most hated man in the British army. From 5 A.M. every day he thrashed, marched and drilled his men into the ground. The slightest mistake by any of his soldiers would turn the Duke into a seething psychopath. Naturally, the floggings multiplied. When news filtered back to England that the Gibraltar garrison was at the point of mutiny, the darkly disturbed Duke was quietly removed and sent to Canada.

Unfortunately he had learned nothing from his mistakes at Gibraltar and viewed his new posting as a fresh opportunity to inflict even more unnecessary cruelty. Once again he drove his troops to the very brink of mutiny with a regime of outrageous punishments. In Canada he also renewed his acquaintance with a French-Canadian prostitute, Madame Julie de St. Laurent. She had originally been procured to provide sexual services for him in Gibraltar in 1790. The Duke's relationship with his "French Lady," as she became known to the family, developed into something deeper than a business relationship as they stayed together for the best part of thirty years.

In 1802 the Duke was bizarrely returned to Gibraltar, this time as Governor-General. On the barren rock there was little for his dispirited Royal Fusiliers to do except drink, so it was only a matter of time before the Flogging Duke banned alcohol. To any sane man, the danger of mutiny would have been obvious. One day, one of the frequent desertions from the Duke's garrison resulted in a soldier being caught. The Duke sentenced him to the maximum number of lashings the army rule book would allow—one short of a thousand. This time the troops mutinied. Many men lost their lives; many more were seriously wounded. Three ringleaders were executed; others were flogged. The Duke was quickly recalled to England, lucky to have escaped with his life.

Madame St. Laurent was distressed to read an article in the *Morning Chronicle* about her boyfriend's duty to marry and provide an heir, as the rest of the British royal family were having some difficulty in doing so. The Duke was perfectly content with his existing arrangement, but a wife within the terms of the Royal Marriages Act and the consequently increased share of the Civil List was a career move he was unable to resist. Madame St. Laurent was pensioned off with a lump-sum settlement.

The Duke of Kent had nearly as much trouble finding a bride as William IV. Eventually, a short list of two prospective brides was drawn up, from which Victoria of Saxe-Coburg, the thirty-one-year-old widow of the Prince of Leiningen-

Dachsburg-Hardenburg, was selected. They lived at Leiningen for the sake of economy, but the Duke borrowed £5,000 to bring his wife home so that their baby could be born in England. She gave birth to a daughter, and they named her Victoria.

7. FIRST, CATCH YOUR KING

The Tragic History of the Fairy-tale Monarchy

THE PRIVATE WITTELSBACH family archives in Munich contain over forty leather-bound volumes detailing the full medical history of Otto I, King of Bavaria from 1886 to 1913. Although Otto spent his entire reign locked up in Castle Fürstenried guarded by a few medical attendants, he remains one of the unsung heroes in the pantheon of royal mental instability. King Otto was as mad as the next monarch, and had the documentation to prove it. Unfortunately, in this case the next monarch happened to be his brother Ludwig. The uncelebrated Otto was at least as crazy as Ludwig and probably a great deal crazier, but, while his big brother was busy altering the Bavarian skyline and organizing pan-European bank robberies, Otto's illness manifested itself in the relatively anonymous pursuits of barking like a dog, pulling faces, shouting abuse and occasionally taking potshots at people with a rifle through his bedroom window.

THE ROYAL HOUSE
OF
WITTELSBACH

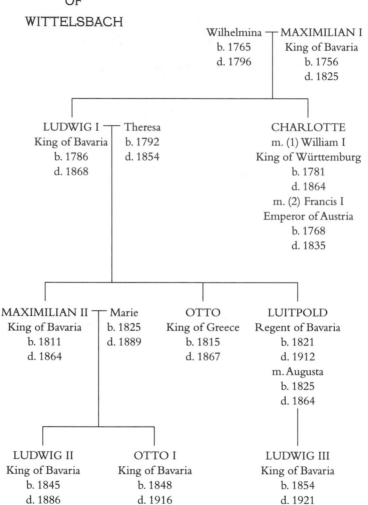

Wilhelmina ⊤ MAXIMILIAN I
b. 1765 │ King of Bavaria
d. 1796 │ b. 1756
d. 1825

LUDWIG I ⊤ Theresa
King of Bavaria │ b. 1792
b. 1786 │ d. 1854
d. 1868

CHARLOTTE
m. (1) William I
King of Württemburg
b. 1781
d. 1864
m. (2) Francis I
Emperor of Austria
b. 1768
d. 1835

MAXIMILIAN II ⊤ Marie
King of Bavaria │ b. 1825
b. 1811 │ d. 1889
d. 1864

OTTO
King of Greece
b. 1815
d. 1867

LUITPOLD
Regent of Bavaria
b. 1821
d. 1912
m. Augusta
b. 1825
d. 1864

LUDWIG II
King of Bavaria
b. 1845
d. 1886

OTTO I
King of Bavaria
b. 1848
d. 1916

LUDWIG III
King of Bavaria
b. 1854
d. 1921

The history of Bavaria's monarchy is the story of the Wittelsbachs, Europe's most dysfunctional royal family. Their un-broken rule of Bavaria, which spanned more than 700 years from 1140 to 1918, despite mental instability spanning forty generations, gave them blood ties with almost every other royal family in Europe, including Holland, Luxembourg, Belgium, Spain, France, Austria, Prussia and Portugal. Three of them became kings of Sweden. They were related to the British royal family via King George I's mother. In the late nineteenth century, the Bavarian Wittelsbachs also inher-ited the Jacobite claim to the throne of England.

Every now and then the confluence of Wittelsbach blood with that of one of Europe's other mentally unstable ruling fam-ilies had infamous and unfortunate consequences. One of the most dramatic examples of this occurred in eighteenth-century Spain with the accession of the oversexed madman King Philip V: part Wittelsbach, part Bourbon. It was in the nineteenth cen-tury, however, that Wittelsbach family eccentricity most strik-ingly tripped over the borderline into insanity. The history of the Wittelsbachs during this period is shot through with madness and violent death. At least twenty members of the Bavarian royal family and their collateral branches were insane.

THE POET KING

The first Wittelsbach to assume the title King of Bavaria was Ludwig II's great-grandfather Maximilian I. He lived a drab and uneventful life by Wittelsbach standards, unlike his eldest son, Ludwig I. Maximilian's heir was thirty-nine years old and already eccentric when he came to the throne, a stone-deaf, shabby, par-simonious little man, generally considered by his subjects to be a harmless lunatic. He was often seen wandering the streets of Munich late at night with his highly idiosyncratic zigzagging walk, wearing tatty threadbare clothes, carrying a battered umbrella— which was considered a great novelty at the time. Most of Bavaria's historically significant buildings owe their existence to the generosity, the religious devotion or the insanity of a Wittelsbach. Ludwig I built extensively and was responsible for Munich's Feldherrnhalle, the Alte Pinakothek and the Ludwigsbrücke.

One of Ludwig's eccentricities was his lifelong hobby of composing outstandingly bad poetry. His muse compelled him to put every experience he ever had, no matter how trivial or mundane, down in rhyme. Once when the King was badly gored by a bull in Italy, he sat down and recorded the event in rhyming couplets. The string of actresses he bedded throughout his reign were all to discover that the only gifts the tightfisted old King was likely to lavish on them were reams of execrable poetry.

His wife, Queen Theresa, was by repute outstandingly attractive. The King was a lover of great beauty, especially when it occurred in women other than his wife. He commissioned a series of thirty-six portraits of beautiful women and used them to decorate the walls of his palace at Nymphenburg. The subjects of his Schönheits Galerie were not famous or aristocratic: they were just women he fancied, irrespective of class, from countesses to laundry women, from actresses to chambermaids, even women he had passed on the street.

After years of dedicated marital infidelity, the odd but otherwise unremarkable King suddenly achieved notoriety by making a fool of himself over an Irish dancer young enough to be his granddaughter. Ludwig was sixty-one years old when he met Lola Montez. She was twenty-eight, a dazzling raven-haired femme fatale with an assumed name, an invented background (she claimed she was twenty-two and born to Spanish nobility) and a string of famous lovers behind her, including Franz Liszt. It was said that Lola introduced herself to the old King one day by ripping open her bodice and revealing her breasts. The story is probably apocryphal, but her general effect on the aging King's libido was nonetheless seismic.

Ms. Montez was acknowledged as one of the most beautiful women in Europe. Her elderly lover on the other hand had few teeth, less hair, and a disproportionately large head which drew attention to a huge cyst in the middle of his forehead. Ludwig pledged his undying love to Lola in long poems and fatally started to seek her opinion on important matters of state. Since Ludwig had never bothered to hide his personal indiscretions, his subjects soon got to know of the affair. At any other time the press would have turned a blind eye to his obsession with the nubile Lola, but this was 1848, the year of European revolution. The King's mistress became a convenient focus of unrest. The press called her "the Apocalyptic Whore."

King Ludwig was subsequently forced by pressure from the mob and his ministers to banish her from the country; some suggested she went willingly to escape another burst of the King's poetry. Soon afterward, Ludwig was driven to declare his abdication in favor of his son Maximilian. Ludwig never met his Lola again, but continued to harass her with his love poems by mail. He outlived her and died in 1868 aged eighty-two.

LUDWIG THE MAD

Ludwig's eldest son, King Maximilian II, and his daughter-in-law Queen Marie were first cousins—an unwise arrangement,

232 ♛ ROYAL BABYLON

as there were many known cases of mental instability on both sides of the family. Maximilian built extensively and brought many prominent scientists and artists to Munich. He also suffered from severe headaches, flogged his children and kept them so hungry that they sometimes had to beg food from the servants. Otherwise he was in a lot better shape than his sister Princess Alexandra, who had become the star turn at Wittelsbach family reunions thanks to her sincere and unwaverable conviction that she had accidentally swallowed a grand piano made of glass. Another of her idiosyncrasies was her desire to wear white at all times, which was perhaps just as well, for poor Aunt Alexandra was to spend a large part of her confused life in a straitjacket.

Ludwig II's Prussian mother, Marie, was seventeen when she married. When it later became apparent that both of her sons were insane, the Wittelsbach family closed ranks, looked around for someone else to blame, and pointed the finger at Marie, alleging that she had brought a streak of Prussian madness into the family. Her cousin Frederick William IV had recently died insane, the latest example of insanity in the Hohenzollern bloodline. One of her ancestors, the Landgrave Ludwig IX of Hesse-Darmstadt, was also mad, and both he and his daughter Karoline experienced hallucinations. The Landgrave and his unfortunate daughter were also noted for their peculiar nocturnal lifestyles. It was of course a fairly outrageous accusation: compared to the Wittelsbachs, Marie's side of the family was almost boringly conventional.

Queen Marie had good reason to be concerned for her two young sons, Ludwig and Otto. She was aware of the family history of madness and inbreeding, which she had recently and carelessly contributed to, and if she ever forgot about it there was always her sister-in-law Alexandra to remind her. She grew more concerned when Ludwig took to dressing up as a nun. When Ludwig was fourteen years old he complained of strange voices in his head. The court doctor reassured the Queen that he would grow out of it. When he was sixteen, Ludwig was allowed to see a performance of Wagner's *Lohengrin*. His tutor noted that Ludwig was so moved by the experience that he almost became hysterical: a portent of things to come. He was a sensitive and highly strung child, but there were no other obvious signs of peculiarity, although it was thought prudent at one stage to deprive young Ludwig of the company of his pet tortoise, with the enigmatic explanation that the boy was becoming rather too fond of it.

Of all Europe's insane monarchs few have ever achieved the sobriquet "mad." One of the best known was the unhinged Spanish Queen Juana la Loca ("the Mad"), who had a complete mental breakdown when her faithless and mostly absent husband died. She made up for lost time by insisting on keeping his embalmed body by her side, even at the dining table and in bed at night—a trial for those around her at the best of times, and especially during the summer. But the most famous of all was King Ludwig II.

The mythical Ludwig has become something of a cult. To some he was an innocent romantic, a misunderstood creative genius who suddenly discovered himself with untold wealth and power but little sense of responsibility to go with it—a nineteenth-century rock star, a royal Keith Moon. To others Ludwig was God's gift to tourism—he is now marketed as a benevolent latter-day Walt Disney. A recent German Tourist Board promotional campaign is typical: "Once upon a time in a faraway land there lived a king called Ludwig, whose dearest wish was to make all his subjects happy, so he built them fairy-tale castles."

These fanciful interpretations of Ludwig are far from accurate. The collection of architectural follies that over a million people a year pay to visit are monuments to schizophrenia, the work of a man whose mental decay was accelerated by a softening of the brain caused by cerebral syphilis. As for his wish to make people happy, Ludwig had no time for people at all, especially his Bavarian subjects. During the last eleven years of his reign he didn't make a single public appearance. He was a miserably self-obsessed misanthrope who despised his countrymen, a king who confessed that he couldn't even bear sleeping in air contaminated by commoners.

In 1864 Maximilian II died and Bavaria found itself with a new king, barely eighteen years old. At first everyone was fascinated by the young monarch. His ministers thought him bright, although immature. His Minister of Justice, Eduard von Bomhard, was the first to hint that the young King might have a screw loose when he noted that Ludwig was "mentally gifted in the highest degree, but the contents of his mind are stored in a totally disordered fashion."

Ludwig's appearance was best described as theatrical. He was self-conscious about his looks to the point of narcissism. He wore a stylised goatee beard and his hair long. His headful of carefully arranged brown curls was attended to daily and at great length by his court barber: without this regular coiffure, the King claimed, he couldn't eat. He was very tall, and moved slowly with a mannered, sweeping gait. As he walked he jerked his knees very high, then stamped his feet down on the ground. When he visited Versailles, Ludwig attracted a crowd of French youths who followed him down the street imitating his walk, and were promptly arrested. This slightly surreal general appearance was enhanced by the huge fur coat that Ludwig always wore outdoors, even in summer.

In the early days Ludwig was hugely popular with his people, especially his female subjects. His immaculate grooming and flamboyant style earned him the nickname "King Charming." Women adored him, wrote him sonnets, sent him flowers, and swooned as he swept past in his coach. He was curiously unmoved by these displays of affection, because for one thing he was far too self-obsessed to even notice, and for another he was homosexual.

Ludwig suppressed his sexuality for most of his life. It was not until he was in his late thirties that he began openly sleeping with his male servants. He embarked on a long-lasting affair with one Alfonso Wecker, who was to eventually betray Ludwig by giving evidence to a commission investigating the King's sanity. Wecker also testified that Ludwig liked to watch young soldiers being whipped. The King also had a long and intimate relationship with Prince Paul von Thurn und Taxis, which ended when the latter married a commoner. Another of the King's lovers, a twenty-six-year-old equerry named Richard Hornig, eventually married as well.

Ludwig thought long and hard about doing his duty by his country and providing it with an heir, and very nearly did something about it. He went so far as to announce his engagement to Princess Sophie, sister of his lifelong friend the Austrian Empress Elisabeth, but as the wedding day approached Ludwig panicked and, rather like a schoolboy begging his mother for a note to excuse him from sports, he persuaded his court doctor to produce a certificate stating that the King was unfit to marry. When Ludwig's court secretary, Lorenz von Düflipp, made a last-ditch appeal to the King to see it through, Ludwig replied, ironically, that he would rather drown. This was to be Ludwig's sole attempt at a relationship with a woman: after the broken engagement Ludwig became overtly misogynous, and even banned all females from the vicinity of his palace.

News of Ludwig's rejection of the Princess Sophie and the sudden and unexpected breakdown of the royal engagement caused quite a sensation. Thirty years later, poor Sophie hit the headlines for the last time when she strayed too near an unguarded gas lamp at a charity bazaar in Paris and became identifiable only by her dental chart.

LUDWIG'S OBSESSIONS

King Ludwig II's reign can be roughly divided into two parts, each dominated by an irrational and ultimately destructive obsession. The first of these resulted in one of the oddest and most intense royal patronages ever known. In his early teens, Ludwig developed a fascination for the composer Richard Wagner. The young Prince found Wagner's fantasy world of operatic medieval legend much more interesting than the real world he lived in. In the giant structures of Wagner's operas, and later of Christopher Jank's castles, Ludwig retreated into a cloud-cuckoo-land of myths and legend, of Tolkienesque giants and gods.

It was a complicated obsession, for Ludwig was completely fixated by both Wagner the man and his works. Wagner at this time was living in obscurity and hiding from his creditors, lurching from one financial crisis to the next. His life had reached such a low ebb that he had considered suicide. As soon as Ludwig heard that Wagner was broke and in danger of being thrown into debtors prison, he rushed to his rescue. The King had long been looking for an excuse to meet his hero. When the King's secretary, Pfistmeister, came knocking at Wagner's door, the middle-aged composer could hardly believe his good fortune.

It was an unlikely alliance. The King was eighteen years old and homosexual; Wagner was about twice his age and a notorious womanizer—one of his more famous affairs was with Franz Liszt's illegitimate daughter, Cosima von Bülow, a girl twenty-four years his junior. Wagner wasn't the easiest of men to get along with and was notoriously sensitive to criticism: he often invited his friends to listen to his new work and to offer their opinions, but his friends soon found out that a less than enthusiastic response was likely to earn them a punch in the mouth. Ludwig was hardly a great music lover; in fact his interest in music was exclusively Wagnerian.

The impulsive young King treated Wagner with incredible generosity. He began by handing over huge gifts of cash to clear Wagner's backlog of debts. Once the debts were settled, it became clear that Wagner's muse required him to live in a state of permanent luxury, including a rent-free house in Munich and an annual salary of 4,000 gulden, far more than many of Ludwig's most senior government ministers could expect to earn. Ludwig was prepared to bankroll Wagner's every whim. He put up the money for many of his most famous and extravagant works, staged his operas in Munich and built for his exclusive use the first model opera house, the Festival Theatre at Bayreuth.

Wagner's apparently limitless greed and his life of opulence made him unpopular. The increasingly hostile Bavarian press depicted him as a sinister old charlatan whose hold over the young King was bleeding the country dry. Ludwig's ministers, especially his chief minister, Baron von der Pfordten, were horrified by the one-way flow of large amounts of money straight out of the Bavarian treasury and into Wagner's back pocket.

Ludwig's sexuality inevitably raises questions about the relationship between the two men, especially as the correspondence that flowed between the composer and his patron, even allowing for the fashionably sentimental prose of the day, was emotionally charged and could easily be taken for love letters. Ludwig couldn't bear to be parted from his idol for long, and whenever Wagner was away the King pined pathetically for his return. Wagner must have known that his friend was mentally unstable, but he also knew how not to look a gift horse, or in this case a lunatic king, in the mouth.

As the popular clamor against Wagner grew, the King of Bavaria was given an unusual ultimatum by his chief minister: discontinue your relationship with Wagner or lose your crown. Ludwig briefly toyed with the idea of abdicating but quickly caved in to public opinion. As the composer left for exile in Switzerland, Ludwig wrote to him, "My love for you will never die, and I beg you to retain forever your friendship for me."

Years later Wagner confessed that he was as mystified by Ludwig's attentions as anyone else—in his opinion Ludwig hadn't a clue about opera or any sort of music. Wagner, it seemed, had somehow hit upon the formula for becoming extremely popular with megalomaniac German rulers. One of

Adolf Hitler's most cherished possessions was a letter written by Wagner's royal patron.

King Ludwig then threw himself into a new passion. It was one that was to earn him immortality, but which in the short term threatened to wreck the Bavarian economy, and ultimately became his downfall. The building urge occurred in several of the Wittelsbachs. King Ludwig I, although renowned for his personal stinginess, spent public millions on grandiose new building projects in his desire to beautify Munich. His second eldest son, Otto, was another compulsive builder who also enjoyed a brief and eventful career as the first King of Greece. Otto was even more unpopular than the Ottoman Turks. He took up the throne at the age of seventeen and quickly bankrupted the national treasury by turning Athens into a building site. For the best part of thirty years he attempted to rule the locals by pointing Bavarian fixed bayonets in their direction, until in 1862 he and his wife, Queen Amelia, were finally forced to flee back to Bavaria with just a sackful of jewelry. Oddly enough, Otto's reign did leave one enduring legacy, although it was not, as he might have hoped, architectural. One of his Bavarian entourage was a brewer named Fuchs: the Greeks changed the name of his product to Fix and have been drinking to his name ever since.

It was in 1868 that King Ludwig II first began to hatch plans to build a series of fantastic mock-medieval castles. For the last eighteen years of his life, these surreal, artificial palaces were an all-consuming hobby which absolutely nothing was allowed to interfere with, certainly not the Bavarian economy or the small matter of the Franco-Prussian War. Unlike other famous builders, Ludwig didn't put up monuments for personal aggrandizement: he built for sheer escapism and the personal satisfaction of seeing his irrational whims become reality. These castles came to be known as his "sick children."

Ludwig started building Neuschwanstein, the smallest but most sensational of his castles, on an inaccessible Bavarian peak in 1869. Neuschwanstein is now at least as much a picture-postcard cliché as London's Tower Bridge and is possibly the most photographed building in the world. He eccentrically gave the job of designing it not to an architect, but to his court scene-painter, Christopher Jank. The mysterious ivory-white castle with its Romanesque windows, battlements and spindly turrets was a ready-made children's fantasy. Walt Disney used it twice, once when he based his *Sleeping Beauty* castle on it, and again in his film *Chitty Chitty Bang Bang*.

Work began on Linderhof, Ludwig's homage to his idol, King Louis XIV, the following year. It was a giant villa, complete with an artificial grotto furnished with cast-iron stalactites coated in cement. It has an underground lake fed by a waterfall, colored lighting and artificial waves created by machinery. On the waters floated a boat shaped like a cockleshell. The King liked to sail across it dressed in his famous swan-motif armor.

Herrenchiemsee, built on an island in the middle of Lake Chiemsee, was intended as a Bavarian version of the Palace of Versailles, but Ludwig didn't live long enough to see it finished. Unlike his previous creations, Herrenchiemsee was a folly, an expensive private joke. Many of the rooms in the great horizontal building were never meant to be lived in—they were empty shells hidden behind a surreal facade. Ludwig planned to build many more castles. His next project was to have been at Falkenstein, and the plans left behind by Jank show it to be even more fantastic than the others. But Ludwig ran out of money.

Part of the fun of being mad was that you didn't have to worry about the bill. The King treated Bavaria's treasury as though it was a private kitty which existed to fund his building program. The total sum expended on his three castles alone was about 31 million marks. Of this, 7.5 million marks were his personal debt. These were tiny, insignificant amounts of money in comparison to the castles' earnings for Bavarian tourism since then, but in the 1870s they were quite enough to make the veins stand out on his finance minister's forehead. The Bavarian cabinet convened to tactfully put it to the King, as a cholesterol-conscious doctor would to his overweight patient, that he might "cut down" on his castles, but economizing was not a concept that Ludwig was familiar with.

LUDWIG'S DECLINE

Ludwig's mental condition, meanwhile, began to deteriorate, and his behavior became more markedly aberrant. The hallucinations that had afflicted him since childhood became more frequent, as did the voices in his head. Ludwig would often ask his servants where the voices had come from. The servants learned to humor him and would apologize for making the noises. Like his father, he was plagued by violent headaches. Ludwig's headaches, however, tended to coincide with days when protocol demanded his presence at some important court function, or when he was obliged to meet a visiting head of state.

As the years went by, the King's barely concealed disdain for government and affairs of state became embarrassingly conspicuous. He was never around when his ministers needed him, and he went out of his way to make sure that they couldn't track him down. He once vanished for a secret meeting with Wagner on the eve of war. When war finally broke out, after his ministers had spent days desperately scouring Bavaria in an attempt to find him, their precious Commander-in-Chief resurfaced to explain that he was terribly sorry but he had been engrossed in a really good fireworks display—he was sure they would understand.

Ludwig was disinterested in international affairs, especially the Franco-Prussian War, which he was supposed to be fighting on Prussia's side. As a military man he was less than convincing. He hated warfare and was contemptuous of anything to do with it. Nothing could persuade him to even take time out to visit his troops. Once he saw a tired-looking sentry outside his palace and had a sofa sent out for the man to lie on.

Ludwig was familiar with his family history of mental instability and feared for his own sanity. One day he was seen staring into a mirror, shaking his head and muttering, "Really, there are times when I wouldn't swear that you are not mad." He was notoriously touchy about remarks on his mental health. Whenever news of the King's eccentricities leaked out to the press, Ludwig threatened to imprison any editor who dared to put them into print. The ban extended to any mention of his brother Otto, who by 1876 had become certifiably insane.

Ludwig's increased withdrawal from the real world more or less coincided with his brother's confinement. The King became almost completely reclusive. He built his own church at Berg so that he could hear Mass alone. Considerably more eccentric were his private command performances at the Hof and Residenz Theatres in Munich. Between 1871 and 1885 he commanded over 200 private performances of his favorite plays. During these eerie events he would recline alone in his royal box above the empty auditorium, occasionally heckling.

He ate alone, but always had dinners prepared for three or four persons so that he didn't feel lonely. Once he invited his favorite horse to dinner, and watched silently as the gray mare wrecked his dining room. Ludwig developed a fixation about the French Bourbon kings and liked to pretend that he was in the company of his heroes, Louis XIV and Louis XV, and their mistresses, Madame de Pompadour and Madame de Maintenon, occasionally making conversation with his imaginary guests in broken French. He became so obsessed with the legend of the Sun King that he took to imitating his walk and his handwriting and forging his signature. On his nightly excursions in winter through the snowbound countryside, his attendants were obliged to wear Louis XIV period costume.

He slept by day and lived by night. He had artificial moons installed in his bedrooms under which he and his lover Prince Paul von Thurn und Taxis would cavort dressed as Barbarossa and Lohengrin. The King's nocturnal jaunts in the valleys of the Bavarian alps in his fantastically gilded, rococo horse-drawn sleigh were legend. In the depths of winter he occasionally found himself caught in a blizzard and would seek refuge in a peasant's hut in the middle of the night—a never-to-be-forgotten experience for his surprised hosts. Weirder yet were his regular nocturnal trips around the Court Riding School in Munich. He rode his horses round in circles all night. Ludwig would pretend that he was traveling, for example to Augsburg, then calculate how many laps round the riding-school perimeter it would take to cover the equivalent distance. At the halfway point of his theoretical trip, he would stop to take refreshment, then remount his horse and complete the journey.

Meanwhile, Ludwig was showing other, more dangerous, signs of mental instability. Working for the King became increasingly hazardous for his servants. He imposed a code of conduct that made their daily routine almost impossible. The slightest offense would provoke severe punishment. Ludwig was a big man and often he would lash out at his servants with his own hands and feet. He ordered that one servant be transported for life for failing to catch a bird that had escaped from the royal aviary; another was ordered to wear a dress and ride around the palace on a donkey. Ludwig despised all forms of imperfection: an ugly valet was found guilty of accidentally making eye contact with the King as he passed him in a corridor, and was made to wear a black hood over his face whenever he was in the presence of the King for more than a year. The hood, Ludwig explained to a bemused guest, was "so that I don't see his criminal countenance."

As Ludwig's grasp on reality diminished, the list of court regulations grew. It became illegal in the royal presence to clear a throat, sneeze or cough. Bavarian dialect was also banned on pain of death. Many of his servants pretended to be ill rather than wait on him. He became obsessed with Chinese court etiquette and made his aides wear oriental dress and ordered them at all times to approach him on all fours. His servants were finally reduced to communicating with him through locked doors by tapping out an agreed code on the woodwork.

Luckily, his palace staff merely pretended to carry out his more inappropriate commands. Ludwig ordered his stable quartermaster, Hesselschwerdt, to travel to Italy, recruit some bandits, then capture the Prussian Crown Prince, who was on holiday there, and keep him chained up in a cave fed only on bread and water. The stable quartermaster chose to overlook the King's orders, thereby avoiding a potential war. Ludwig casually ordered floggings and executions, none of which ever took place. His orders were ignored, and in any case the executions were nearly always commuted by the King himself, who in his quieter moments remembered that he hated violence.

His building program meanwhile carried on apace, and he doubled his personal debt to 14 million marks—about $39 million today. The King then hit upon his most insane scheme of all, one which he confidently believed to be the perfect solution to his cash-flow problems. He would sell the entire state of Bavaria, and with the proceeds buy himself another kingdom where he would find less resistance to his castle-building problem.

In 1873 the Director of the Bavarian State Archives, Franz von Löher, was summoned by the King. Löher, a minor middle-aged civil servant, was instructed to go away and find a few thousand square miles of foreign land on which Ludwig could start up a new kingdom from scratch and live undisturbed, "completely independent of seasons, men and needs of all kinds."

Löher applied himself to his assignment with a great deal of enthusiasm. His first voyage took him to Spain and the Canary Islands, along the Mediterranean, around the Greek Islands to Constantinople, then back again—a trip which he reported upon in pedantic detail to the King. He had conscientiously inspected many sites and looked closely into the legal implications of purchasing a new Bavaria: there was, however, nothing much worth buying. Two years later, Löher was off on another expenses-paid jaunt at the King's behest, this time to Cyprus, Crete and finally Turkey, with a view to buying part of the Crimea. Once again he wrote up a meticulous report on his investigations. The quest was still not satisfied. Löher turned his sights to Egypt, then South America, Persia and Norway. By this time, Löher's lifestyle, which had already landed him three holidays of a lifetime and authorship of a best-selling travel guide, was attracting the jealous attentions of the press and government alike. Löher sensibly conceded that he'd probably pushed his luck far enough, and advised the King that it was his regrettable conclusion that he was probably stuck with Bavaria for life.

Ludwig reluctantly abandoned his dream of Utopia, but took solace in the fact that he had a couple more castles on the drawing board. There was talk of his building a replica of Versailles at Graswangtal. He desperately needed to lay his hands on more cash immediately—another 20 million marks would do. His request for more money was politely but firmly turned down by the Bavarian government.

If Ludwig's ministers wouldn't give him the readies, he would simply have to look elsewhere. Ludwig had read about an incredibly rich Persian who could lend or donate him all the money he needed. The King dispatched an aide to beg for money from him, confident that his request would not be denied. The request was never made: Ludwig's embarrassed aide simply hid himself away in Munich for a plausible length of time, then presented himself back at the Bavarian court to break the news that, sadly, the Persian gentleman had died of cholera before he had a chance to speak to him.

Ludwig was not to be put off by this minor setback and redoubled his efforts. Another aide was ordered to travel to England to ask the Duke of Westminster if he could spare 10 million marks (about $27 million). He sent begging letters to the Austrian Emperor, to the King of Norway and Sweden, to the Turkish Sultan in Constantinople, and to the Shah in Tehran. In the meantime, Ludwig was ready with an alternative plan: he would recruit thieves to burgle the major banks in Stuttgart, Frankfurt, Berlin and Paris. A group of his servants, with no previous experience of armed robbery between them, were dispatched to Frankfurt with instructions to hold up the Rothschild bank. They traveled to Frankfurt, hid themselves away for a few days, then went back to the King to explain that their elaborate plans had been thwarted by a last-minute hitch.

At this point his ministers agreed that the King was obviously unfit to rule and drastic action was required. It had long since become impossible to get him to attend to State affairs, and he had recklessly neglected his duties. Moreover, his begging letters had turned Bavaria into an international laughingstock. Even his subjects began to resent this remote King whom they never saw, and who according to rumor spent much of his spare time buggering his cavalrymen.

For several years Ludwig had been preoccupied by a prophecy, attributed to Nostradamus, that he believed alluded to the House of Wittelsbach. On his father's deathbed, the old King Maximilian II had whispered in Ludwig's ear the seer's prophecy: "When Good Friday falls on St. George's day, Easter on St. Mark's day and Corpus Christi on St. John's day, all the world will weep." As St. George was also the patron saint of Bavaria, this prophecy was thought to have a special significance for the royal family. In 1886 all of the conditions listed in the prophecy were fulfilled. This was also the year in which King Ludwig II was officially declared insane.

The King's chief minister, Johann von Lutz, consulted a leading Bavarian psychiatrist called Bernhard von Gudden and asked him to diagnose the King's mental condition. Von Gudden set about tracking down witnesses who would offer testimony about his sanity. The evidence was entirely anecdotal: Ludwig had forced his young soldiers to strip naked and dance together for him in the moonlight; he had nocturnal picnics in the woods, and insisted on eating al fresco in the middle of a winter blizzard with temperatures at well below freezing point; he made his servants play children's games such as Hunt the Slipper with him until dawn; he wanted to soar over the Bavarian Alps in a car drawn by peacocks, and ordered the construction of a flying machine; there was a holly tree to which he bowed low whenever he passed it, a hedge that he greeted ceremoniously, and a pillar at Linderhof that the King cuddled at the beginning and end of every visit there; he had ordered that his father's body be exhumed, years after Maximilian's death, so that Ludwig could give him a long overdue thrashing; he had twice dispatched one of his ministers to check that the water in his artificial grotto at Linderhof was precisely the correct shade of blue.

Without ever once personally examining his patient, von Gudden produced a lengthy medical report which concluded that the King was suffering from advanced paranoia and was incurably insane. This was enough for the Bavarian government to declare that Ludwig II was mad and incapable of exercising his duties.

CATCHING LUDWIG

The legal pronouncement of insanity was one thing; in order to enforce it, they first had to catch their King. In June 1886 a group of soldiers, led by von Gudden and his assistant and several male nurses, set out for him with a straitjacket and a bottle of chloroform. However, Ludwig had been forewarned and was expecting their imminent arrival. They arrived at Neuschwanstein to find the castle doors bolted and guarded by local gendarmes who refused to let them in. They were then attacked by one of Ludwig's supporters, an irate old woman with a brolly. The humiliated delegation decided upon a tactical retreat. At this point the King took the offensive and sent a detachment of local police to arrest them. They were interred in his castle lodge, with orders that they should be tortured and their eyes gouged out. The order was quietly ignored. One of the commissioners was able to escape, and persuaded the local police to let them out. Once freed, the embarrassed posse slunk back to Munich. Ludwig meanwhile contemplated suicide, but his aide refused to go out and buy poison for him, so the King paced up and down his castle considering other methods of killing himself.

When they came for the King a second time it was very different. There was no sentry to bar them, and they found Ludwig inert, dazed, and offering no resistance. They led him quietly away to his castle at Berg, on the shores of Starnberger Lake. The ex-King appeared to take this turn of events with unexpected good humor. He was in such a relaxed mood that he was given permission to take an evening stroll round the lake, accompanied by his physician and captor, Dr. Gudden. At around 6:45 P.M. on

June 12, Ludwig and Gudden set out for their walk. Two hours later, Ludwig and the doctor had failed to return and the alarm was sounded. Servants and local police searched the area around the lake and the castle grounds. At around 10 P.M. the bodies of Ludwig and Gudden were found floating facedown in shallow muddy water. Gudden's face was marked, showing possible signs of a struggle.

The deaths of both men remained a mystery. It is generally assumed that the King had decided to take his own life. Gudden had either drowned accidentally while struggling to prevent the suicide, or else had been deliberately drowned by his prisoner. A cross marks the spot where King Ludwig II drowned. He was forty years old.

With hindsight the straitjacket earmarked for Ludwig by his countrymen was not only a monstrous act of ingratitude but also very bad planning. They should have simply let him get on and finish the job of turning his country into a giant Wagnerian theme park. If only his contemporaries could have guessed at what their dear demented King was going to do for their balance of payments, they would have undoubtedly struck a medal in his honor. Unfortunately it took Bavaria more than a century to see the funny side.

MERRY OTTO

The declaration of Ludwig's insanity by the Bavarian government was a grave embarrassment not only for Bavaria but for every royal household in Europe. Almost every one of them had close blood ties to a man who had just been branded a dangerous lunatic. For Bavaria the constitutional problem was far

from over. The day Ludwig II died, his brother Otto was pronounced King of Bavaria, with his uncle Luitpold acting as
Regent. The government had in effect organized a coup d'état
to overthrow one mad king and replace him with another. A
messenger was dispatched to Castle Fürstenried, where Otto
had been incarcerated ever since he was declared incurably insane in 1878, with instructions to inform him that his brother
was dead and he was now King. Otto listened, but registered
no emotion and changed the conversation to another subject.

Otto was three years younger than Ludwig. Although he
had always been regarded as odd, in his teens he was an affable,
rather excitable youth widely known in Munich as "the Merry
Otto." Almost overnight, however, he changed from a lively
young man into a depressive hypochondriac who suffered from
panic attacks and would burst into tears for no reason. Otto's
first and last major appearance on the international scene was at
the Versailles Conference, after Prussia and the other German
states had defeated the French Emperor Napoleon III. Ludwig
had refused to leave Bavaria on the grounds that his teeth hurt,
and sent Otto to represent him instead. It was in the middle of
one of history's most important conferences, in front of the
crowned heads of Europe, that Otto first manifested obvious
signs of mental instability. Bavaria's representative sat through
the entire proceedings with his shoulders hunched, his eyes
glazed, his body shaking, giving everyone the distinct impression that he hadn't taken in a single word that was said. The
Prussian Crown Prince, who was seated next to him, was
alarmed at how pale and strangely distracted Otto appeared.

Ludwig had been tempted on occasions to abdicate in favor
of Otto, and was relying on his younger brother to produce
sons and continue the dynasty. If only he could be left alone to

play with his castles, Ludwig was quite happy to let someone else take charge. After Versailles, Ludwig was forced to concede that this option was no longer open to him.

Otto's condition deteriorated rapidly. In 1871 Ludwig wrote to a friend:

> It is really painful to see Otto in such a suffering state which seems to become worse and worse daily. In some respects he is more excitable and nervous than Aunt Alexandra, and that is saying a great deal. He often does not go to bed for forty-eight hours, and did not take off his boots for eight weeks, behaves like a madman, makes terrible faces, barks like a dog, and, at times, says the most indecorous things.

By 1872 Otto had become so dangerously unstable that his doctors advised that he be temporarily locked up for his own safety. He was removed to Nymphenburg and detained under mild restraint. The rare occasions when Otto was let out became a major embarrassment to the family. By 1875 his hallucinations had taken a religious turn. One day during High Mass he burst into the church dressed in a shooting jacket, threw himself at the feet of the Archbishop and began an extremely loud and hysterical confession that he had sodomized several local choirboys. After this episode it was agreed that it was time to deprive him of his liberty on a more permanent basis, and Otto was pronounced incurably insane and led away, smiling and clutching one of his favorite childhood toys, to a castle near Munich. The man who signed the certificate was Dr. Bernhard von Gudden. At first Ludwig was a frequent visitor to Fürstenried, but the sight of his brother in a straitjacket was too much for his own troubled mind to cope with and soon he stopped visiting altogether.

For twenty-seven years after Ludwig's death, Otto reigned in name only from his cell in Castle Fürstenried, while his uncle Luitpold took charge of Bavaria as Prinzregent. Prinzregent Luitpold interfered little in the day-to-day running of the kingdom, leaving state affairs in the hands of his ministers, and during this period Bavaria enjoyed unprecedented growth and stability. A discreet veil of silence was thrown over the mad King. He was indulged with a mock court comprising guards, doctors and jailers who always addressed him as "Your Majesty." Otto spent his days growing enormously fat and playing with his toys. It was said that the King's screams could occasionally be heard outside the castle. Three years after he ceased to be King, Otto died aged sixty-eight.

THE END

King Ludwig III, Luitpold's son, was already elderly and in poor health when he came to the throne in 1913, and was the last Bavarian monarch. After World War I, Bavaria was declared a workers' republic. The royal family fled Munich on the advice of the new government, which could not guarantee their safety. After 783 years in power, the rule of the Wittelsbach family in Bavaria was at an end.

Royal titles still exist in Germany, although they no longer carry any legal status. In 1945, monarchist sympathizers formed a movement to put Rupprecht, King Ludwig III's son, on to the throne, but nothing came of it. Rupprecht died in 1955, and the Wittelsbach claim now resides with his grandson Franz. The Wittelsbach family still counts approximately fifty members, among them Kaltenbach brewery owner Prince Luitpold von Bayern.

8. THE STUD FARM OF EUROPE

The Rise of the House of Saxe-Coburg

ONE DAY, WHILE Queen Victoria was boring a minor Prussian royal on the subject of marriage, she advised that it was not wise to dig too deeply into the royal families of Europe because one would discover many "black spots." In her case it would have revealed more of a black hole.

While the obvious points have often been made about the disastrous effects of the decadent Hanoverian heritage on the genetic makeup of the British royal family, a fact often overlooked is that Queen Victoria and her descendants were equally the products of an even more extraordinarily debauched German family, the Saxe-Coburgs. They were an obscure clan of Saxon princelings who ruled over a poor and insignificant German principality, one of thirty-nine similar domains which existed in northern Europe in the eighteenth century, but in their relentless and occasionally comical crusade to aggrandize

THE SAXE-COBURGS
ON THE THRONES
OF EUROPE

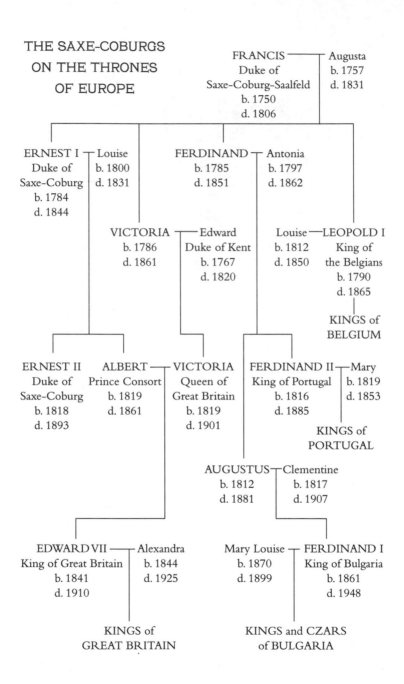

FRANCIS ——┬— Augusta
Duke of   b. 1757
Saxe-Coburg-Saalfeld   d. 1831
b. 1750
d. 1806

ERNEST I ——┬— Louise
Duke of   b. 1800
Saxe-Coburg   d. 1831
b. 1784
d. 1844

FERDINAND ——┬— Antonia
b. 1785   b. 1797
d. 1851   d. 1862

VICTORIA ——┬— Edward
b. 1786   Duke of Kent
d. 1861   b. 1767
d. 1820

Louise —— LEOPOLD I
b. 1812   King of
d. 1850   the Belgians
b. 1790
d. 1865

KINGS of
BELGIUM

ERNEST II   ALBERT ——┬— VICTORIA
Duke of   Prince Consort   Queen of
Saxe-Coburg   b. 1819   Great Britain
b. 1818   d. 1861   b. 1819
d. 1893   d. 1901

FERDINAND II ——┬— Mary
King of Portugal   b. 1819
b. 1816   d. 1853
d. 1885

KINGS of
PORTUGAL

AUGUSTUS ——┬— Clementine
b. 1812   b. 1817
d. 1881   d. 1907

EDWARD VII ——┬— Alexandra
King of Great Britain   b. 1844
b. 1841   d. 1925
d. 1910

Mary Louise ——┬— FERDINAND I
b. 1870   King of Bulgaria
d. 1899   b. 1861
d. 1948

KINGS of   KINGS and CZARS
GREAT BRITAIN   of BULGARIA

their family name they hawked their sons and daughters, nieces and nephews around the courts of Europe with all the subtlety of time-share salesmen. They became, in effect, Europe's first professional dating agency for monarchs.

By the time of King Edward VII's accession in 1901, four European thrones were occupied by the male descendants of the House of Saxe-Coburg, a statistic that caused Germany's Chancellor Otto von Bismarck to sneer that they were "the stud farm of Europe." If the Saxe-Coburgs were nothing more than royal breeding stock, they at least injected a bit of German industry and strength of character into the veins of the main ruling houses, who had shown themselves to be good only at churning out a procession of fat libertines. Unfortunately the Coburg DNA also carried a few less welcome traits.

ERNEST THE RAKE AND THE "CLOWN FROM COBURG"

The Saxe-Coburg lust for glory began with the Duchess Augusta, grandmother of Queen Victoria and her husband, Albert the Prince Consort. The old Duchess was insanely ambitious for her three sons and four daughters and she spent a lifetime scheming how to get them married into the biggest and best courts in Europe. The eldest of Augusta's sons, Duke Ernest, was the father of Prince Albert.

The Duke had a violent temper and an extraordinary lifestyle. "There are few deviations from morality or convention," wrote his biographer Giles St. Aubyn, "that he had not pioneered." Ernest spent much of his youth randomly seducing mistresses by the dozen, siring bastards both at home and abroad. His sister Juliane had married into the Russian royal family, and the Duke found a firm friend in his new brother-in-law, the sinister and brutal Grand Duke Constantine, a grandson of Catherine the Great. It was said that the Dukes Ernest and Constantine amused themselves by kicking hussars to death and firing live rats from cannons in the Marble Palace.

He was a huge embarrassment to his elderly mother, who eventually persuaded him to settle down and produce a legitimate son, if only to prevent Saxe-Coburg from passing to the heirs of his younger married brothers. Duke Ernest was subsequently wed to his pretty sixteen-year-old cousin Louise, daughter of Duke Augustus of Saxe-Coburg-Altenburg, and she gave him two sons, Ernest Junior and Albert.

Neither married life nor fatherhood dulled the Duke's rapacious appetites, and within two years of Albert's birth he had returned to the regular company of prostitutes. His wife, a vivacious but very lonely young woman, was discovered having an affair with an army officer. Ernest cited his wife's adultery as grounds for a divorce, and in 1824 Louise was banished from court, leaving four-year-old Albert without a mother. Seven years later she died of cancer, aged thirty-one. In 1832 Ernest was married again, this time to his own niece, Mary.

Duke Ernest's burgeoning reputation throughout Europe as an unscrupulous rake reached a hiatus when one of his earlier affairs returned to haunt him. In Paris the Duke had seduced a sixteen-year-old French girl, Pauline Panam. He smuggled her into Coburg dressed as a boy and kept her hidden in a safe house where he could meet her when the fancy took him. Within a year she was pregnant with his child, another Ernest Junior. When the Duke grew tired of his Lolita, both she and his child were discarded.

But the Duke had not heard the last of Miss Panam. Inconveniently, she became a successful actress, known in Paris as "La Belle Grecque." Her fame enabled her to travel extensively and soon she found herself on first-name terms with some of the most powerful men in Europe. Wherever she went she made sure that everyone heard about her terrible treatment at the hands of the vile Duke of Saxe-Coburg, and she would point to his bastard, poor little Ernest Junior, who was naturally always in tow. Her story attracted a considerable amount of sympathy.

Duke Ernest decided to silence his ex-mistress. His first plan was to kidnap his illegitimate son and threaten Pauline Panam that she would never see the boy again unless she joined a convent and remained quiet about her past. When this plot failed he tried to arrange for their deaths in a fake coach accident, but both mother and son survived.

The old Duke of Saxe-Coburg continued to be a major source of embarrassment long after his son married Queen Victoria. He stayed on in London after Prince Albert's wedding in 1840 and scandalized the royal household by attempting to seduce most of Queen Victoria's ladies-in-waiting. The old Duke Ernest was not the only unwanted guest at the British royal wedding. Prince Albert's degenerate older brother, Ernest, also stayed on for about three months after the event, and fell seriously ill with venereal disease while he was under the Queen's roof.

The Prince Consort's brother, Ernest, very nearly became Queen Victoria's husband, for it was he, rather than Albert, who was the original marriage candidate proposed by their father. A senior Anglican churchman who met Ernest said later that the only thing that could ever increase his liking for Albert was the thought of what would have happened to England if Victoria had married Ernest. The "clown from Coburg," as Albert's brother came to be known, was a profoundly ugly man with a large underbite and bloodshot eyes, which gave him the appearance of a bulldog with a hangover. In time, Albert's brother revealed himself to have an even greater talent for profligacy than his father. Ernest progressed from molesting his servant girls to an adulthood given over more or less entirely to indiscriminate adultery and lavish spending on his droves of mistresses. No woman was safe from his advances. Married diplomats were advised to leave young or pretty wives at home if they had to visit his court.

In 1842 Ernest was married to Princess Alexandrine of Baden, a once pretty woman who in later years sported a gray beard. Although Ernest infected her with his syphilis and generally treated her ungallantly, she remained strangely loyal to her husband, always referring to him as her "dearly beloved, good Ernest." When he died in 1893, Alexandrine even gave financial support to his most recent mistress. Even more magnanimous was her instruction that the little park villa that her late husband had openly used as a love nest to seduce a long line of girlfriends should become a shrine and be left exactly as it was, on the grounds that Ernest had spent some of his happiest hours there.

THE AMBITIONS OF LEOPOLD

Prince Albert and his brother had an uncle Leopold, the youngest of Duchess Augusta's three sons. He had been briefly married to Princess Charlotte, the only legitimate heir of

George IV, but had seen his chance of sitting on the British throne as Prince Consort vanish when his young bride died in childbirth. Before his marriage to Charlotte he had been virtually penniless. When he arrived in London for the victory celebrations after Waterloo he stayed in rented lodgings over a butcher's shop in Marylebone High Street. At his wedding at Carlton House, when Leopold promised to endow his bride with all his worldly goods, Princess Charlotte burst out laughing. Parliament voted him a share in a joint income of £60,000, and a pension of £50,000 a year if he outlived the Princess. After her funeral Leopold returned to Germany wifeless, but with his pockets lined by the British taxpayers and his appetite for the good life whetted by his brief membership of the British royal family.

Leopold was by far the most nakedly ambitious of the Duchess Augusta's sons. With a Saxe-Coburg single-mindedness, he determined to regain royal status for himself and his family. In order to do that he needed to acquire a throne, and he didn't particularly care where it came from. In early-nineteenth-century Europe, this was by no means an unrealistic ambition for a young duke to have. The new map of Europe, redrawn in the aftermath of the Napoleonic and Balkan Wars, had created many opportunities for minor royals with the right political connections. When the throne of Greece became vacant, Leopold was the first to send in his C.V. On this occasion, however, his application failed. He had better luck when the Great Powers met in London in 1830 to consider the future of the newly unified Belgium. They were turned down by Louis Philippe's son the Duc de Nemours, but found in Leopold a willing second choice. As the new and ostentatiously styled King of the Belgians, Leopold found himself in an excellent position from which to build an empire for the House of Saxe-Coburg.

Leopold was a little man who wore a feather boa and three-inch heels. His androgynous appearance belied the fact that he was a compulsive womanizer. In 1832 he married for the second time, to Louise, a daughter of France's Louis Philippe. His new wife, although very young, suffered frequently from poor health, and found that she was unable to satisfy her oversexed husband or keep him remotely faithful. When Leopold took to openly sleeping with her ladies-in-waiting, she chose to overlook his behavior with some relief. Her husband had also somehow managed to convince her that by taking lovers he was doing her a big favor.

The King continued to sate his appetites wherever, and whenever, he could, and there was never any shortage of Belgian mistresses willing to accommodate him. His most enduring affair was with the young Arcadie Claret de Viescourt, who liked to flaunt her position in public, even when it meant having her coach pelted with rotten vegetables on the streets of Brussels. The King maneuvered her into his palace by arranging for her to be married to one of his stewards, and she took the title Madame Meyer von Eppinghoven. The steward was then persuaded to make himself scarce. Arcadie gave Leopold two sons. Although he was infamously parsimonious (according to one mistress, Karoline Bauer, the King went to bed with two little clamps between his back teeth to prevent wear on the enamel while he slept), he always made generous provision for his bastards: illegitimate daughters were taken care of by arranged marriages, and sons received diplomatic postings or army commissions.

In his youth, Leopold was regarded as both handsome and

virile, but he aged prematurely. His physical decline accelerated at an alarming rate as he took on a cadaverous appearance, but he refused to grow old gracefully: he painted his sunken cheeks with rouge, penciled in his eyebrows and hid his bald head under a jet-black wig. Leopold spent the last couple of years in agony with a bladder stone. The pain was so severe that he had to sleep upright, wedged between two horsehair mattresses. But to the bitter end he continued to surround himself with his small harem of mistresses. The stone was finally crushed by the celebrated urologist to the crowned heads of Europe, Sir Henry Thompson, but Leopold was soon dead, in the thirty-fourth year of his reign, aged seventy-five.

Leopold is generally regarded as the midwife of the modern British monarchy, for as uncle to both Prince Albert and Queen Victoria he was the matchmaker and architect of their wedding. Although Leopold had seen his own chance of becoming Prince Consort cruelly snatched away from him by the death of his first wife, he had never given up on the idea of installing a close male relative on the British throne. His favorite nephew, Albert, was effectively groomed to succeed where he had failed. Leopold and his mentor, Baron Stockmar, head-hunted Victoria as a future bride for Albert with almost military precision.

QUEEN VICTORIA'S "ODD" COUSIN— LEOPOLD THE UNLOVED

The blackest stain on the reputation of the Saxe-Coburg dynasty was undoubtedly Queen Victoria's cousin Leopold II, King of the Belgians, a monstrous man who lived only for money, sex and power. He cared neither for Belgium nor his subjects. "I am King of a small country," he said, "and a small-minded people." This was the sort of inspired diplomacy that helped generate a hatred of him not only among his own people but also eventually throughout the Western world.

Leopold II was tall, cadaverous, and walked with a sciatic limp. In his youth he was known for his long, beaky nose. "It is such a nose," Disraeli remarked, "as a young prince has in a fairy tale, who has been banned by a malignant fairy." The nose was later upstaged by a long, white fantail beard. Queen Victoria thought her sullen cousin "very odd." In spite of his emaciated appearance he was a hard man and a fitness fanatic. In the Belgian royal palace at Laeken he slept in a hard camp bed, from which he roused himself at 6 A.M. by dousing himself with buckets of ice-cold seawater. The only drink he ever took was a cup of hot water. Throughout his life he was intensely proud of his physical condition, and even when he was in his seventies he took pleasure in making visitors stand for long periods so that he could prove he was in better shape than they were.

Like every male member of the House of Saxe-Coburg, he was driven by ambition. This particular Coburg, however, was a megalomaniac, consumed by crazy colonial ambitions which were eventually to have him condemned by the whole world as "the butcher of the Congo."

Although his fledgling country was a bantamweight beside the great colonial powers of the Victorian era, Leopold dreamed of creating a Belgian Empire in Africa. "I do not want to miss the opportunity," he wrote in 1877, "of our obtaining a share in this magnificent African cake. In order to turn his fantasy into reality without arousing the suspicions of his more powerful European neighbors, Leopold set up a bogus missionary organization called the International African Association. The IAA, he announced, would take the teachings of Christ to the dark continent. In fact, it was all part of an incredibly ambitious scam—a front for Leopold's personally sponsored expedition to the Congo Basin, for which he also enlisted the services of the great explorer and journalist Henry Morton Stanley. Stanley was unfortunately slow to realize that Leopold was not quite the innocent philanthropist he claimed to be, and that his sponsor simply wanted to acquire the Congo Basin for himself.

In 1885 Leopold was declared King-Sovereign of the Congo Free State. It was an astonishing coup. Under the noses of the British, including the ruthless land-grabbing Cecil Rhodes, the French and the Germans, and without any assistance from his own government, he had personally acquired a country eighty times the size of Belgium. He was now absolute ruler of over 1 million square miles of Africa that were rich in rubber, copper and ivory, and had a population of about 10 million people.

Whenever King Leopold's colonial adventure ran short of cash he invented bizarre fund-raising schemes. When one of his applications to the Belgian government for a personal loan was turned down, he succeeded in embarrassing them into paying up by pawning his foreign medals and his servants' livery bit by bit. Eventually a complicated deal was struck whereby Leopold leased the Congo back to his government for a considerable fortune. As the only obvious benefactor from the deal was the King himself, he had in effect pulled off a gigantic swindle.

Not content with merely owning most of central Africa, Leopold's ambitions became even more fantastic. His next plan was to extend his lands north along the Nile by acquiring Sudan and even Egypt. Thus the House of Saxe-Coburg, he hoped, would become the new dynasty of Pharaohs. Leopold casually hinted to the British Prime Minister, Lord Salisbury, that, if he would allow him to lease the Sudan from the Khedive of Egypt, he would lend Britain his Sudanese subjects to do with whatsoever they wanted. They could even be used, Leopold suggested helpfully, to create an army with which Britain could annex China. When Salisbury told Queen Victoria about her cousin's plan, she noted that the Belgian King had "taken leave of his senses." The full extent of Leopold's insane greed was yet to be revealed.

Unaccountably, over a period of fifteen years, the population of the Congo had fallen by about 3 million. By the turn of the century, disturbing rumors leaked out of Leopold's Congo that began to make sense of this shortfall in numbers. Missionaries spoke of atrocities carried out by Leopold's state officials against the local population. These reports were later damningly confirmed by the American journalist Ed Morel. The phrase "Congo horrors" was heard for the first time.

In ten years, between 1896 and 1906, King Leopold made £3 million in clear profit from his private fiefdom in central Africa by using his monopoly to ruthlessly strip the country of its natural resources. The local population was forced to collect rubber by Leopold's government agents, usually cannibals from local tribes who were chosen by the Belgians for their expertise in human butchery. As no new rubber vines were ever planted to replace the old ones, resources were very quickly depleted. The Congolese, no longer able to supply rubber quickly enough, were forced on pain of death to work even harder.

Leopold's agents were motivated by a grisly bonus scheme: to prove that they had done their job properly they were expected to return with a quota of human hands severed from the dead. Missionaries reported seeing baskets full of human hands being inspected by Belgian officials. When the agents were accused of being too wasteful with their bullets, they simply hacked off the hands of the living. The terror tactics escalated: whole villages were razed to the ground and tribes were wiped out. Women were raped and beaten; their children were thrown to the crocodiles. Those who lived were worked to death. Leopold, meanwhile, pocketed the spoils from the massacre and spent it on the beautification of Ostend.

The international community, including Conan Doyle and Mark Twain, lined up to condemn the King of the Belgians. Twain wrote in a virulent attack:

> In fourteen years Leopold has deliberately destroyed more lives than have suffered death in all the battlefields of this planet for the past thousand years . . . this moldy and piety-mouthing hypocrite, this bloody monster whose mate is not findable in human history anywhere, and whose personality will surely shame hell itself when he arrives there—which will be soon, let us hope and trust.

King Leopold's response to the storm of criticism was to handle it as a public-relations exercise. He set up a secret press bureau to distribute favorable propaganda and spent a fortune trying to buy the support of leading public figures.

As if the damage to his reputation by his involvement in the Congo wasn't enough, the King of the Belgians continued to shock with his astonishing private life. Within days of making his marriage vows to his Austrian wife, Marie Henrietta Leopold, he was sleeping with a famous actress, Aimée Desclée. In an attempt to justify his behavior he sportingly put it about that he had caught his wife sleeping with the coachman. He went on to create a series of sex scandals, which earned him the nickname "Le Roi des Belges et des Belles." Leopold scandalized his countrymen, as his father had done, by driving through the streets of Brussels with his mistresses in his royal carriage.

While the King threw himself into a spiraling life of debauchery, Queen Marie Henrietta filled the hours by teaching animals to do tricks. Visitors to the royal palace at Laeken became used to the sight of horses trotting up and down the grand staircase: her magnum opus was a pet llama that had been taught to spit in the face of anyone who stroked it.

The London *Pall Mall Gazette* published a damning article about child prostitution in the capital that named the Belgian King as a regular client of a Mrs. Jeffries, whose brothel specialized in the procurement of young girls for pedophiles. The allegations were never refuted by Leopold, nor did he sue. His biographer Ludwig Bauer wrote: "It cannot be said that any moral scruples would have restrained the King of the Belgians from the offenses attributed to him . . . he paid for what he wanted and took it."

When he was in his seventies, Leopold II began a very high-profile affair with a sixteen-year-old prostitute, Caroline Lacroix, whom he met in a Parisian brothel. The sight of the white-whiskered old King parading around the fashionable spas of Europe with a teenage brunette on his arm provoked outrage and disbelief. There was wild speculation about the tricks she surely employed to hold on to an old man whose appetite was jaded by a lifetime of prolific sexual excess. There were rumors of perversion, of strategically placed mirrors and "special" equipment. Whatever she did for him, it kept her in pole position, as it were, to his death.

Abroad, the Belgian King's reputation reached epic proportions. The German Emperor's wife found him so personally repugnant that after his state visit to Germany she ordered her court chaplain to exorcise the apartment in which Leopold had been staying. President Theodore Roosevelt, unmoved by the gift of a silver-framed picture of Leopold personally sent to him by the Belgian King, refused to invite him to visit the St. Louis Exposition, dismissing him as a "dissolute old rake." Even Victoria's son Bertie thought it wise to give him a wide berth.

Leopold regarded his two daughters, the Princesses Louise and Stephanie, as bait to reel in even more European royal houses, in his drive to push the Saxe-Coburg name up the European royal ladder. In so doing, he condemned one to several years in a lunatic asylum, and the other to relentless marital infidelity and syphilis.

Princess Louise was betrothed at seventeen to the voluptuary thirty-one-year-old Prince Philip of Saxe-Coburg. When Philip dragged her off to live in his rat-infested castle in Hungary, Louise sought affection outside her loveless marriage with a young lieutenant, Count Geza Mattatic-Keglevic, and, unwisely, paraded her new boyfriend in public. Louise quickly found out the Belgian royal family's position on divorce: when she asked her father for permission to begin the process of legal separation from her degenerate husband, her request was dismissed out of hand. The King advised her that, provided she kept up the appearance of a respectable royal marriage, she could sleep with whoever she liked.

The cuckolded Prince Philip was determined to make Mattatic pay for making him look foolish, and was able to engineer trumped-up charges of forgery to send his wife's lover to prison. Leopold offered Princess Louise an ultimatum. She could either return to her husband and keep up the appearance of a good and loyal wife, or he would have her committed to a lunatic asylum. Without hesitating, Louise chose the latter. The Princess was duly certified insane and flung into an asylum in Linderhof, Saxony. In a touching display of fatherly concern, King Leopold advised the superintendent of the asylum: "Keep a strict watch upon the madwoman." Neither he nor his wife visited her throughout her incarceration.

When news leaked that the perfectly sane Belgian Princess was being held in a lunatic asylum, there was public outrage. The Belgian royal family responded by having her moved to a more low-profile mental home. Four years later, Count Mattatic was released from prison and was able to organize Louise's escape and subsequent flight to Paris. She spent the next two decades penniless, relying on handouts begged from friends. Princess Louise finally obtained a divorce in 1906.

King Leopold anticipated a struggle to find a husband for his second daughter, Stephanie, who was described as having the figure of a Danube tugboat. What Stephanie lacked in looks and personality she compensated for by misplaced self-confidence. The younger Belgian Princess was, according to her mother-in-law, the Empress Elizabeth, "an obelisk of tactlessness." One of Princess Stephanie's accomplishments was an execrable singing voice which she would inflict upon every member of her family and which would cause the family dog to flee for cover. Although her marital prospects were considerably improved by the fact that eligible princesses were unusually scarce in 1879, her father couldn't believe his luck when, at the age of fifteen, Stephanie—or the "Rose of Brabant," as she alone was fond of calling herself—was betrothed to Crown Prince Rudolf, heir to the Austro-Hungarian throne.

Rudolf's father, Emperor Franz Josef, was desperate to get his son married off as soon as he possibly could, as Rudolf appeared to be hell-bent on defiling every woman in Vienna. His sexual experience, even for a healthy young prince with time on his hands, was extraordinary. Princess Stephanie may have had some inkling of this when he turned up in Brussels to formally request her hand in marriage with his girlfriend in tow.

At her wedding she walked down the aisle, according to an eyewitness, with "all the daintiness of a dragoon," but went to her marital bed that evening, like her elder sister, as a lamb to the slaughter. "What a night," she wrote later. "I thought I should die!"

Leopold II later severed all connections with the two daughters he had so maliciously misused, and cut them out of his will. When Queen Marie Henrietta died, the two Princesses joined forces to claim their inheritance from Leopold's incredible fortune, and Brussels witnessed the unprecedented business of a king being sued by his daughters. Leopold won his case against a tide of public outrage. Both daughters later took their revenge in scathing autobiographies.

When Leopold was seventy-four years old and dying, he married his teenage prostitute, now ennobled as the Baroness de Vaughan. When the ceremony was over, he turned to one of the witnesses and said with a prophetic slip of the tongue, "Let me introduce you to my widow." The following day he had an abdominal operation. Forty-eight hours later, on the forty-fourth anniversary of his accession to the Belgian throne, Leopold "the Unloved" died. The first act of the late King's family was to kick the Baroness de Vaughan out of the house, from where she fled screaming back to Paris. On December 22, 1909, Queen Victoria's cousin was dispatched with a full state funeral. It was noted that the pamphleteers peddling salacious exposés of his private life along the funeral route outnumbered the official mourners by three to one.

9. DUTY, DIGNITY, DECENCY

The Windsors

GEORGE V

THE CULT OF the monarchy as upholders of British morality was Prince Albert's invention, but the British royal family didn't fully become identified with solid middle-class family values until the arrival of the two great royal icons of the early twentieth century, King George V and Queen Mary. There are few figures in the British royal family whose public images are so sharply—or, as it transpires, so misleadingly—defined.

George V became King by default in 1910 because his elder brother, Albert Victor, had long since died of pneumonia, to the great relief of many. The new King was far from gifted. Robert Lacey noted:

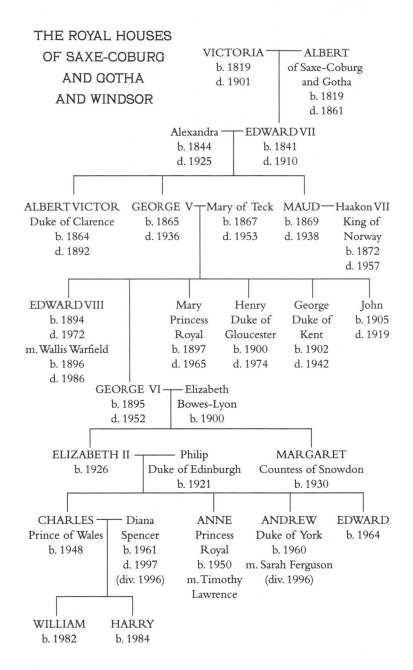

THE ROYAL HOUSES
OF SAXE-COBURG
AND GOTHA
AND WINDSOR

VICTORIA ——— ALBERT
b. 1819 | of Saxe-Coburg
d. 1901 | and Gotha
b. 1819
d. 1861

Alexandra ——— EDWARD VII
b. 1844 | b. 1841
d. 1925 | d. 1910

ALBERT VICTOR | GEORGE V ——— Mary of Teck | MAUD ——— Haakon VII
Duke of Clarence | b. 1865 | b. 1867 | b. 1869 | King of
b. 1864 | d. 1936 | d. 1953 | d. 1938 | Norway
d. 1892 | | | | b. 1872
| | | | d. 1957

EDWARD VIII | Mary | Henry | George | John
b. 1894 | Princess | Duke of | Duke of | b. 1905
d. 1972 | Royal | Gloucester | Kent | d. 1919
m. Wallis Warfield | b. 1897 | b. 1900 | b. 1902
b. 1896 | d. 1965 | d. 1974 | d. 1942
d. 1986

GEORGE VI ——— Elizabeth
b. 1895 | Bowes-Lyon
d. 1952 | b. 1900

ELIZABETH II ——— Philip | MARGARET
b. 1926 | Duke of Edinburgh | Countess of Snowdon
b. 1921 | b. 1930

CHARLES ——— Diana | ANNE | ANDREW | EDWARD
Prince of Wales | Spencer | Princess | Duke of York | b. 1964
b. 1948 | b. 1961 | Royal | b. 1960
| d. 1997 | b. 1950 | m. Sarah Ferguson
| (div. 1996) | m. Timothy | (div. 1996)
| | Lawrence

WILLIAM | HARRY
b. 1982 | b. 1984

As his official biographer felt compelled to admit, King George V was distinguished "by no exercise of social gifts, by no personal magnetism, by no intellectual powers. He was neither a wit nor a brilliant raconteur, neither well-read nor well-educated, and he made no great contribution to enlightened social converse. He lacked intellectual curiosity and only late in life acquired some measure of artistic taste." He was, in other words, exactly like most of his subjects. He discovered a new job for modern kings and queens to do—representation.

In truth, the King's lifestyle was one that few of his subjects would have been able to identify with, unless you happened to be a superrich country squire. George's day was one long shooting party punctuated by visits to his stamp album and by his fanatical obsession with royal etiquette. He saw his job as an irritating intrusion into his private life. He hated anything to do with matters of state, especially the business of opening a new Parliament, even though all that was required of him was once a year to read aloud a few words prepared for him by a speechwriter.

George V was, like George III, a royal paradox. He was pathologically resistant to change, yet it was during his reign that many of the rituals we associate with the modern British royal family were invented. He and his wife were the first King and Queen to trade on the comfortable myth of the royal family as stalwarts of marital fidelity and the middle-class values of hearth and home. George V was the first British sovereign to recognize that the royal family needed to be popular to survive. He was the first King to hire a public-relations officer, the first to make use of the talking cinema newsreel, the first to make use of the Christmas radio broadcast to the nation, and the first to insist that his relatives do something to make themselves look slightly more useful to help justify their gilded existences. It was George V who gave the royal family its modern name, the House of Windsor. However, the new name and the new image, like nearly everything else about George V, was largely based on falsehood and crippling hypocrisy.

George V was not a shrewd and manipulative image maker; in fact he was largely incapable of planning anything. In contrast to his grandmother Queen Victoria, who strove to exert political influence in the tradition of Elizabeth I, and his father, Edward VII, who aspired to manipulate the balance of power in Europe, George's ambitions were humble. The King was happy to have his opinions on all matters of state formed for him by his palace "think tank," an inner circle of personal assistants and civil servants. But he was a particularly attentive listener when it came to matters concerning his own self-preservation.

He was a desperately poor scholar. Before he could pass the exam to become a cadet aboard *Britannica*, the navy had to fiddle it by lowering the minimum entrance standard. He was the only senior member of a European royal family unable to speak a second language with any degree of fluency. Although he spoke English with a slight German accent, he couldn't actually speak German, the mother tongue of his father, his grandparents and his wife. The British Consul-General in Berlin wrote in 1913: "It is hardly credible that George cannot speak a solitary word of German, and his French is atrocious."

His lifelong hobby was stamp collecting. When a British representative in the Middle East heard of a suspected case of smallpox in the local printing works, he was worried in case the royal tongue became contaminated and had 400 stamps boiled in a saucepan before dispatching them to London. A courtier innocently inquired at breakfast one morning, "Did your Royal Highness read that some damned fool has just paid one thousand four hundred and fifty pounds for a single stamp?" George replied, "I was the damned fool."

Like his father before him, George V had no time for the arts and wore his ignorance like a badge. His favorite opera was *La Bohème* "because it is the shortest." His social gaffes were legion. On one of his rare and grudging trips to an art exhibition, when he found himself before a French Impressionist painting, he shouted to his wife across the gallery, "Here's something to make you laugh, May." (Queen Mary was called May by her family.) He once confided to the director of the National Gallery, "I tell you what, Turner was mad. My grandmother always said so." The King's small talk was loud and cheerfully witless. He greeted Charles Lindbergh, who had just become the first man to fly solo across the Atlantic, by asking him, "What did you do about peeing?" In 1935 the King met the author John Buchan and told him how much he enjoyed reading his books, especially *The Thirty-Nine Steps*. Later, Queen Mary took Buchan aside and confided, "The king does not get much time for reading but when he does I'm afraid he reads the most awful rubbish." (George VI inherited his father's cheerful ignorance of art. He once saw the paintings of John Piper, who was known mainly for his storm scenes, and stammered, "Pity you had such bloody awful weather.")

One of King George V's gallant contributions to the war effort was an alcohol ban in Buckingham Palace, although it was quietly understood when he took the pledge that it did not apply to the King himself. His choleric temper and ruddy face belied the official palace line that he drank very little. Prayers were said in the East End of London for Queen Mary and her children, "begging the protection of heaven on their unhappy drunkard's home." The Palace had to instruct the Dean of Norwich to publicly refute the allegations of alcoholism. The Dean did as he was required and the rumors died down.

THE KILLING FIELDS OF SANDRINGHAM

Shooting was George V's sole accomplishment: he was an ecological disaster made flesh. He slaughtered animals with a zeal that far exceeded the social demands of his day. He acquired the killing habit from his father, and his first shotgun at the age of twelve. From that day on he organized his life around the shooting calendar. George V's idea of a good day was to blast away at comatose birds with his twelve-bore shotgun until he was ankle deep in spent cartridges. His targets were usually pheasants, partridges, woodcock, snipe and duck, mostly hand-reared, tame and barely mobile. The shoots were designed so that the killing was ridiculously easy. The King wasn't in the least embarrassed about wiping out scores of driven birds, most of which, according to a shooting companion, were "ridiculous in their slow flight." Nor, unlike his father, was George in need of such easy targets. Endless target practice had made him one of the best shots in the world. While British troops were being shot in droves by the Boers in 1899, the royal shooting party was busy exterminating about 12,000 pheasants in Norfolk.

Throughout World War I he continued to shoot at Sandringham, excusing it as his patriotic contribution to the nation's food supplies. During his reign, more than 20,000 head
of game were mowed down on the fields of Sandringham each
year, not counting the hundreds of shoots he was invited to attend. In a single December day, George and his friends killed
4,000 pheasants; the King personally killed about a thousand.
Even some of his guests were shocked by the scale of the carnage. Lord Lincolnshire wrote: "Can this terrific slaughter possibly last much longer?"

Winston Churchill was an appreciative hunting guest but
he winced at the King's slaughterhouse tactics. "I shot three
and could have shot more," he told his wife later, "but re-
frained, not wishing to become a butcher." One day the King
was heard to observe to his eldest son, as the pair waded
through heaps of spent cartridges, "Perhaps we went a little far
today." On his trip to Nepal, in less than a fortnight he personally killed twenty-one tigers, eight rhino and one bear. The
shoots were managed so that none had any chance of escape.
"A record," the King gloated later, "and one I think will be
hard to beat."

One of George V's fellow big-game hunters was the Indian
Maharaja Jay Singh of Alwar. Although the Maharaja was a notorious pedophile and a part-time psychopath, he was the
King's personal friend and his guest at Buckingham Palace in
1931. The Maharaja also liked to play polo. One day in 1933 he
had a bad game and decided to blame his horse, which had
stumbled and thrown him. As an audience of British V.I.P.'s
watched, the Maharajah poured a can of petrol over the polo
pony and set fire to it. The King may not have been aware that

his friend also liked to use live babies and elderly widows as tiger bait.

In spite of overwhelming evidence to the contrary, the King wouldn't tolerate any suggestion that he was cruel to animals. In his defense he would point to his much loved pet parrot. To George this was proof enough that he was an animal lover. To everyone else it was merely proof that he hadn't yet taken to shooting parrots.

His son George VI was also a compulsive shot, indulging his hobby almost every day of the week. In 1924 he and the Queen Mother went on a four-month big-game shooting holiday in Africa, and with her Rigby rifle she shot a variety of wild animals, including rhinoceros, buffalo, waterbuck, antelope, Kenyan hartebeest, steinbuck, water-hog and jackal. In Uganda her husband shot an elephant whose tusks weighed ninety pounds each. "It was very lucky," he said later, "as there are not many very big ones left." When Britain declared war on Germany he expressed concern that the crisis might interfere with the Balmoral grouse season.

ALIEN ROYALS

George V was a xenophobe, albeit a very confused one. "Abroad is awful," he once said. "I know. I have been." He particularly hated Naples, noting that the harbor was full of dead dogs. But, for a German living in England, where exactly was "abroad"? Although he had centuries of undeniably German ancestry and not the slightest trace of English blood, he liked to pretend that he was wholly English. Others, including Lloyd George, were not fooled. Before visiting the Palace in 1915, the Prime Minister remarked to his secretary, "I wonder what my little German friend has got to say to me." Later on during World War I, the King explained to Asquith that his cousin Prince Albert was "not really fighting on the side of the Germans," but had only been "put in charge of a camp of English prisoners." "A nice distinction," Asquith observed.

When the King heard about H. G. Wells's comment that the royal family was "uninspiring and alien," he was indignant. "I may be uninspiring," George snarled, "but I'm damned if I'm alien." He had presumably forgotten that he was currently honorary colonel of a German regiment, and that he and most of his family were German to the marrow.

Since the Battle of Hastings, England has been ruled by six families, none of them English. Queen Elizabeth II claims descent from William the Conqueror, but then, statistically, so do most of the inhabitants of Western Europe. Indeed, ever since they arrived from Hanover, Britain's current solidly German royal family have made few concessions to their adopted country. King George I, born on and buried in German soil, showed barely disguised contempt for his new homeland and would scurry back to Hanover whenever the opportunity arose. A myth arose that George I couldn't speak a word of English. In fact his English was good enough for him to communicate with his ministers, and it improved as his reign progressed: the point was that for most of the time he didn't consider it necessary. Conversation with his English courtiers was not a problem anyway because the language spoken in court was French.

His son George II was a similarly reluctant Briton, but was at least careful to play down his origins in public, once announcing in thick, guttural tones, "I have not one drop of blood in my veins that is not English." Later, however, Prince Albert would pronounce, "Every part of my being is German," and Edward VIII boasted in the 1930s, "I have not one drop of blood in my veins which is not German."

If Princess Diana had made it to the throne she would have been the first Englishwoman to sit there since Catherine Parr. The Royal Marriages Act of 1772 was designed to keep the British royal family German. The architect of the legislation, King George III, was also desperate, nevertheless, to be known for his pro-British sentiments, a situation eloquently put when he pronounced from his throne, "Born unt educated in zis country, I glory in ze name of Briton." In private conversation with his wife, however, he always spoke German, and once admitted, "My heart will never forget that it pulses with German blood."

Invariably, the British royals took German wives. George II's grandmother thought that a native mistress might improve his English, which he spoke inadequately throughout his life, but his Queen was very German. George II's prospective daughter-in-law, Princess Augusta of Saxe-Coburg, arrived in England in 1736 without a single word of English at her command. She had been assured by her mother that this would not be a problem because the Hanoverians had ruled England for twenty years and surely everyone by now would speak German. From the moment that George III's new German bride, Queen Charlotte, said, "Ich will," she struggled to converse with any of her subjects, although in time she acquired a competent grasp of English. King William IV's German wife, Queen Adelaide, couldn't speak a word of English, and the order of service at her wedding had to be written in phonetics for her.

By the time of Queen Victoria's reign, the British had become so used to generations of foreign royals that the line between German and English royalty had become blurred. Prince Albert was perceived as patently German—indeed he was open and unambiguous about his loyalty to his fatherland. Yet his wife, although regarded as essentially British, was no less a German than he was. Both of her parents were German and they spent the early part of their married lives in Germany, even though they were living on an income granted to them by the English Parliament. Victoria's mother couldn't speak a word of English when she was first married and had to make public speeches from phonetic scripts prepared for her. Victoria and Albert disliked London and chose to live at Balmoral because it reminded them of the north German countryside. Victoria often insisted that her family wrote and even conversed in German. Their son Edward VII spoke English with a German accent, which became much more pronounced when he lost his temper.

In fact, George V's wife, Queen Mary, was the first Consort for over 400 years to speak English as a first language, but she was 100 percent German and took pride in her pure Hanoverian descent, always quick to point out that her family was not tainted by any of Prince Albert's inferior Saxe-Coburg blood. Yet Queen Mary wasn't in the least bit embarrassed to claim in her German accent that she was "English from top to toe," the oft-repeated claim of foreign royals living at the expense of British taxpayers.

When George V delivered his first Christmas Day radio broadcast, many of his subjects were bemused to find that he also spoke with a slight German accent. Today that slight

German accent has been so subtly assimilated into the dialect of the British royal family and so widely imitated by the establishment that it has long been accepted as an exclusive variant of received pronunciation.

MORE GERMAN THAN THE KAISER

The slumbering conundrum of the royal family's nationality was brought suddenly to life in 1914 when the start of World War I saw an outbreak of xenophobia. German traders in the East End had their shops looted and their goods destroyed. People refused to drink German wine and kicked dachshunds in the street. The press hinted at a fifth column at work, and anyone with a German-sounding name was interned without trial. Betrayed by his ancestry and his strong accent, Lord Louis Mountbatten's father, Admiral Prince Louis von Battenberg, although a naturalized Briton, was hounded by the popular press and forced to resign. The war also invited people to look long and hard at their "British" royalty.

It was left to George V's palace counselors to point out to him that he and his family were more German than the Kaiser. Ever since the marriage of Victoria to Prince Albert, the royal family had reigned in the stoutly Teutonic name of Saxe-Coburg-Gotha. In 1917 it became a bigger embarrassment when German Gotha airplanes began to bomb London. The royal family were naturally only too eager to distance themselves from their German cousins. There was nothing like a World War or the Civil List to bring out the English in them. It was agreed that George V and his family should undergo a swift rebranding exercise and adopt a name more "naturally English." The King considered restyling his dynasty the House of Wipper, then the House of Wettin, before settling for the House of Windsor.

The last name was suggested by Lord Stamfordham when he learned that Edward III had been known as Edward of Windsor. The change was not confined to the King's immediate family. Collateral branches of royal family were also de-Germanized. The von Battenbergs became the consumer-friendly Mountbattens, and Queen Mary's family, the Tecks, became Cambridges. The King's first cousins, the Coburgs, far too obviously from the wrong side of the Seigfried line for comfort, were ostracized completely. Thereafter, the true identity of the British royal family was officially suppressed.

The royal name changes were not a lightly taken decision, because in most royal circles, especially German, heraldry was more important than life and death. Many minor "British" royal personages regarded the move as a dreadful betrayal of their true German roots and were furious that their ancient family names had been changed to silly made-up Anglo-Saxon ones simply because of the King's cowardice. Royal relatives abroad were similarly scandalized. The Bavarian Count Albrecht von Montgelas observed gravely, "The royal tradition died on that day . . . when, for a mere war, King George V changed his name." George's cousin Kaiser Wilhelm joked that he was looking forward to a performance of *The Merry Wives of Saxe-Coburg-Gotha*. (Another version of this anecdote has it that he said he was looking forward to *The Merry Wives of Mecklenburg-Strelitz*.)

Ironically, while the British royal family was being criticized for its German origins, the Kaiser was being berated at
home for being too English. He was accused of having too
many English ideas, and was criticized for his English habits,
even his many English clothes. The Kaiser was popularly believed, quite wrongly, to be half-English, because his mother
was a daughter of Queen Victoria. Yet the Kaiser's mother
didn't have a drop of English blood in her veins: she was pure
German stock, half-Hanoverian, half-Coburg.

As a first cousin of King George V, the Kaiser's attitude toward his British family connections was schizophrenic. It was
in the Kaiser's arms that Queen Victoria eventually died, and
when he appeared on the streets of London for her funeral he
was heartily cheered as "one of ours." However, he loathed his
uncle Edward VII, and treated his British-born mother very
badly. When war loomed he became rabidly anti-British. Yet
most of the time he liked to play at being a British aristocrat.
He told Theodore Roosevelt in 1911, "I adore England."
Dressed up in his tweed suits or racing his yacht at Cowes, he
certainly looked the part. When Wilhelm was exiled to Doorn
in Holland after the war, his life became essentially that of the
archetypal English country squire. Young German officers who
made the pilgrimage to his home were confused to find their
ex-Kaiser surrounded by the works of P. G. Wodehouse and
sipping cups of imported English tea.

The British royal family never forgot that the Kaiser was
family, and sent him congratulatory telegrams when he reached
his eightieth birthday. When Hitler's army marched on
Holland, Wilhelm was even offered sanctuary in England. The
Kaiser refused because he was too proud to accept charity from
former war enemies.

The business of embarrassing German relations was an issue that would return to haunt the British royal family many times. Queen Elizabeth II's husband, the Duke of Edinburgh, ostensibly a member of the former Greek royal family, is seven-eighths German with a dash of Dane. When the blue-eyed and blond Prince Philip proposed to the young Princess Elizabeth in 1946, King George VI was worried that his daughter marrying a German so soon after World War II would be hugely resented by the British public. He ordered them to delay the engagement until she was twenty-one the following year.

Prince Philip brought with him a few other problems. His brother-in-law, Prince Christopher of Hesse, for example. Prince Christopher, married to Philip's sister Sophie shortly after her sixteenth birthday, was a high-ranking Nazi. Originally head of Goering's secret phone-tapping service—the forerunner of the Gestapo—he went on to join the Luftwaffe. Prince Christopher died in a plane crash in 1943 while on a top-secret Nazi assignment. (The Palace prefers a different, "official" version of his death in which this hitherto active and very enthusiastic Nazi was killed for bravely denouncing the Third Reich.) Prince Christopher's brother, Philip of Hesse, was Obergruppenführer in the SS and a personal friend of Herman Goering. Another of the Duke of Edinburgh's sisters was also married to a German army officer. None of Prince Philip's sisters received an invitation to his wedding.

When the young Princess Elizabeth got engaged it was decided that Philip's surname, Schelswig-Holstein-Sonderburg-Glücksburg, would have to be anglicized in the time-honored tradition, since it sounded too much like Borussia Munchen-Gladbach's back four to be passed off as typically British. The Duke of Edinburgh's Uncle Dickie, Mountbatten, revealed himself to be an old-fashioned, scheming royal matchmaker in the mold of Queen Victoria's Uncle Leopold. He saw an opportunity of aggrandizing his family name by establishing a Mountbatten on the British throne, and persuaded his nephew to adopt his surname. The ease with which he was able to do so, and the close physical resemblance, inevitably led to speculation that Prince Philip might in fact be his illegitimate son.

As it turned out, Mountbatten was wasting his time, because the Queen flatly refused to drop the name Windsor. The legitimacy of her decision is questionable. Queen Victoria, a daughter of the House of Hanover and born with the surname Guelph, set a precedent when she took the name Saxe-Coburg-Gotha upon her marriage to Albert. Arguably, Queen Elizabeth II should have taken her husband's name. Logically therefore, Britain should now be celebrating the reign of neither the House of Mountbatten nor Windsor, but the House of Schleswig-Holstein-Sonderburg-Glücksburg.

The royal-family disinformation service was even less convincing in a more recent case of Nazi skeletons in the family wardrobe. In 1977 the Queen's cousin Prince Michael of Kent was married to a Catholic divorcée, Baroness Marie-Christine von Reibnitz, who was eventually forced to admit that her father had also been a member of the SS, albeit only, according to a heroic Palace statement, "an honorary member." The royal family knew all about the Nazi connection long before Princess Michael was married into their family, and there was therefore no possibility that she herself was unaware of her father's position. When the news broke, however, the Palace announced that it had come as a terrible shock to all concerned, especially to Princess Michael herself.

Britain is not alone when it comes to unfortunate German connections. The nearest thing that the current Dutch royal family have had to a full-blown media scandal occurred in 1966, when Queen Beatrix, then heir to the throne, wedded a German diplomat, Claus von Amsberg, who had served in the Wehrmacht during the war and been a card-carrying member of the Hitler Youth. This was a particularly insensitive marriage considering that a little over twenty years earlier the Germans had invaded Holland, bombed Rotterdam and forced the Dutch royal family to flee overseas. The wedding ceremony was boycotted by about half the invited officials and there were violent protests outside; orange swastikas were daubed over the palace walls.

After World War I, against a backdrop of desperate economic hardship, George V found that his fake British coat of arms was still not quite enough to make the former House of Saxe-Coburg-Gotha entirely palatable to the public. The King was warned by his advisers that, although his family were now less obviously alien, they still needed to make themselves more conspicuous if they wanted to be loved.

George responded by throwing himself and his family into a frenzied round of visits to industrial areas, thus inventing the royal tradition of factory tours. It was a revolution in royal behavior. The provinces of the United Kingdom, especially the industrial north of England, were completely uncharted territory for them. No Hanoverian monarch until George IV had ever bothered to set foot in Wales, Scotland or Ireland. Queen Victoria never troubled the royal transport system unless there was the prospect of someone showering her with jewelry. She often refused to even greet visiting heads of state, let alone show her face to her subjects. To George V's eldest son, the Prince of Wales, who normally only left the safety of his St. James's bachelor pad for the nightclub or the gaming table, Walsall and Wolverhampton would have seemed like Mars.

DITCHING THE ROMANOVS

George V was ample proof that the royal family, over and above any notions of being representative of duty, dignity and decency, was and always had been in the extremely practical business of retaining its position of privilege. After disowning the German part of his heredity, George V turned his back on another close part of his family. He shared an apparent firm friendship and an uncanny physical resemblance with another first cousin, the Russian Emperor Nicholas II. The King's affection for his "dear Nicky" did not extend to saving his cousin's life when it was clearly within his power to do so.

In 1917, Imperial Russia was torn apart by revolution, and three centuries of Romanov rule were ended when Nicholas II abdicated in favor of his brother Michael. The younger Romanov sensibly declined the Crown unless it was formally offered to him by an elected assembly, but events swiftly overtook him when the Bolsheviks suddenly seized power. Shortly after the abdication, Russia's provisional government inquired whether Britain was willing to receive Nicholas and the imperial family. George V immediately agreed to let them settle in Britain. The proposal was approved by Prime Minister Lloyd George and the British government, and asylum was offered.

It was at this point that the natural royal instinct for survival at all costs took over. If there was one thing that could wholly concentrate the King's limited faculties it was the threat of republicanism. The presence of the ex-Czar in Britain, his palace advisers persuaded him, would be resented by the public and could undermine the monarchy. George V very quickly changed his mind about saving his cousin.

The King had a problem: asylum had already been offered to the Romanovs, and he was desperate to distance himself from what could be seen as a cowardly U-turn. However, he found a way out by letting his government do the dirty work for him. From that point on, the King repeatedly begged Lloyd George to rescind the offer and leave the Russian royals to their fate, thus denying his cousin's family their only chance of escape. In July 1918 the Czar, his wife and their five children were taken to Ekaterinburg and ruthlessly eliminated. In effect, George V had passed a death sentence on his near relatives rather than risk damage to his own popularity.

The real threat to the King's own skin was slight. Precedents set under far more difficult circumstances had made England the traditional bolt-hole for unwanted monarchs and their families for centuries. "The much more serious threat of imported revolution from France did not prevent Britain from giving sanctuary to the detested Bourbon Louis XVIII. The British government even paid the throneless French King £7,000 a year pocket money to allow him to establish a pseudo court in Buckinghamshire. When Napoleon was defeated, Louis was amused to receive an invitation to Carlton House to meet the Prince Regent, who had hitherto been too scared to acknowledge the Frenchman's existence. As recently as 1910, the remnants of the Portuguese royal family, including the last ruling Portuguese King, Manuel II, had also followed the well-worn path to retirement in England after King Carlos and his brother Prince Louis Filipe were cut down by republican assassins.

Despite his own involvement in the refusal of asylum for the Czar, George V later compounded this naked act of self-preservation by allowing his Prime Minister to take the blame for his cousin's death. For decades afterward, the British royal family allowed everyone to believe that Lloyd George denied the Romanovs asylum in England, and that he was therefore partly to blame for Nicholas II's assassination. In fact, Lloyd George had no part in it at all. He saw the King's failure to save the lives of his cousins as a private family matter; in the end he had simply done as George had asked.

Until the truth about George V's betrayal was publicly disclosed fifty years after his death—when government papers, scrutinized for the first time in 1986, confirmed it beyond doubt—the Windsors allowed Lloyd George's name to be abused every time the subject of the Romanovs arose. Lord Louis Mountbatten in particular lied extensively and often about how the King had gallantly striven to rescue Nicholas from the Bolsheviks, only to be thwarted by his evil Prime Minister. The Windsors also exploited the Czar's demise for their own personal gain when Queen Mary took to snapping up Russian royal-family jewelry at bargain prices. In 1933 she paid £60,000 (about £2 million today) to buy the jewels of the Empress Marie Feodorovna, the mother of her husband's dead cousin Nicholas.

SANCTIFIED BIGAMY

King George V has always been regarded as a limited but virtuous King, more interested in philately than philandery, his private life held up as a shining example that today's royals cannot match. But this aspect of his public persona was a sham. George V was not the first British king for nearly a century without a mistress, but he was the first to keep it a secret. According to his authorized biographer, Kenneth Rose, as a young man he used to visit "high-class tarts," and in his early twenties he kept one mistress at Southsea, while sharing another with his bisexual brother Eddie (Albert) in St. John's Wood, London. There were also alarmingly persistent stories concerning his alleged bigamy. It was widely rumored that as a young man George had secretly married the daughter of a British naval officer, Sir Michael Culme-Seymour, in Malta. As the years passed, these rumors refused to go away. A newspaper called the *Liberator*, published in France but freely circulated in England, featured an article written by E. F. Mylius under the headline "Sanctified Bigamy."

According to Mylius, George had indeed married Miss Culme-Seymour in 1890, and his young wife had borne him several children. As soon as the Duke of Clarence died and George unexpectedly found himself in line for the throne, George cruelly abandoned his wife and children and entered into a bigamous relationship with the daughter of the Duke of Teck, later Queen Mary. Mylius was arrested and sued for libel. He was found guilty and sentenced to a year in prison. But, although George's honor was apparently vindicated, Mylius was unrepentant and repeated the story a year later in a new pamphlet published in America entitled "The Morganatic Marriage of George V."

QUEEN MARY

In times of crisis the British royal family has required a steady supply of younger brothers to fall back on. When the impotent playboy George IV failed to produce an heir, his inadequate brother William was promoted to King. When Edward VIII was exposed as the black sheep of the 1930s, his reluctant and desperately unprepared brother "Bertie" was required to fill his shoes. But for George V, a generation before, was reserved the rawest deal of all. Not only was he expected to replace his elder brother as heir to the throne: he was also required to marry his deceased brother's fiancée. *The Times* solemnly expressed the hope that "a union rooted in painful memories may prove happy beyond the common lot." It was anything but, although George V and Queen Mary were to spend the rest of their lives successfully presenting to the world an image of domesticated matrimonial contentment.

George V's subjects would have been shocked indeed had they known that their King's regular trips to Bognor and other seaside resorts on the South Coast, according to A. N. Wilson, were discreetly arranged for him so that he could seek brief refuge from his wife with prostitutes.

Queen Mary, known to her family as "May," was born into the House of Teck, one of Germany's more impoverished minor royal dynasties. Her brother Frank was kicked out of Wellington School for assaulting his headmaster and spent the rest of his life as a reckless gambler, rarely out of debt. In 1895 he found himself owing £1,000 to an Irish bookmaker, and attempted to get himself out of his predicament by pledging £10,000 he didn't have on a ten-to-one-on "cert" in order to win just £1,000.

Fortunately, his brother-in-law George and several other members of the British royal family found the money to bail him out. Frank's punishment was exile to India. When his mother died, he embarrassed the family yet again by lavishing all of the Teck family jewels on his very elderly mistress. He died unmarried in 1910.

Queen Mary herself was a walking metaphor for the moribund institution she represented. She showed nothing of herself; she gave nothing away. Her image, including a dress sense that was already dated when she was a young woman, was frozen in time. Her personality was a well-kept secret. The court diarist "Chips" Channon noted that having a conversation with her was "like talking to St. Paul's Cathedral." Prime Minister Asquith agreed: making conversation with her, he complained, was much harder work than a debate in the House of Commons.

Like Queen Victoria before her, Queen Mary was a grasping and predatory collector of jewelry. Although she spent her entire reign trying to present an image of down-to-earth middle-class respectability, she would cover her monolithic frame with an ostentatious display of gems at every opportunity. At the wedding of Kaiser Wilhelm II's daughter in Berlin in 1913, she simultaneously wore nine diamond necklaces, six diamond brooches, two diamond bracelets and diamond earrings.

SPONGING FOR BRITAIN

The economy of the House of Windsor was based on their ability to beg for money faster than they could spend it. They did this by periodically pretending they were broke. When George IV, an obscenely extravagant Prince of Wales, was asked to trim his running costs after blowing £49,000 on soft furnishings and £17,000 in a day on trinkets, he huffily sacked his servants, pawned his jewelry, closed up his London palace and flounced off to Brighton with his mistress. Before Prince Albert left Coburg he swore, "I shall never cease to be a true German," then persistently sent begging letters to Her Majesty's Government for more British money. His eldest son wrote an anonymous letter to *The Times* recommending that that fine fellow the Prince of Wales deserved much more money from the Civil List. Thanks to Queen Victoria's cunning and a succession of deferential governments who virtually absolved the royal family of all taxes, by the time her grandson arrived on the throne the Windsors were—second only, perhaps, to the Romanovs—the wealthiest royal family in the world. Yet George V once threatened that if he didn't receive more money he would have to go to open Parliament in a taxi cab. Prince Philip continued the tradition in 1969 when he complained that things were getting so tight he might have to give up playing polo, and again in 1995 when he bemoaned the impending loss of the royal yacht.

Not all royals were complete spendthrifts. Although life in his day at Sandringham was royally extravagant, George V could also be very miserly. He filled his home with cheap reproduction furniture. When his old mother, Queen Alexandra, impulsively sent out gifts to friends and deserving causes, the King sent out servants to retrieve them. His expensive sporting life on the fields of Sandringham was a world apart from the plight of the people who helped sustain his hobby. The wages he paid to his estate workers—about fourteen shillings a week—caused a scandal in Norfolk.

Unlike other European monarchs and heads of state, the British royal family do not surrender gifts, including jewelry, given to them on state occasions. This has provided a situation that they have been able to exploit many times over. Edward VII and George V made trips to India that were no more than excuses to shoot tigers and take advantage of the natural generosity of their Indian subjects, thus increasing their personal wealth. For the Delhi Durbar in the winter of 1911, at which King George and Queen Mary were to be crowned Emperor and Empress of India, the Crown jeweler was commissioned to make a new crown at the cost of £60,000. The people of India paid for it, but they never even got to see it, because it has been stored away in the Tower of London ever since. The Indian Princes, true to form, showered the British royal couple with gems. The King and Queen were very coy about disclosing the contents of their haul and even today the jewelry they were able to stash away from their Delhi trip is one of the royal family's best-kept secrets.

ROYAL KLEPTOMANIA

A republican would argue that all royal property is theft, but Queen Mary has the unique distinction of being the only known royal kleptomaniac. Apart from her obsession with jewelry, she was a prolific collector of anything associated with her dynasty, especially ornaments, family portraits and miniatures. The Queen had little notion of good taste and during her reign she amassed a huge and eccentric private collection. However, what made this one quite different from other royal collections were the dubious and often criminal methods she employed to put it together.

Whenever Queen Mary wanted to make an addition to her haul of expensive bric-a-brac, her first tactic was to fall back on

the royal tradition of browbeating the owners into freely handing over their possessions. This she did with a well-honed technique that involved staring long and hard at the item that took
her fancy, while sighing aloud, "I am caressing it with my eyes."
Inevitably, the embarrassed donor, unwilling to offend with a
refusal, would be cowed into submission. Soon, word got
around the stately homes of Britain and her impromptu visits to
wealthy friends were generally preceded by a panicked hiding
of anything she might take a shine to. When it finally dawned
on Queen Mary that she had been rumbled, she took to turning up uninvited.

Her next tactic was less subtle. She stole things. If she found
an ornament small enough, she would slip it into her handbag.
In her biography of Queen Mary, *Matriarch*, Anne Edwards
records that on her frequent visits to London's antique dealers
"the Queen was prone to take what she wanted and they
would go without payment." Edwards notes, "This led to a
story that Queen Mary was a kleptomaniac, an accusation
never substantiated and thoroughly untrue." While it is correct
to point out that taking things without paying for them doesn't
necessarily make her a kleptomaniac, there does appear to be
quite a good case for calling Queen Mary a common thief.

Buckingham Palace became aware of Queen Mary's problem when some of her victims complained about the thefts, and
the Queen's ladies-in-waiting were quietly instructed to keep
a close eye on her. From then on her stolen goods were usually
retrieved by an aide and mailed back to the original owner
with a covering letter explaining that there had been a "mistake." Inevitably, stories about Queen Mary's compulsive thiev-
ing leaked out from time to time. The Palace, obliged to come
up with some sort of explanation, lamely expressed it as

her natural keenness to save anything worthwhile for the nation.

BUGGER BOGNOR

George V didn't exist outside the time-consuming but utterly useless framework of royal etiquette. The King had an obsession with old rituals which was both comical and absurd. He got involved in bitter disputes with his sons over their choice of trousers and would personally scold government ministers for wearing the wrong type of hat. He once rebuked a U.S. ambassador for failing to wear knee breeches at evening court. A worried and confused official from the newly created Soviet Union heard about this and sent a telegram to the Kremlin asking whether he ought to wear knee breeches to Buckingham Palace. "If necessary," the Kremlin wired back, "you will wear petticoats." While Field Marshal Haig was planning the Battle of Paschendale, George V's advisers agonized over whether or not women workers in a Northern munitions factory should wear gloves when they shook hands with Queen Mary.

The King always wore his crown when he signed official papers to remind himself, he explained, of the importance of it all. Queen Mary always wore her tiara at mealtimes at home, even when she and the King dined alone. Every day the King and the Prince of Wales sat down to eat wearing the Windsor uniform, a costume designed by George III comprising a dark-blue tailcoat with red collar and cuffs, white breeches and a white tie and waistcoat. The meal was accompanied by music provided by a string orchestra, which was hidden out of view behind a grille. Originally they had been required to play from inside a small cupboard, but this had resulted in some of them fainting in the middle of a selection from *No No Nanette*. The mealtime entertainment would always end with George V standing rigidly to attention for "God Save the King," even though there was no one other than his own wife and children watching.

It is apt that a king who lived such a regimented and superficial life, dominated by court etiquette, should also have died at the convenience of the court almanac. Depending on whether you believe the official version or not, George V's last words were either "How is the Empire?" or, as is slightly more likely, "Bugger Bognor." One fact concerning his death that is beyond dispute is that the King was killed by his doctor to meet a newspaper deadline.

Lord Dawson of Penn served as royal doctor to four sovereigns—Edward VII, George V, Edward VIII and George VI— and although he was the best-paid doctor in the country it didn't necessarily follow that he was the best at his job. One of the more vicious stories that circulated about his alleged incompetences was how he treated a man for jaundice for six weeks until he realized his patient was Chinese. On the evening of January 19, 1936, the King lay dying, having already lapsed into a coma. At his bedside were Lord Dawson, Archbishop of Canterbury Cosmo Lang, Prime Minister Ramsay MacDonald and Queen Mary. In another room the King's two eldest sons and his private secretary were planning a royal funeral. The arrangements were already well advanced: all that was missing was a corpse.

According to the Duke of Windsor's autobiography, later that evening Lord Dawson took Queen Mary and him aside and asked them rhetorically, or so they believed, if they wished the King "to suffer unduly." The Queen and the Prince replied that they did not. Years later the King's eldest son said that it never for a moment occurred to him that Dawson was asking for permission to end his father's life. The doctor took pen and paper and composed the line "The King's life is drawing peacefully to its close." Then, shortly before midnight, to make absolutely sure his prose wasn't premature, he slipped a hypodermic syringe containing a lethal injection of morphia into George V's jugular vein.

Dawson's medical notes confirm that he hadn't in fact terminated the King's life to end his suffering. The King was unconscious and therefore not in any pain. It was done for the sake of the morning papers. The moment of death was deliberately timed to ensure that the news, in Dawson's words, "received its first announcement in the respectable morning papers, such as *The Times*, rather than the rather less appropriate field of the evening journals." Dawson even phoned *The Times* to warn them to hold the front page and to expect an important announcement shortly. "Effectively," the Duke of Windsor reflected in his authorized biography, "Dawson murdered my father." The regicidal doctor received a viscountcy in that year's Honours List for his troubles.

Gordon Winter, co-author of the book *Secrets of The Royals*, made a convincing case that Queen Mary was similarly killed. Winter was working as a Fleet Street journalist in 1953 when he interviewed a senior unnamed royal servant who accurately predicted that Queen Mary would die between 10 P.M. and 11 P.M. two days later. Queen Mary was at the time terminally ill, and both she and her family had expressed a desire that her death should not in any way impede Queen Elizabeth's forthcoming coronation ceremony, which had been planned for June 2. According to the Palace insider, her death had been scheduled so that a decent mourning period could be observed and the coronation would go ahead as planned. The odds against this prediction coming true by accident, notes Winter, were about 2,000 to 1.

WINDSOR FAMILY VALUES

Between the Queen's collection of objets d'art and the King's stamp album there was little time for the royal offspring. George V and Queen Mary were disastrous parents, neither of them willing to show, or capable of showing, affection toward their children. The King's father, Edward VII, had seen little of his wife but even less of his children. George V was so frightened of him that he once fainted at the prospect of being told off, and his own philosophy on the subject of fatherhood was similarly enlightened. "I was terrified of my father," he explained to a friend, "and I am determined that my children will be terrified of me." While the King terrorized his children, bullying them into cowering wrecks, his wife believed she had an excuse for looking the other way. "I have to remember," she said, "that my husband is also my sovereign."

Queen Mary's emotional sterility was demonstrated most chillingly in her relationship with her youngest child, Prince John. Queen Elizabeth II's Uncle John was rarely mentioned by the royal family even when he was alive, because he was regarded as an embarrassment. Born in 1905, he displayed early signs of mental disability, and from the age of four he also suffered from epilepsy. When the fits grew worse it was decided that he should be segregated from his family, and at the age of twelve he was removed from his home and exiled to Wood Farm, Wolferton, in the permanent care of a nurse. One day the young boy was informed that his mother and father were going to be crowned King and Queen. He understood, but was not allowed anywhere near the coronation festivities. Although he was only a short distance away, Queen Mary never once visited him and hardly ever spoke of him after he was taken away from his family. A final epileptic attack in January 1919 caused fatal heart damage and he died suddenly.

The death was greeted with relief by his parents and indifference by his brothers. Prince George, the future George VI, was in France and did not return home for the funeral. The Prince of Wales, according to his biographer Philip Ziegler, saw his youngest brother as "little more than a regrettable nuisance." The fact that Prince John was handicapped and epileptic was not reported in any of his obituaries, nor was any explanation offered as to why Prince John was separated from his family.

THE PINK SHEEP OF THE FAMILY

In the 1920s and 1930s, thanks to a deferential British press, George V's sons were able to run amok in public with impunity. The Windsors have to this day declined to cooperate in any official biography of Queen Elizabeth II's Uncle George, the Duke of Kent. His papers are locked away in the Royal Archives at Windsor, closed to historians. Even after all the problems they have encountered in recent years, the royal family consider George just too embarrassing. Prince George was the fifth child born to George V and Queen Mary. He was bright, artistic and very effeminate, always drenched in strong perfume. When he wasn't blowing his share of the Civil List on an expensive cocaine habit, the Prince indulged his bent for blond, blue-eyed Aryan-type German boys.

He spent much of his time in the seedier West End nightclubs, where he enjoyed the company of stage entertainers of either sex. In 1926 he began an affair with the black cabaret singer Florence Mills which continued well after his marriage to Princess Marina. He also had a string of affairs with the daughters of aristocrats, including the banking heiress Poppy Baring. Any hopes she may have had of marriage were dashed by her careless confession that she found the royal family unbearable. George even had at least one illegitimate son, who was adopted by a well-known American publisher of the day.

Although his scandals were unreported in the press, his bisexual conquests were well known in court circles. One night he was arrested by police in company with a known homosexual in a nightclub, the Nut House, and held in cells until his identity could be confirmed. In 1932 he wrote love letters to a young man in Paris: they eventually had to be bought back by a palace courtier for a large sum of money. There were also affairs with an Argentinian diplomat and an Italian aristocrat.

But his most famous homosexual affair was with the actor and playwright Noel Coward. The latter's extraordinary private life, in the context of his friendship with the royals, is described in Kenneth Rose's *Kings, Queens and Courtiers* as "unorthodox though discreet," with the additional twinkling observation that "Coward's romantic devotion to the royal family was lifelong." They met in 1923 when the Prince was twenty and Coward was three years older. According to the actor, he seduced the Prince in the dressing room at the Duke of York's theater in St. Martin's Lane, London. Years later, Coward would boast about his "little dalliance," proud that he had made a sexual conquest of a member of the royal family. His acquaintances noted that he even became something of a bore on the subject.

Drug abuse was fairly commonplace in the circles inhabited by the young British royals. When the Prince of Wales visited the Muthaiga Club in 1929, cocaine was openly offered around under his nose at dinner. His younger brother George was a serious cocaine addict. George had been introduced to cocaine and morphine in 1932 by an American girlfriend named Kiki Preston, known as "the girl with the silver syringe." His addiction was also fed by another dealer, a young South American man, whom the Prince of Wales later personally had kicked out of the country. Friends noted that one of the few truly useful things that the Prince of Wales ever did was to try to wean his brother George off drugs. He even had the young Prince kept under house arrest in an attempt to cure him of his problem.

However, Prince George was still a drug addict at the time of his engagement to Princess Marina of Greece in November 1934. The arranged marriage of the pink sheep of the family, hailed publicly as an ideal love match, came as a huge relief to the Windsors, but it didn't signal any notable change in his lifestyle.

George died in August 1942, when the plane in which he was flying crashed in mountains in northern Scotland, killing fifteen passengers. His death, even sixty years after the crash, remains a royal mystery. The official report of events, read to the House of Commons, placed the blame squarely upon the plane's captain for taking the wrong flight path. Others have claimed, however, that the Prince himself was at the controls that day, drunk after a heavy session with crew members. The lack of evidence concerning the crash and the failure to make the report public fueled darker rumors that the Prince had been assassinated because of his debauched lifestyle.

Curiously, Noel Coward went on to establish a long friendship with Princess Marina. It was, insiders noted, a strange relationship: they became so close that after Prince George's death a friend joked that Coward was trying to become the Dowager Duke of Kent.

"UNCLE DICKIE" AND HYPOCRISY

As a cadet at Osborne, Lord Louis Mountbatten was branded a German spy, but in his lifetime came to be popularly regarded as the royal family's most heroic figure—a fearless destroyer captain, a Supreme Allied Commander in World War II, a statesman in India, and later a benign, wise old father figure to the nation. He was also promiscuously bisexual, although you won't find any mention of it in Philip Ziegler's 786-page official biography, *Mountbatten*—other than a terse four-paragraph dismissal of rumors that he was gay.

Mountbatten's marriage was arranged, a cynical pact designed to make the most of the combined assets of his royal connections and his wife's money. In 1921 he suddenly announced his engagement to the incredibly wealthy heiress Edwina Ashley, granddaughter of Sir Ernest Cassell, the son of a Jewish moneylender in Cologne who had gone on to make a fortune in banking. Cassell was a financial adviser to Edward VII and one of the richest men in Europe, and on his death his granddaughter inherited £2 million. For Mountbatten, ostensibly surviving on a naval salary of about £350 a year, it was love at first sight. His new wife was dazzled by the fact that he was a minor royal. Mountbatten admitted later that the couple had spent their entire married lives hopping in and out of other people's beds.

Polite society was scandalized by their complicated affairs. What little time Edwina had left over from her extravagant shopping excursions she spent alone with her lesbian sister-in-law, or pursuing her much sensationalized interest in black men. The revelation in *The People* that she had been "caught in compromising circumstances" with the singer Paul Robeson was one of the great tabloid scandals of the day. The idea of a white, titled lady sharing a bed with a black man was, in the 1920s, too shocking for words, and Buckingham Palace advised her to sue. For the first time since Edward VII, a member of the British royal family took the witness stand and brazenly lied in a court of law. Edwina Mountbatten completely denied that she had ever met the singer and, to Robeson's astonishment and everlasting hurt, convinced the jury. *The People* was ordered to pay damages of £25,000.

Mountbatten had been part of a gay circle at Cambridge that included the socialite Peter Murphy, who eventually moved into the Mountbatten home. At one point the young Mountbatten was sternly rebuked by Queen Mary for spending too much time "hanging around actors," especially Noel Coward. Mountbatten brought Murphy, Coward, Somerset Maugham and many more of his gay acquaintances into Edward VII's circle of friends, and, according to some sources, Noel Coward slept with the then Prince of Wales. "The Duke [of Windsor]," wrote Coward in his memoirs, "although he pretends not to hate me, he does because I'm queer and he's queer. However, unlike him, I don't pretend not to be."

Rumors about the nature of the relationship between the Prince of Wales and his cousin Mountbatten first began during the Prince's Empire tours, during which time they were hardly ever apart, causing the ship's crew to swap crude jokes about how Mountbatten was monopolizing the Prince's time. Dickie wrote to his mother, "You've no idea what a friend David [the Prince of Wales was known as David to his family] is to me . . . how I wish he wasn't the Prince of Wales and then it would be so much easier to see lots and lots of him." Later he wrote, "I don't know if I have ever told you exactly what friends David and I are . . . I have told him more about myself and he has told me more about himself than either of us have ever told anyone before in our lives." None of this would be remarkable if it weren't for the Windsors' pretense of archetypally "straight" family values.

The Prince's preference for gay male friends continued well into married life with Wallis Simpson. In 1951, his wife, by then the Duchess of Windsor, had an affair with a famously disreputable American bisexual, Jimmy Donahoe. The grandson of the chain-store founder Frank W. Woolworth, Donahoe was a flamboyant transvestite who liked to embarrass his mother by floating around the house in drag while his parents entertained important guests. He mixed with male prostitutes and drug addicts in New York, and subsequently died of alcohol and barbiturate poisoning. Both Windsors enjoyed his company and, for three years, the trio were so inseparable that there were rumors of a ménage à trois. "The fag hag must be enjoying it," Coward observed. "Here she's got a royal queen to sleep with, and a rich one to hump."

THE BLACKEST SHEEP OF ALL

George V's eldest son, David, the Prince of Wales, was born on June 23, 1894. He reigned briefly as Edward VIII, then skulked at length in self-imposed exile as the Duke of Windsor. He was arguably the blackest sheep in 300 years of royal-family history. His daily routine was that of a useless libertine, enjoying all the benefits that life on the Civil List carried, but unwilling to offer anything in return. Born and bred to be the King of England, and still unmarried at forty-one, the Prince of Wales was the world's most eligible bachelor, attracting adoring females wherever he ventured. North America danced to the popular song: "I've danced with a man who danced with a girl who danced with the Prince of Wales . . ."

All four of King George V's surviving sons were heavy drinkers, but Edward's relentless thirst astounded people around him. In the 1920s there were frequent public sightings of him drunk, although none was ever reported in the press. His Private Secretary Alan Lascelles confessed bluntly, "I can't help thinking that the best thing that could happen to him, and to the country, would be for him to break his neck."

He was also seemingly incapable of keeping out of the beds of married women. His first adulterous affair was with Lady Marion Coke, wife of Viscount Coke, heir to the Earldom of Leicester, and the cuckolded husband eventually had to warn the Prince to stay away from his wife. In the spring of 1918 the Prince began an affair with a Liberal M.P.'s wife, Mrs. Freda Dudley Ward, which lasted for about sixteen years. At around the same time he was sleeping with the twenty-five-year-old American Thelma Furness, whose husband was head of the Furness shipping line. In January 1931, the Prince of Wales attended a party with Lady Furness where he met for the first time Mr. and Mrs. Ernest Simpson. The Prince dropped Lady Furness when he discovered that she had also slept with an Indian, Prince Aly Khan. The jilted mistress took her revenge by informing everyone within earshot that the Prince of Wales was very poorly endowed and useless in bed.

For most of her life, Wallis was investigated, for one reason or another, by just about every intelligence-gathering agency in the Western Hemisphere. She was born on June 19, 1896 (although Queen Mary's personal private investigation into her background put the birth date years earlier), and was raised in Baltimore in a three-story house on East Biddle Street. She was brought up by her mother, Alice, after her father died of tuberculosis when she was five months old. In 1916, aged nineteen, she married Earl Winfield Spencer, a naval pilot and a violent alcoholic. In 1924 she and her husband traveled to China and Hong Kong. According to the so-called China Report, a spurious dossier prepared by MI5, in the mid-1920s Mrs. Wallis Spencer indulged in "deviant" sexual activities in the high-class brothels popular with senior naval personnel stationed in Hong Kong. It is now generally accepted that the China Report was fiction, a smear campaign to blacken her name.

Earl Spencer kicked his wife out of their home when he discovered she was having an affair with a naval ensign. In 1927 they were divorced, and in the following year she was married to Ernest Simpson. On November 29, 1934, she made her first major appearance at a formal court occasion, the wedding of Prince George and Princess Marina. Over the next two years, the Prince often entertained the Simpsons at his country retreat, Fort Belvedere, outside London. Soon Ernest slipped into the background, and the Prince met Wallis alone. "He was the open sesame to a new and glittering world," she would later reflect. "Yachts materialized; the best suites in the finest hotels were flung open; airplanes stood waiting . . . It was like being Wallis in Wonderland."

Although she was still married, Wallis Simpson had been the Prince of Wales's mistress for some time when he became King. The British newspapers knew all about it, but the press barons kept the story under wraps until the abdication crisis forced it into the open. Consequently you could read all about the King's affair just about anywhere in the world except Britain. The U.S. press found it particularly amusing that the King of England was copulating with an American divorcée and none of his subjects was allowed to know anything about it.

Ultimately, the heir to the throne bought Wallis for £100,000. This was the amount he gave Ernest Simpson, via a secret bank account, partly to compensate him for the theft of his wife, and partly to get him to appear to be the adulterer in subsequent divorce proceedings. When the Prince of Wales told Louis Mountbatten in 1936 about his intention to marry Mrs. Wallis Simpson, his cousin took him to one side and quietly reminded him of the tradition of kings. He should do what his grandfather Edward VII had done: marry a suitable royal princess while continuing to fornicate with whosoever he chose for the rest of his life. Mountbatten's advice was ignored and the British royal family found itself with the first abdication crisis in 500 years. Nearly forty years later, he offered exactly the same advice to his great-nephew Prince Charles.

For a while, Wallis Simpson held the position of Britain's Most Hated Mistress, a title later held by Camilla Parker Bowles in a fine tradition stretching back to George IV's paramour, Lady Isabella Hertford. In keeping with the aforementioned royal mistresses, Mrs. Simpson was far from beautiful. The photographer Cecil Beaton described her as "attractively ugly, *une belle laide.*" "She was a dominatrix type," commented author Gore Vidal, "and he [the Prince], having been beaten up by nannies and governesses all his life, needed a strong woman to bawl him out." By many accounts, Wallis was content with the status quo and was happy to stay as royal mistress. According to Donald Spoto's book *The Decline and Fall of the House of Windsor*, by this time Wallis Simpson "was bloody bored with the King and wanted out."

When the Prince announced his plans to marry her, the situation was on the brink of constitutional crisis. The Church censured divorce; Parliament refused to grant Wallis Simpson a title, and English law had no precedent for a wife of the King with no title or official capacity; the British public hated her. Prime Minister Stanley Baldwin forced the Prince to choose marriage or the monarchy. Edward was widely perceived as a charming gadabout, weak-willed and incapable of making up his mind, but when he finally came to a decision it astonished the English-speaking world. He chose to abdicate. On December 11, 1936, in a radio broadcast that reached millions, the newly proclaimed King announced: "I have found it impossible to carry the heavy burden of responsibility and to discharge my duties as King as I would wish to do, without the help and support of the woman I love."

When her connection with the King was first revealed to the British public, Wallis Simpson received hate mail and even death threats, and bricks were thrown through her windows. Considering some of the things that the royal family had got up to, the backlash against her was both extraordinary and unfair. Her family background was checkered, but not as shocking as the King's. In the final analysis, Edward VIII was not forced to abdicate because of any Act of Parliament or royal precedent. There is nothing in the British constitution that prevents royal marriages to divorcées: it only forbids marriages to Catholics. The precedent of marrying a divorced woman was set by Henry II's marriage to Eleanor of Aquitaine. Edward VIII's government were simply able to get rid of him by appealing to old-fashioned British snobbery. Neither the public nor the establishment could stomach Wallis Simpson. She was perceived as vulgar, common, ambitious and, worse still, American. The prospect of this bejeweled Aunt Sally appearing on Britain's postage stamps, Winston Churchill reflected after the abdication, was "too horrible to contemplate." But there was, however, another angle on this story that neither the American nor the British press got hold of.

At best, Edward's links with Nazi Germany on the run-up to, and during, the war were ill-advised and insensitive. Many historians believe, however, that there is enough circumstantial evidence to prove that his actions were treasonable and that if he hadn't been a member of the royal family he would have been arrested, tried, and most probably executed. In fact, Churchill seriously considered charging him with treason in 1940, but resisted.

There is substantial evidence that both the King and his

mistress were unashamed Nazi sympathizers. In this they were not of course alone. At that time a substantial minority of leaders felt that war with Germany would be a tragedy and that Britain should be uniting with Hitler against the Soviet Union. Even in 1940 some members of the British establishment believed that there were still sufficient grounds for a compromise peace. German secret documents published after World War II show that the Duke of Windsor was an admirer of Hitler as early as 1935.

Both the Duke and his wife were surrounded by Fascist friends and influences. Their mutual lifelong friends were the British Fascist Sir Oswald Mosley and his wife Diana, who kept framed bedside pictures of her idols Hitler and Goebbels. Diana Mosley said later that Edward VIII's politics were "far to the right" of even her husband's. Edward's cousin, the British-born Duke of Coburg, who was Hitler's personal emissary before the war and who turned up at his father's funeral wearing a Nazi uniform, described Edward as "an ardent Nazi."

The German documents detailed Wallis Simpson's friendships with leading Nazis and Fascists, including Joachim von Ribbentrop. Indeed, Stanley Baldwin had received a security report that showed she was in contact with several leading German Nazis, many of whom had befriended her quite independently of Ribbentrop. Before she met the Prince of Wales, she had had an affair with Mussolini's son-in-law.

The Prince of Wales was under constant surveillance by MI5 and Scotland Yard, separately and independently, long before he married Wallis Simpson. MI5 agents learned quite by chance (at the time they were following Errol Flynn) of the couple's infamous visit to Germany after the abdication. The

Duke and Duchess met Hitler at his mountain home at Berchtesgaden. A German aide present at the meeting recalled that the Duke appeared throughout to be in awe of Hitler and grovelingly eager to please: he so overdid the "Heil Hitlers" and the Prussian heel-clicking that it even embarrassed his Nazi hosts. "It was all a little bit ridiculous," recalled von Ribbentrop's secretary, "but no one dared to tell him." The Duke later had private meetings at his home in Paris with Hitler's deputy, Rudolph Hess, and with Martin Bormann. "There is no need to lose a single German life in invading Britain," Hess reported back to the Führer. "The Duke and his clever wife will deliver the goods."

Edward married Bessie Wallis Warfield at the Chateau de Cand, France, on June 3, 1937, and they set up home in Paris. When the French capital was occupied by German troops, they fled to Portugal. Churchill sent three flying boats to bring the Duke and Duchess back to England, but the Duke refused to return. Churchill had to threaten him with a court-martial. The Duke eventually agreed to go to the Bahamas, where they spent the rest of the war. There the British royals were befriended by the murderous Mafia boss Meyer Lansky, a man personally involved in about 800 gangland killings. Meanwhile, in German-occupied Paris, Hitler made sure that the Duke's home, his personal possessions and even his bank account were left exactly as he had left them. The Duke was still in touch with the Germans, via a Spanish intermediary, until shortly before Berlin fell. Whether he was aware of it or not, the Duke of Windsor was Hitler's puppet-king in waiting. According to British intelligence, in the event of a German victory the Duke was to have been kidnapped by Hitler and restored to the British throne.

The Duke of Windsor was unrepentant about his Nazi connections to his death. "Of course, if I'd been King," he once chillingly observed, "there'd have been no war."

The participants in the so-called Romance of the Century were to live lifestyles of epic vacuity. After the abdication, the Duke and Duchess would step on to a treadmill of endless partying and free-spending drifting. Very few British taxpayers were aware that they were actually paying to keep the playboy ex-King and his American wife in the jewelry to which she had become accustomed. When he abdicated as Edward VIII and emerged a humble Duke of Windsor, he decided that it was time to fall back on the family tradition of pleading poverty. Although he already had the equivalent of about £24 million accrued from his earnings as Prince of Wales, he told the British government that he was almost broke, and was subsequently awarded £21,000 a year on the Civil List. The money was sent to him via his brother's bank account to make it look as if it was coming directly from the royal family's purse. The French government had also given them a rent-free mansion and declined to charge them any income tax. This meant that the exiled couple were able to live at the expense of the taxpayers of two countries, on a scale that was probably even more lavish than the one Edward had tasted as King.

The one outstanding accomplishment of the Duchess of Windsor, people noted, was her ability to wear about three times her own body weight in jewelry. Her most memorable bon mot was "You can never be too rich, or too thin." Throughout the austere post-war years she staggered around Europe smothered from head to toe in diamonds, rubies and emeralds. In one month her husband spent the equivalent of about £500,000 on her jewelry. The Duchess once complained that she had been reduced to an allowance of only $4,000 a year on new dresses—about $240,000 today.

The royal family shunned the Duchess until her husband's death in 1972, when Queen Elizabeth finally invited her to stay in Buckingham Palace. Wallis survived Edward by fourteen years, spending the last eleven of them wasted and bedridden, unable to walk or eat. Finally, in 1986, the Duchess of Windsor discovered that it was possible to be too thin after all. One day, Churchill predicted, the British people would erect a statue to her.

KEEPING BELOW THE PARAPET

Some of Britain's most successful monarchs were dull, lackluster men and women who kept their heads below the parapet at times of change and emerged unscathed. The fight for democracy which swept Europe in the nineteenth century had dire consequences for royalty, but King William IV's complete lack of charisma was probably instrumental in the British monarchy passing through the era unscathed. In fact, William was the only European monarch of the age to survive republicanism. George VI was desperately ill-equipped to lead his country into a world war, but his weaknesses and his lack of charisma worked in his favor, and it is now generally accepted that his succession was the best thing that could have happened in the circumstances.

As his father had done before him, the King visited troops, munitions factories, supply docks, and bomb sites.

The actions of the new King and Princess Elizabeth during the war years built the prestige of the monarchy to a new high. The pressure of public life left the highly strung King physically and emotionally drained by the time of his death, but he left the monarchy in better condition than he found it.

Elizabeth II's enigmatic style is more or less straight from Queen Mary's copybook: to show nothing of her private self and to give nothing away. Winston Churchill, who had served four monarchs, said he found her to be knowledgeable, witty, and capable of a rare sense of humor seldom exhibited in public. A later Prime Minister, James Callaghan, on the other hand, found her to have little direct experience of anything at all apart from racing and breeding horses.

WWW.WINDSOR.CO.UK

By the early 1990s, half a century of adulation had led the British royal family into a fossilized complacency. The litany of disasters that followed for the beleaguered House of Windsor is still fresh in the memory. Three of the Queen's children were divorced, with the fourth reluctant to get married; Windsor Castle burned; the tabloid press published photos of the Duchess of York having her toes sucked by a man who was not her husband; the heir to the throne revealed in a six-minute taped telephone conversation that he fantasized about reincarnation as his forty-five-year-old mistress's tampon. Then, in August 1997, the woman once intended to be Britain's Queen died in a Paris underpass with her lover.

This was the single most important event in the history of the British monarchy since the abdication of Edward VIII in 1936. Mass demonstrations of public grief turned to anger, much of the bitterness directed at an apparently unbending and uncaring royal family. For a few nail-biting days, support for the monarch among the majority of the British population, taken for granted for more than a century, was apparently on the wane. The reputation of the Prince of Wales seemed beyond rescue. There was talk of the Queen "skipping a generation" by passing over Prince Charles and handing the Crown, when the time came, to Prince William (never an option as it is not within the gift of the Queen to decide who succeeds her). Shorn of their star attraction, the British royal family, once the greatest show on earth, suddenly began to look like an outmoded, almost purely ceremonial, unpopular and discredited institution. The Windsors were briefly but totally eclipsed by the cult of Diana: the supreme manipulators had found themselves outmaneuvered and outclassed by a commoner, the girl they employed to provide them with an heir.

The House of Windsor had presented themselves as guardians of family values. They had been slow to perceive that therefore they were obliged to at least pretend to lead respectable lives. However, they had always survived times of crisis by skillful presentation, and seldom had there been a better time for a spot of rebranding. The Queen appointed a "spin doctor" to take strategic control of the royal image; Buckingham Palace also acquired a web site. Charles the adulterous husband was reinvented as Charles the caring single parent. Royal weddings, royal jubilees, even royal funerals, breathe new life into the cult of monarchy. Diana's death, far from having seriously weakened the monarchy, may have even reinforced its place at the heart of British nationhood. It was business as usual—at least for another generation.

EPILOGUE

ROYAL IGNOMINY HAS a long pedigree, and this book has revealed some, but not all, of the personal tragedy, gross sexual license, madness, wickedness and plain naivety that has bedeviled the history of European monarchy.

World War I cast a shadow over the career prospects of many a prince, and monarchy as an institution had largely disappeared in Europe by 1945. Today, only ten monarchs remain, seven of whom have familial ties to the House of Windsor. The British monarchy alone continues to reign by a set of rules written in the late-seventeenth century.

Sentimental attachment to monarchy is a singularly British institution, like drizzle, fox hunting, soiled beaches and nostalgia for hangings. Two hundred years after the American and French Revolutions, even the far left in British politics retains a mysterious soft spot for their royal family.

Whether you take the view that monarchy is a useless and dysfunctional remnant of dynastic inbreeding, or that at best it is an iconic symbol of national unity and identity, at worst, eccentric artifice, bringing in the tourists and giving comfort to many while harming no one—there is no doubting the continuing fascination with royalty. No one can predict how many of Europe's royal families will survive the twenty-first century, or even the next twenty-five years; the institution is, however, far from dead.

BIBLIOGRAPHY

Acton, H., *The Bourbons of Naples*, Methuen, 1956.

———, *The Last Bourbons of Naples*, Methuen, 1961.

Aronson, T., *The Coburgs of Belgium*, Cassell, 1969.

———, *A Family of Kings*, Cassell, 1976.

———, *Grandmama of Europe*, Cassell, 1973.

Ashdown, D., *Royal Weddings*, Robert Hale, 1981.

Barber, N., *Lords of the Golden Horn*, Macmillan, 1973.

Bauer, L., *Leopold the Unloved*, Cassell, 1934.

Bennet, D., *King Without a Crown*, Heinemann, 1977.

Blunt, W., *The Dream King*, Hamish Hamilton, 1970.

Bradford, S., *George VI*, Weidenfeld & Nicolson, 1989.

Carlton, C., *Royal Childhoods*, Routledge & Kegan Paul, 1986.

Chapman-Huston, D., *Bavarian Fantasy*, John Murray, 1955.

Constant, S., *Foxy Ferdinand, Czar of Bulgaria*, Sidgwick & Jackson, 1979.

Coughlan, R., *Elizabeth and Catherine*, Macdonal & Jane's, 1975.

Crankshaw, E., *The Fall of the House of Habsburg*, Longmans, 1963.

———, *The Habsburgs*, Weidenfeld & Nicolson, 1971.

Cullen, T., *The Empress Brown*, Bodley Head, 1969.

Davies, N., *Europe, A History*, Oxford University Press, 1996.

Davis, W., *Punch and the Monarchy*, Hutchinson, 1977.

de Polnay, P., *A Queen of Spain: Isabel II*, Hollis & Carter, 1962.

Duff, D., *Alexandra Princess and Queen*, Collins, 1980.

Edwards, A., *Matriarch: Queen Mary and the House of Windsor*, Hodder and Stoughton, 1984.

Friedman, D., *Inheritance*, Sidgwick & Jackson, 1993.

Gainham, S., *The Habsburg Twilight*, Weidenfeld & Nicolson, 1979.

Gillen, M., *Royal Duke*, Sidgwick & Jackson, 1976.

Gooch, G. P., *Louis XV*, Longmans, 1966.

Green, V., *The Madness of Kings*, Alan Sutton, 1993.

Gribble, F., *The Royal House of Portugal*, Nash, 1915.

Hall, P., *Royal Fortune*, Bloomsbury, 1992.

Haslip, J., *Madame du Barry*, Weidenfeld & Nicolson, 1991.

——, *Marie Antoinette*, Weidenfeld & Nicolson, 1987.

Hatton, R., *George I*, Thames & Hudson, 1978.

Hedley, O., *Queen Charlotte*, John Murray, 1975.

Hibbert, C., *George IV, Prince of Wales*, Longman, 1972.

——, *George IV, Regent and King*, Penguin, 1973.

Holme, T., *Caroline*, Hamish Hamilton, 1979.

——, *Prinny's Daughter*, Hamish Hamilton, 1976.

Howarth, T. E. B., *Citizen-King: The Life of Louis Philippe*, Eyre & Spottiswoode, 1961.

Hubatsch, W., *Frederick the Great*, Thames & Hudson, 1973.

Hunter, R., and Macalpine, I., *George III and the Mad Business*, Penguin, 1969.

James, R., *Albert, Prince Consort*, Hamish Hamilton, 1983.

Jones, S., *The Language of the Genes*, Flamingo, 1993.

Judd, D., *Prince Philip: A Biography*, Michael Joseph, 1980.

Katz, R., *The Fall of the House of Savoy*, George Allen & Unwin, 1972.

Lewis, W. H., *The Scandalous Regent: A Life of Philippe, Duc d'Orléans*, Deutsch, 1961.

Lincoln, W. B., *The Romanovs*, Weidenfeld & Nicolson, 1981.

Listowel, J., *A Habsburg Tragedy*, Ascent, 1978.

Longford, E., *The Oxford Book of Royal Anecdotes*, Oxford University Press, 1989.

Louda, J., and Maclagan, J., *Louda and Maclagan*, Orbis, 1981.

Lynch, J., *Bourbon Spain 1700–1803*, Blackwell, 1989.

Macartney, C. A., *The Habsburg and Hohenzollern Dynasties in the Seventeenth and Eighteenth Centuries*, Macmillan, 1970.

Marek, G. R., *The Eagles Die*, Hart-Davis, MacGibbon, 1975.

McIntosh, C., *The Swan King*, Allen Lane, 1982.

Middlemas, K., *The Life and Times of Edward VII*, Weidenfeld & Nicolson, 1993.

Mitford, N., *Frederick the Great*, Hamish Hamilton, 1970.

————, *The Sun King*, Hamish Hamilton, 1966.

Mortimer, P., *Queen Elizabeth: A Life of the Queen Mother*, Viking, 1986.

Morton, A., *Diana: Her True Story*, Michael O'Mara, 1992.

Noel, G., *Ena: Spain's English Queen*, Constable, 1984.

Norton, L., *The Sun King and His Loves*, Hamish Hamilton, 1983.

Oakley, S., *The Story of Denmark*, Faber & Faber, 1972.

Pakula, H., *The Last Romantic, A Biography of Queen Marie of Roumania*, Weidenfeld & Nicolson, 1985.

Parker, J., *King of Fools*, Macdonald & Co., 1988.

Petrie, C., *King Charles III of Spain*, Constable, 1971.

Porter, R., *English Society in the Eighteenth Century*, Penguin, 1982.

Reddaway, W. F., *Cambridge History of Poland*, Cambridge University Press, 1950.

Rice, T., *Elizabeth, Empress of Russia*, Weidenfeld & Nicolson, 1970.

Roby, K., *The King, the Press and the People*, Barrie & Jenkins, 1975.

Rose, K., *King George V*, Weidenfeld & Nicholson, 1983.

Saxe-Coburg-Gotha, Duke, E., *Memoirs of Ernest II, Duke of Saxe-Coburg-Gotha*, Remington & Co., 1888.

Seward, D., *Naples, A Traveller's Companion*, Constable, 1984.

Smith, D. M., *Italy and Its Monarchy*, Yale University Press, 1989.

Somerset, A., *The Life and Times of William IV*, Weidenfeld & Nicolson, 1980.

Stevenson, R. S., *Famous Illnesses in History*, Eyre & Spottiswoode, 1962.

Tapie, V., *The Rise and Fall of the Hapsburg Monarchy*, Pall Mall, 1971.

Thomas, H., *Madrid: A Traveller's Companion*, Constable, 1988.

Trench, C., *George II*, Penguin, 1973.

Troyat, H., *Alexander of Russia*, New English Library, 1982.

van der Zee, H. and B., *William and Mary*, Macmillan, 1973.

Warwick, C., *George and Marina*, Weidenfeld & Nicolson, 1988.

Weintraub, S., *Victoria: Biography of a Queen*, Unwin Hyman, 1987.

Whittle, T., *The Last Kaiser*, Heinemann, 1977.

Williams, G., *The Age of Agony*, Constable, 1975.

Wilson, A. N., *The Rise and Fall of the House of Windsor*, Sinclair-Stevenson, 1993.

Winter, G., and Cochran, W., *Secrets of the Royals*, Robson, 1990.

Woolf, S., *A History of Italy 1700–1860*, Methuen, 1979.

Ziegler, P., *King Edward VIII*, Collins, 1990.